THE WORLD
IN 2020

HAMISH McRAE

THE WORLD IN 2020

Power, Culture and Prosperity

Harvard Business School Press
Boston, Massachusetts

First published in the United States
by the Harvard Business School Press
in hard cover, 1995; in paperback, 1996

First published in Great Britain
by HarperCollins *Publishers* Ltd, 1994

Library of Congress Cataloging-in-Publication Data

McRae, Hamish.
    The world in 2020 : power, culture, and prosperity / Hamish McRae.
      p. cm.
    Includes bibliographical references and index.
    ISBN 0-87584-604-1(hc)
    ISBN 0-87584-738-2(pbk)
    1. Business forecasting.   2. Twenty-first century—Forecasts.
3. Economic history—1990—   I.Title.
HD30.27.M385   1994
388.5'443—dc20   94-24545
                                                                  CIP

TO MY FAMILY

Contents

Tables and Graphs

Preface

THE IMPETUS FOR WRITING this book came from a conversation at an Oxford conference in September 1991. I had been talking about future developments in international finance and was asked if I could recommend any good books on the subject. I couldn't . . . and so I thought I had better try and write one.

What I have written differs from most exercises in futurology. These either take the form of scenario building, where different possibilities are outlined and the reader is left to choose between them, or they paint a picture of exaggerated optimism or pessimism. The first approach is a useful one for businesses as a way of outlining the range of possibilities for which they might plan – excellent work is done in this field by Shell, which pioneered the approach, and by the Organization for Economic Co-operation and Development (OECD) in Paris, which held a conference in the summer of 1991 on long-range prospects for the world economy, and to whom I owe a considerable debt. But scenario-building is unsatisfying: some may well be more or less right, but others will be spectacularly wrong. The second approach is equally unsatisfactory because the authors tend to have a powerfully opinionated view of the future which readers are obliged to accept: the future will be wonderful, or it will be dreadful, and all the evidence is piled up to support the view. I recognize the genre – I have contributed to it myself in the past.

I have tried to find a middle way, first by looking at the world as it is now, then by examining the various forces for change and trying to judge how these forces will alter the world over the next generation, and finally by drawing attention to some choices the industrial world in particular has to make. I know this book has weaknesses of its own – many of the details will turn out to be wrong, but it would worry me more if, through some flaw in the analysis, I had failed to spot some really big global change.

I have focused principally on the present developed countries and those which are likely to become developed within the next thirty years. The division of the world into the three main economic regions of North America, Europe and East Asia means that large parts of the globe – Latin America, Africa, the Middle East and the Indian sub-continent – are treated in a relatively sketchy manner. This is not a serious omission for the horizon I have taken of 2020. These areas are of course extremely important in human, social and political terms, but they are not yet (with the specific exception of the Middle East's oil fields) particularly important as economic producers – nor will they be within one generation. Even if India, the world's second most populous nation, enjoys a better economic performance in the next thirty years than it has in the last, it is unlikely to be a great world economic power by 2020. China, by contrast, will probably become one, though its progress may prove more uneven than many people in 1994 assume.

Anyone seeking to write a book on a subject as wide as the future development of the world knows that one can only hope to build a small cairn on top of the mountain of other people's ideas. I am aware of some of these ideas and the people who have developed them, or introduced me to them, but I also know that there are other ideas I have simply absorbed and developed during the twenty years in which I have been interpreting and writing about the world economic change on two British national newspapers, without knowing how they came to my attention in the first place. As a result I am not only unable to thank everyone who has helped me with this book, but unable to explain fully why I may have reached my conclusions. I have tried in the source notes to explain as far as possible how each chapter was constructed – whether largely from interviews with experts, or from published material.

Writing for the *Independent* has proved a fine base from which to set out on the journey into the future. Not only have I been able to test-market a number of the ideas through my column, but I have also been surrounded by a group of thoughtful and robust people on whom I could try them out, and who were quick to tell me when they thought I was wrong. Several have fed ideas into the book: Mary Dejevsky has been a wise adviser on change in Russia, as has Tim Jackson on Japan; David Robson and Jane Taylor have repeatedly asked, 'Interesting idea, but is it right?'; Matthew Symonds has injected ideas on the relationship between economics and social change; and Andreas Whittam Smith, the editor, has encouraged me throughout the project.

A second group have been directly involved in the book. At Harper-

Collins, Michael Fishwick has been the model publisher, enthusiastic, supportive and critical by turns, and Juliet Van Oss has edited the script with care and craft. Andrew Evans has designed the cover and Philip Lewis the book. Justin Arundale at the *Independent* and Patrick Cunningham have checked the proofs, and the index has been compiled by Christine Bernstein. I have also been helped by Anne Hathaway, who has acted as researcher, encourager, checker and editor, digging out facts and figures which I rather hoped would exist but had been unable to discover, and by Frances Cairncross, my wife, who read and edited the entire draft. Quite aside from catching some embarrassing howlers, she has disentangled many of my thoughts and set them in a more logical order. For this, and so many other things, I will always be grateful.

HAMISH MCRAE
London, February 1994

I

WHERE THE WORLD STANDS NOW

ONE

WHAT MAKES COUNTRIES GROW

The efficient society

THE SUCCESS OR FAILURE of any country over the next thirty years hinges on growth. By the next generation, some countries are likely to have improved substantially both their standard of living and their quality of life; some will have muddled along, becoming a little richer, but feeling distressed that they have in relative terms slipped back; and some seem destined to fail, with all the misery that falling living standards inflict on their people.

To give a sensible judgement about which countries will flourish and which fail, it is necessary to be able to explain the present and the recent past: why some countries have managed to outpace others, not just in improving their living standards, but in increasing their power and influence in the world. This involves examining the competitive position these countries start from now, which to a large extent is still a function of the strengths and weaknesses of their manufacturing industries. It also involves making some judgements about the efficiency of their service industries (banking, hotels, health care, education and so on): how competitive these are at the moment, and how their relative competitiveness might change over the next generation. Most important of all, it involves making judgements about the efficiency of their societies as a whole, and in particular assessing the very different approaches to social organization evident in North America, Europe and East Asia.[1]

The ways in which these three regions organize their societies are best compared by looking at three measures: the proportion of GDP (Gross Domestic Product)[2] going through the state, which gives a feeling for the extent to which the state has taken responsibility for social affairs; the level of savings, which gives a feeling for the

3

availability of funds for investment; and the proportion of young people in higher education, which gives a feeling for the willingness to invest in human development.

In both North America and East Asia public spending is significantly lower as a percentage of GDP than it is in Europe, suggesting that Europe is unusual in the extent to which it relies on state-financed education, health and social security systems – which account for some 60 per cent of Europe's total public spending. East Asian countries have some of the highest levels of savings in the whole world, while the US has the lowest. On the third measure, both North America and the richest countries of East Asia seem to lay more stress than any European country on ensuring that as many of their young people as possible receive tertiary education, though if one were to measure levels of attainment rather than the crude numbers, the figures would be closer together. The North American education system, despite the resources put into it, does not necessarily deliver higher quality results than the European or East Asian systems. It is important when comparing service industries, like education, to look at the quality of the output rather than the quantity of the input.

A more detailed assessment of the starting point of the big three centres of economic activity is made in the following three chapters, but a caricature at this stage might help explain the different choices each society is making.

North America believes in a relatively low level of public spending on social matters, leaving individuals to pay much of the bill directly or through insurance. It does not believe in saving, preferring to consume a high proportion of present income. And while it believes in providing widespread access to education, the quality of the output of that education has been poor.

Europe, by contrast, is wedded to a high level of state intervention: in western Europe the state takes a much higher proportion of the decisions about allocating resources than in North America or the East Asian industrial societies. Most European countries believe in saving, though the commitment is not universal. They also believe in education, though again standards vary widely from country to country.

In East Asia a variety of different countries of widely different political backgrounds, from democracies to dictatorships (and including a colony, Hong Kong) reach similar practical decisions about the way their countries should be run. They believe the state should have a relatively modest role in social affairs, they are determined savers, and they are dedicated to education.

Assessing the extent to which each of these regions will prosper means guessing how countries in each region will change the way they organize themselves. All developed countries do not need to be exactly alike. But we know enough about what drives economic growth to be fairly sure that there are certain things that countries must do if they are to deliver a good economic performance. For example, to what extent will the United States increase its savings? How will European countries refashion their welfare systems? Will the social overhead costs of most East Asian societies be able to remain so low?

Countries learn from each other – the information about how countries run themselves is universally available. Since the Second World War there seems to have been a tendency for the economic performance of countries of broadly similar levels of wealth to converge, while those of different wealth levels seem to diverge. In other words, the rich industrial countries tend to draw closer together while the poorer, less developed countries find that the gap between them and the rich widens. Only a handful of countries, almost entirely in South-East Asia, have jumped the gap.

How has one group of countries been able to succeed in leaping the gap between income levels in developing countries and industrial countries in just one generation, something which has never before been achieved anywhere else in the world? It is an immensely important question, to which, unsurprisingly, there is no single easy answer. An authoritarian politician like Lee Kuan Yew of Singapore would explain the region's success in terms of self-discipline and hard work, whereas in Japan success has often been attributed to the cultural and genetic homogeneity of the country. (This causes grave offence in the US, which, by implication, is condemned to relative decline by its cultural and racial diversity.) Economic theory, on the other hand, would focus on the investment in education that all the countries in the region have made.[3] But none of these approaches really helps much, for they do not really answer the 'why?' questions. Why is East Asia self-disciplined? Why does cultural homogeneity help growth – if it does, which is questionable? If education is so important, why does investment in it bring such varying results? We know that rapidly-growing societies have characteristics in common, and these are particularly evident in South-East Asia: things like emphasis on education, high savings, and sheer hard work.[4] But we understand little about why these societies have developed these characteristics.

In making predictions about the future one has to make a judgement about the ability of the established industrial world to adapt. One of the great lessons of the last quarter of the present century was that the 'old' industrial world, North America and Europe, had something to learn, often painfully, from the industrial processes developed in the new, in particular from Japan. One of the great issues of the first quarter of the next century will be whether countries can learn from each other not just how to make their industries efficient but how to make their whole societies more efficient.

The importance of growth

To put so much emphasis on efficiency is not to claim that efficiency – or rather the growth that increased efficiency delivers – is the only thing that matters. That would be absurd. Indeed one of the main arguments developed here is that if economic growth is to increase human wellbeing (in the words of the Declaration of Independence, 'Life, Liberty and the pursuit of Happiness'; in economists' jargon 'welfare') it must also take into account social and environmental concerns. While it is certainly true that solving many other problems, even including environmental ones, can become much easier if there is the wealth generated by growth to pay for solutions, the quest for growth alone can lead to catastrophe, as the experience of the former Soviet bloc's economic policies has shown: here, the blind pursuit of quantitative economic goals led to excessive pollution, falling life expectancy, corruption and misery. And of course in the United States the emergence of an underclass shows that even very rich societies may find it hard to ensure that all people get some share of the nation's wealth. However, even if growth itself does not solve all problems, the absence of growth makes the problems infinitely more difficult to tackle.

Growing richer is not just a matter of improving living standards – buying more consumer durables, or spending more on education and health. Growth is also power, for it changes the world political order. The twentieth century is thought of as the American century, for the economic power of the United States has thrust upon it the task of global political leadership. In fact, the extraordinary rise in the relative size of the US economy and its equally striking fall mirrors the rise of the US in political influence, and its subsequent decline. In 1914 the US accounted for roughly 34 per cent of the industrial world's output; by 1955 this had risen to 58 per cent; by 1990 it had fallen back to 33 per cent. The US started the century as an important political force, but one which stood alongside the main European powers of Germany, Britain and France. It ended the Second World War dominating the globe. Now, with the demise of the Soviet Union, it remains the only superpower and the largest economy in the world, but the margin of dominance over the EU, Japan and, increasingly, China has been eroded. By the early years of the next century, the proportion of world output generated by the US will be back to the proportion it held in the first years of this one. It may not even remain, as it has for more than a century, the world's largest economy. China will probably overtake it.

During the 1980s China quite suddenly set itself on the path to becoming the largest economy in the world. The Chinese leaders were very well aware that outside the mainland of China, Chinese people had become among the most successful in the world: the expatriate communities in Taiwan, Singapore and Hong Kong had discovered the key to economic growth, and were chasing Japan in increasing their wealth and influence. Yet on the mainland these same people were failing. It was not just that economic growth was stagnating; the country had the greatest difficulty feeding itself. This was deeply humiliating. It was this sense of national failure which led to a conscious decision to reject the economic system which had not worked and to allow into China the one which had. In 1979 Deng Xiao Ping introduced a series of economic reforms which lifted it out of economic stagnation and enabled it to become the fastest growing region of the world during the 1980s.

The introduction of market reforms was cautious and partial: the government began by creating special economic zones in which some of the freedoms of the market economy could operate, but such was the surge in growth which resulted that by the end of the 1980s it was clear that these would be extended gradually to the whole of China. If the pace of momentum is kept up, China, with its 1.2 billion people, will have a larger GDP than the United States by 2003.[5] Even if its 1980s growth rate halved, it would pass the US in 2014. It is very difficult to see China as anything other than the world's largest economy in the year 2020, a position which will inevitably give it very much more influence in world politics.

In purely economic terms, the position of smaller economies can change even more dramatically. Consider the relative positions of two countries, Argentina and Singapore. Before the outbreak of the First World War, Argentinians were among the richest people in the world, second only to the United States in income per head. Had the country's relative performance been maintained, its economy would now be approximately the size of Britain or Italy, while in terms of living standards it would be ahead of Germany or Japan. As it is, Argentina's economy is roughly the size of Norway's and a tenth that of Switzerland, while Argentinians are poorer even than Hungarians. Argentina's experience stands as an awful reminder of the capacity of bad government to wreck a prosperous economy.[6]

Singapore, on the other hand, was a British trading post and military centre in 1900 with a small population of some 220,000. At the end of the Second World War, following the Japanese conquest, its population was still under a million. Its economy stagnated in the 1950s and early 1960s under British rule, and in 1970 its GDP per head was only $950. Its astonishing transformation into a modern industrial state began after its break from Malaysia in 1965. By 1990 its GDP per head was $12,310,[7] three-quarters that of the UK, achieved with full employment, budget surpluses, low pollution and – by the standards of the most industrial countries – relatively few social problems. By the end of the century Singapore may well pass Britain in terms of GDP per head.

It may have taken three-quarters of a century for Argentina to decline in the world ranking of wealth per head from number two to number fifty, but it took just one generation for Singapore to move from developing world to developed world status. Enormous shifts can take place over quite short periods if countries grow at different rates.

How does growth happen?

If countries understood better the path to higher growth they would take it. Explaining growth is, alas, one of those many problems to which economists have only the most partial of answers.

What we do know, firstly, is that economic growth has been driven

The rich and the poor: GDP per head, at purchasing power parities, in relation to the US[8]

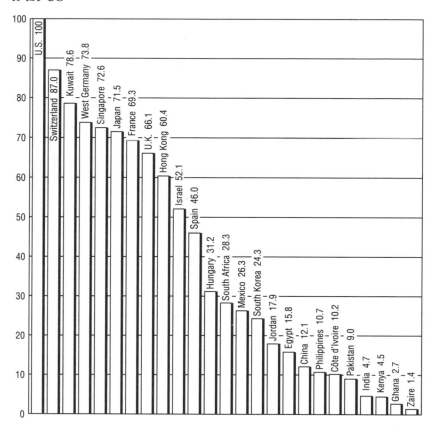

by different things in different countries. Let's look at some examples: pre-industrial France and the city-state of Venice, and modern Hong Kong and New Zealand. Before the industrial revolution, wealth came principally either from land or from trade. In 1500 France was roughly twice as rich as Britain in terms of income per head, thanks largely to more productive agricultural land, but Venice was richer than France without any land at all, its wealth being generated by craftsmanship and trade. Similarly, New Zealand and Hong Kong, which in 1991 had roughly the same GNP per head, generated their wealth quite differently. New Zealand has the asset of plentiful land but very few people, and is therefore a low-cost producer of agricultural goods – nearly 20 per cent of its exports come from primary products (for example timber, minerals); add in meat, dairy products, fish, fruit, vegetables and beverages and the proportion rises to nearly 70 per cent. Hong Kong, on the other hand, has hardly any land and the densest population of any territory on earth, and is therefore a manufacturer and entrepôt trader, with some 90 per cent of its exports being manufactured goods. New Zealand is akin to sixteenth-century France, Hong Kong to sixteenth-century Venice.

Even within Europe, nations with an apparently similar cultural heritage and similar standards of living earn those standards of living in rather different ways. Germany's largest export earnings come from manufactured goods, France's from tourism; Norway receives 33 per cent of its export earnings from oil and gas, Sweden receives virtually none; in 1991 Scotland exported £1,800 million of Scotch whisky alone, while Ireland's entire exports of beverages – whiskey, Guinness, Beamish, bottled water, and so on – were only £145 million. Similar countries are good at different things.

In the industrial revolution, Britain, the first industrial nation to add mass manufacturing to the existing sources of wealth generation, demonstrated to the whole world the power of the factory system. The British model came to be imitated and developed throughout what is still the main industrial world: continental Europe, North America, and Japan. The road to riches seemed to be to industrialize as quickly as possible; in fact, it frequently led to disaster. The forced industrialization of the Soviet Union and eastern Europe, China's Great Leap Forward, the rush to build up industries in many less developed countries did not lead to self-sustaining economic growth but actually inflicted misery on the people and did enormous damage to the environment. What works for one country will not necessarily work elsewhere.

The second thing we know is that the motors of growth change over time, as technical developments increase productivity in, first, agriculture, then manufacturing and ultimately services. As countries develop, their economic structure inevitably changes: agriculture accounts for a smaller and smaller proportion of their output, while industry increases its share; then after a while industry starts to decline proportionately and is replaced by a variety of service industries. Typically, in a so-called 'industrial' country, i.e. a member of the Organization for Economic Co-operation and Development (OECD), services account for 60 to 70 per cent of the GDP.

At the moment there is a curious paradox here. All industrial countries are becoming less and less industrialized, but those which are doing so at the slowest rate seem to be more successful than those which are deindustrializing more quickly.[9] Some figures show this. The process of deindustrialization has gone furthest in the US where, by the end of the 1980s, industry accounted for only 29.2 per cent of GNP; in the UK it was 30 per cent, in France 28.7 per cent. But in Germany and Japan, where deindustrialization has been slower, industry accounted for 38.7 per cent and 41.8 per cent respectively.[10] Germany and Japan are thus generally perceived as more successful, and, in the sense that they have maintained large balance of payments surpluses through the 1980s (until unification in the case of Germany), they have been.

However, despite the view in Britain and the United States that the failure to prevent the run-down of the industrial sector represents a failure of public policy – of education, of the financial services industry, of culture, and of government – the actual answer may be that, although some countries like the US and the UK may have allowed too rapid a switch from industry to services, which has left them with a balance of payments problem (since services tend not to be traded internationally to the same extent as goods), nevertheless strategically these countries will be better placed to benefit from economic growth in the future. Thus Germany and Japan, in seeking to preserve their industry, have a significant structural problem which could put them at an economic disadvantage for at least the next decade.

The main reason why the mature industrial countries cannot preserve an advantage in manufacturing is that the technical developments which increase manufacturing productivity pass with increasing rapidity across national boundaries. The mechanism by which technology transfers varies from industry to industry. In electronics, for example, it may simply be a matter of copying a new product feature, which can take as little as two months. Thus a product developed in the United States or Japan is being made within a matter of weeks in Korea or Taiwan: witness the growth in production of 'clones' of IBM PCs – the majority of the 'clones' are made in Taiwan. Increasingly, however, the multinationals themselves are moving their purchasing and production across national boundaries. The switch of Japanese car production out of Japan and into the US and Europe (particularly Britain) both forces and enables other world producers to copy Japanese technology, and, just as important, Japan's management techniques.

As manufacturing technology moves more and more freely across borders it will become harder and harder for any one country to gain a competitive advantage over another just by making things. Instead, comparative advantage will come from design and marketing, from branding and distribution. In the sense that design and marketing are still manufacturing, even if the goods are actually made elsewhere, so the countries which are good at it will continue to prosper; but their advantage will be narrower in the future than it has been in the past. The more durable way countries will be able to gain an edge over their competitors will be to excel at producing things which are more difficult to copy.

These may not be goods at all; they may be services. One of the really interesting questions for the next generation is whether competitiveness in producing services, rather than producing goods, will take over as the main motor of economic growth. Up to now a country which produces services efficiently may give a higher standard of living to its people, but this standard has had to be built on exports of some form. Because services have been traded internationally to a much smaller extent until recently than goods, a service society has always tended to have difficulty exporting enough of those services to pay for its imports. This has been the problem of the United States and Britain in the 1980s. But international trade in services has been growing faster than trade in goods, and in 1991 Britain became the first country to earn more from invisible exports (services) than from visible ones. This may be a symptom of weak visible exports, but it may also be a sign of the building of a comparative advantage for the future.

During the next century, the gradual shift away from the production of manufactured goods towards the production of services in industrial countries will not happen suddenly or swiftly, and it will not happen at all for the newly industrialized countries, so for the rest of the twentieth century and the first years of the twenty-first, it will remain vitally important to be good at making things. But gradually the comparative advantage will be won by being good at producing services, as the next section argues.

The new motors of growth

The old motors of growth – land, capital, natural resources – no longer matter. Land matters little because the rise in agricultural yields has made it possible to produce far more food in the industrial world than it needs. Capital no longer matters because it is, at a price, almost infinitely available from the international markets for revenue-generating projects; and natural resources in recent times have fuelled economic growth in only a tiny handful of countries, mostly in the Middle East. These quantitative assets, which have traditionally made countries rich, are being replaced by a series of qualitative features, which boil down to the quality, organization, motivation and self-discipline of the people who live there. This is borne out by looking at the way the level of human skills is becoming more important in manufacturing, in private sector services, and in the public sector.

In most areas of manufacturing, the 1980s and 1990s have seen the start of a long retreat from mass production. Superficially not much has changed from the 1950s, when many of the present consumer durable industries grew up. The factories of the motor industry still produce cars, those of the electronics industry still produce TVs. The products are more sophisticated, and the factories, particularly in the electronics industry, may now be located in East Asia instead of Europe or North America, but the way these products are put together is, on the face of it, much the same (many of the plants date back to the immediate post-war or even the inter-war period). But inside the factories of the rich countries there have been enormous changes in the use of labour: instead of large numbers of workers performing repetitive tasks, a much smaller number are performing much more highly skilled jobs.

The effect of these changes is most evident in the motor industry, which is the largest single industry in the world, making the most complicated product which can be mass-produced. Here, three main factors have come together to change radically the type of person which the car companies need to employ:

- Robots now carry out many of the repetitive jobs, but those robots need to be serviced and adjusted
- Consumers demand more variety in the product line and change their tastes more swiftly
- Computers enable the information on changes in consumer taste to be passed directly to factories, which then build to order

As a result, manufacturers are moving part of the way back to the old craft-based manufacturing methods. The aim is to produce individual products to order, but at mass-production costs. The result is that companies need far fewer line-workers, and more people on specialist teams which organize the increasingly complicated tasks that manufacturing processes now require.

In other areas of manufacturing the main theme has been less one of reorganizing production, more one of down-grading the production of goods and upgrading the design, development and marketing of them. It is very easy to make a new consumer electronics product, much harder to think of it in the first place. So the value added is less in execution, more in conception.

In private sector services the need for a well-trained and well-educated workforce is just as important as it now is in manufacturing, but being well-trained is not the same as being well-educated. One of the crucial competitive issues in service industries is whether it is necessary to have a well-educated workforce as well as a well-trained one. It is perfectly possible to provide high-quality services with poorly-educated people, provided that they are well-trained. McDonald's is the best example of the way a high-quality service can be mass-produced, sometimes using people with very little education, to deliver consistent quality in any country in the world, but there are plenty of others. For example, a revolution took place in financial services in the 1970s and 1980s when credit-scoring replaced discretion for most loan decisions. This enabled loan officers to grant credit without needing to make any judgement themselves, and so made it possible to use less experienced and accordingly cheaper staff.

Much the same process is starting to take place in other service areas, like health care, where there is an increase in the use of paramedics and computer diagnostic methods to cut costs. In medicine, however, the process is inhibited by the rigidities of the medical profession, and to some extent by the way health care is financed. The health industry will always need a relatively large labour force simply to care for the large numbers of old and sick, and much of this 'caring' workforce, as opposed to the 'professional' workforce, will always be relatively unskilled. But greater skills should help improve productivity in other areas: the American service industries' genius for training people so that they can deliver quality service at a multitude of delivery points has many further applications in the health industry.

The disadvantage of using poorly-educated, well-trained but not very well-paid people to produce and deliver high-quality services to much richer professionals, as in the American model (evident in its most extreme form in Latin America, rather than the United States), is that the large income and wealth differentials result in high social costs, in particular crime, drug abuse and poor health. The only sensible way forward is to increase the general levels of education of the people in service industries. We know that a better-educated workforce is the way to increased efficiency in manufacturing. It is also the way to increased efficiency in services.

One of the problems in analysing services generally is that there are some services where it is very hard to see any ways in which labour can be used more efficiently, however excellent the education of the people concerned – these might include care of the elderly and taxi-cabs, where the hours simply have to be put in. There are others, such as education and health care, two big, rapidly growing service industries, where more skill *should* increase efficiency, or at least improve the quality of output, but where improving productivity is far more complex.

In education, the more skilled the teacher the better the performance of the taught. Yet the education industry everywhere is using the same techniques that were common 150 years ago: students in groups of ten to forty being taught by a single teacher. The subjects taught have changed, but the teaching method has not. Education has only just begun to think of ways of increasing its output, for example by employing the electronic management techniques which are commonplace in manufacturing. The challenge will be to make education less labour-intensive by using fewer teachers better.

Health care, in the industrial world at least, faces two slightly different challenges to its efficiency. One stems from the way it is financed. As it is largely funded either by insurance schemes or by the state, medical treatment is free to the user at point of delivery. The user pays, of course, but the payment, through an insurance premium or through taxation, is not generally made at the time medical care is received. Since people can absorb almost infinite amounts of health care (even if there is nothing wrong with them, they still go to health farms!), care has to be rationed in some way, but because the consumer does not pay directly it is very hard to force more efficiency into the system at that point. In practice, countries which fund their health care through taxation find it easier to control costs than those which use an insurance system. When the insurance company is paying, bills tend to be scrutinized less closely.

The other challenge is to come to terms with the fact that medicine is reaching the limits of what can be achieved by advances in technology (although genetic engineering and diagnosis may bring new break-throughs). The real advances in public health are coming from changes in people's behaviour – improving their diet, stopping smoking, taking more exercise – rather than by new surgical techniques or new drugs. Up to now, changing people's behaviour – with the exception of anti-smoking campaigns and, post AIDS, the promotion of safer sex – has not been thought of as a responsibility of the health industry.[11] Yet a society in which people lead healthy lives is surely going to have a higher standard of living than one in which resources have to be spent on coping with the illnesses which might have been avoided, had people made different choices.

A motor of growth, therefore – that is, growth in the standard of living, if not in GDP per head – will not just be the productivity of workers in the growing service industries; it will be the lifestyles of whole populations. Societies which work well will get richer not just because their workers work more efficiently, but because their people live their whole lives more efficiently.

Measuring efficiency

So the motors of growth will become efficiency in service industries – the 70 per cent of an economy which is not agriculture or industry. However, being efficient at running service industries is not just a question of doing the jobs as well as possible with the fewest number of people; it also involves not needing to do jobs at all – not needing to spend resources on police or security guards because the streets are safe without them; not needing to spend money on divorce lawyers because people stay married to each other; not needing to spend so much on health care because people lead healthy lives; not needing to spend money on unemployment benefit because a combination of cultural values and education levels enables economies to operate with low unemployment rates.

To illustrate this, let's look at national wealth using GNP as a method of assessing it. There is no other measure, but anyone using it should be aware of its flaws. The main ones are:

– It is distorted by shifts in exchange rates which make countries
   whose currencies are depressed look poorer than they really are

- It counts only economic activity which passes through the money economy, excluding, for example, the labour cost of DIY, or unpaid housework
- It makes it difficult to allow for quality of life, including the costs of pollution and congestion
- It can be inflated by activities which, even if they're necessary, do not increase the standard of living or quality of life in a country, such as court cases

The first flaw can be tackled by taking exchange rates at their purchasing power parity[12] so that rates reflect what the money actually buys. The result is that the differences in GNP are less subject to short term movements in exchange rates. On actual foreign exchange rates Japan ranked in 1993 as the richest large industrial country in the world. But on purchasing power parities the US still had a slightly higher GNP per head than Japan. This more accurately reflects the higher general US living standards.

The second is less of a problem when comparing broadly similar countries than it is when comparing countries at very different stages of economic development. Objectively a developed country like France with a GNP per head of some $20,000 does not seem fifty times as rich as India with a GNP per head of $400, because a lot of activities which go through the money economy in France do not do so in India, such as child care. Within the industrial world itself there are also some problems of measurement: the growth in dual income families within developed countries tends to overstate the size of a country's GNP, because when working spouses pay other people to look after children that appears as economic activity, whereas if they do it themselves for free it does not. However, since the move to dual income families is universal in the industrial world, the distortions are not serious.

For practical purposes it is the third and fourth flaws that matter most. Although adjusting for the third flaw is harder than for the first two, it is increasingly recognized that quality of life matters as much as GNP per head when assessing national wealth, and that, for example, items such as the costs of pollution have to be taken into account when comparing standards of living between countries.

The final flaw of the GNP measure is that it is extremely difficult to distinguish between activities which do increase wellbeing, or what economists call welfare, and those which do not, or which indeed decrease it.

A comparison of two very different activities illustrates this: a rise in crime leading to a rise in the prison population; and more people deciding to take short holiday breaks in luxury hotels. It costs roughly the same to keep someone in a high security prison as it does to stay at a top-flight hotel. Building a new prison or a new hotel appears as economic activity and so adds to GDP. Each extra night spent in either also increases GDP. In that sense both are a form of economic growth; but one decreases welfare, while the other increases it. This flaw is equally well illustrated by the divorce rate in a country. If it rises there will be additional activity for the lawyers who agree the settlements – that shows up as an increase in GDP. But the standard of living in the country has not risen as a result of the rise in the number of divorces; indeed it has almost certainly fallen. A country may *appear* richer if its GDP rises, but the crude measurement of wealth of GDP per head makes no allowance for the way the GDP is generated.

This last problem is enormously important. Any book about growth can only use the measures which exist, keeping firmly in mind that they are only crude measures of welfare. Any book interested in living standards can count the number of cars, telephones or refrigerators and draw conclusions from these statistics, including making an allowance for the costs of pollution and congestion. What is much harder is measuring the value of services, and distinguishing between those services which improve living standards and those which may simply reflect a worsening of them.

If a society is working well, companies do not need to hire security staff to guard their offices; schools do not need to install TV cameras to counter arson attacks by pupils; doctors would not need enormous liability insurance against unwarranted or even frivolous claims, as they do in the US. This discrepancy between GNP per head and welfare goes far to explain why, between 1970 and 1990, when GNP per head climbed by around 30 per cent, living standards in the United States hardly rose.[13] This illustrates one of the central themes developed here: that countries which wish to grow richer will find it much easier to do so if they are able to maintain a more self-disciplined society.

The importance of this theme cannot be overstated, for it reflects a change in the nature of economic competition. Getting societies to run smoothly and cohesively with a well-educated and stable workforce is a different task from running efficient industries or efficient services.

The ability of different countries to shape themselves to this task will determine to a large extent which parts of the world prosper over the next generation; and which, therefore, will be able to exert political influence.

To say this might seem to suggest that order must triumph over chaos. There can be little doubt that order has become a more important element in the competitive mix than it used to be. The frontier spirit of Britain's industrial revolution or of US twentieth-century capitalism, with all its vigour, can make great ships and create giant oil companies, but it does not foster the meticulous attention to detail and marketing that has enabled Japan to flood the world with video-recorders. The top-down control by the bosses of Britain and America in the past has not proved as effective as the bottom-up sense of responsibility generated by the highly-educated workforce of Japan today. But if the added value in societies comes increasingly from services – for example, the programmes which are shown on the video recorders as opposed to the manufacture of the VCRs themselves – then societies must foster creativity alongside order. At one extreme there is a society where people sit in rows and do what they are told. At the other there is one where everybody does their own thing. The key to economic success in the future will be to find a way of balancing the two: group responsibility and individual creativity.

The capacity to learn

If one were to take the changes of the period between 1960 and 1990 and simply project them forward another generation, it would be easy to sketch the world in 2020. In economic terms, the largest economy would be China; the richest large country (excluding the odd off-shore tax haven or oil sheikhdom) would be Japan; East Asia would have become a more important economic region than either North America or Europe; many parts of the developing world, including most of the Indian sub-continent and most of Africa, would continue to be desperately poor. While a majority of North Americans would still be rich, they would be poorer on average than people in equivalent positions in Europe, or East Asia. While most of Europe would be comfortably off – perhaps with income levels on average double that of 1990 – the condition of most of the population of the former Soviet

Union would be bleak. The rich Chinese would be the richest of all, with Hong Kong the financial capital of the world, exporting Chinese savings, which would be borrowed by North America and Europe. (If that seems absurd, consider that in 1992 Hong Kong, with just over 5 million people, was a larger market for a luxury item like cognac than Britain, which has a population eleven times the size.)

In social terms, North America would become an even more divided society, with greater differences of income, even higher crime levels, and large areas of urban deprivation interspersed with pockets of extreme wealth. Society would have become even less stable, with the majority of marriages ending in divorce, so that marriage would become a temporary contract principally to facilitate the upbringing of children. In Europe, social change would have taken different patterns in different countries, but with the common theme of increasing inequalities, and increasing social strains. In northern Europe marriage would have been replaced by consensual union (in Britain in 1991, one-third of births were to unmarried parents)[14]; southern Europe's divorce rates would have risen to North American levels. By contrast, in their different ways, both China and Japan would have remained more socially ordered societies, dedicated to work and (increasingly) conspicuous consumption.

Finally – on present trends – political power would have followed economic power, with China and Japan joining the United States as the dominant political forces in the world. European nations would have a limited voice; Russia – in spite of its nuclear weapons – would have little more influence in the world than Latin America has today.

But it won't happen quite like this. To extrapolate the present is to underestimate the ability of nations both to learn and to make mistakes. Within the industrial world, the private sector is accustomed to the idea of learning best manufacturing practice from others, for not to do so is to risk oblivion, and in traded services a gradual process of cross-border education is also evident. In non-traded services (such as the professions) and in government services, however, this process is more limited.

Nevertheless different countries' practice in non-traded service industries and government, and therefore their economic performance, is likely to converge:

- Some services which are not traded much internationally at the moment are increasingly likely to be (for example: health care, or personal financial services)
- The freedom of action of national governments is being steadily eroded by both commercial forces (like international financial markets) and supra-governmental bodies (like the European Commission)
- Information about the effectiveness of national policies is becoming increasingly widely available, putting pressure on governments to adopt policies which are seen to be successful elsewhere (a good example is the way privatization has spread across the globe)

But countries must be prepared to learn from each other. In places where there is a strong 'not invented here' culture they may not recognize the need to change, particularly if the existing culture seems to be successful in the short-term. Some countries will, for whatever reason, pursue perverse economic policies and as a result make themselves poorer than they need be.

By perverse economic policies, I mean rejecting the market economy. One of the great advantages of writing in the early 1990s is that the supremacy of the market system over the centrally-planned systems is beyond dispute. This was not nearly so clear ten years ago, when the centrally-planned economies seemed to be performing reasonably well – certainly well enough for them still to be considered an attractive model by many developing countries – and there were serious doubts about the ability of markets to work under conditions of high and rising inflation. Viewed from the very long perspective, in 1993 the industrial world is probably still in the quite early stages of re-establishing markets, as opposed to state bureaucracy, as the main method of allocating resources.

This does not mean that there will be little role for governments in economic management over the next thirty years. They will continue to set policy over a large range of issues, and they will continue to provide the basic legal and financial infrastructure under which the markets will operate. They will retain, and maybe increase, their responsibility for ensuring social order and underwriting the lives of the disadvantaged. But they will increasingly look for ways of achieving their aims by regulation rather than intervention: they will see their task as making markets work better, not to replace or even second-guess them.

This implies that national governments will become less powerful. This is already happening for a number of reasons:

- Some power is being passed upwards to supra-national bodies such as the European Union, and more will be passed upwards in Europe if the EU is to gain a common currency
- Some power is being passed downwards to regional authorities to counter regional concerns that their interests are neglected by the centre
- World financial markets set limits for both fiscal and monetary policy for all but a handful of countries
- The need to maintain access to foreign markets determines trade policies, and limits the scope for domestic policies which might interfere with free trade (e.g. subsidies to industry)
- Multinational corporations determine their investment policy partly on the basis of tax treatment, thus limiting the freedom of governments to extract tax from foreign businesses

The process is likely to intensify over the next generation because, in addition to the forces above, an increasing proportion of the highly-skilled will themselves become more mobile. Top talent in many of the world's fastest-growing professional occupations, such as the entertainment business or financial services, can choose where to locate itself, so governments will increasingly find themselves in competition for talent, too. This will not just mean low rates of personal taxation; it will mean creating societies in which mobile talent wants to live.

Where we get to in a generation's time will depend to an enormous extent on where we are now. The rest of this part of the book will look at where the developed world stands in the early 1990s: the different advantages and different handicaps the various regions start with. Part Two will then look at the main forces for change over the next genera-tion, and how these different regions might respond to these. Finally Part Three will sketch how the world is likely to look in 2020. This involves making some judgements on where technological progress will be rapid (such as telecommunications), and where it will be slow (such as construction). It looks at some of the new jobs that will be created over the next generation, mindful of the fact that many of the type of job that were created during the 1980s did not exist in 1960.

Finally, we have to make some assumptions. One important one ought to be made clear at this stage. This is that while there will be catastrophes (natural disasters such as major earthquakes, man-made disasters such as another Chernobyl), there will be no catastrophe on a scale that would threaten for long the wealth-generating process which has continued since the industrial revolution, and certainly no catastrophe that would threaten the existence of humankind – no large-scale nuclear war.

First, however, let's turn to the starting point: where the main regions stand, and what their strengths and their weaknesses are.

TWO

NORTH AMERICA: THE GIANT IN RETREAT

A time of questioning

WHAT HAPPENS TO North America inevitably turns on what happens in the United States, for the US is the locomotive for the entire North American economy. Canada and Mexico, the other two main nations of North America, are interesting in themselves, for both have important political decisions to make: Canada has to decide whether to stay as one country or whether to split into its Anglophone and Francophone parts; Mexico whether to continue down its path of democracy and market reforms. But in economic terms the future of both will be determined elsewhere, by the US.[1]

The early 1990s are seeing a wave of reappraisal sweep across the US, a period of self-examination which has questioned central aspects of the way both the economy and the entire society are organized. It is easy to see why: the 1970s and 1980s were a period of relative economic failure, with living standards hardly rising, and the share of world GNP falling from 48 per cent to 33 per cent over the twenty years.[2] In 1970, US output was 2.6 times as high as that of Japan and Germany combined, but by 1987 the ratio had slipped to 1.3.[3] To some Americans this slippage appears to point to a failure by American business. They do not need to be familiar with the statistics to see the flood of foreign products on their roads and in their homes, or know that Japanese firms have bought such symbols of US capitalism as the Rockefeller Center in New York. Others see a failure by the American financial system, which, they would argue, enriched a few at the expense of the majority. Others blame American education, which produces school leavers who perform badly by comparison with students of the same age in Germany or Japan. And inevitably, many people blame US politicians. However the blame should be apportioned, one stark truth remains: for the first time ever, the present generation of US school leavers cannot expect to have a better material life than their parents. Something has gone wrong.

Yet any balance sheet of the advantages of the United States *vis-à-vis* other nations would still show a large positive. It would show that in absolute terms US workers were still more productive than those of any other nation. The lead is particularly marked in service industries. Although many services are not yet traded internationally – and so America's lead is not yet reflected in her international trade position – services are a larger proportion of US GNP than manufacturing, and so the growth of international services exports should give a significant boost to relative US living standards. In any case the balance sheet would show that real US living standards were still higher than those of any other country. True, using actual exchange rates, the US ranks only tenth in the world, behind Japan, Denmark, Germany, Luxembourg, and all of the EFTA countries bar Austria; but when adjusted to reflect purchasing-power parities – the only sensible way of measuring exchange rates when they fluctuate so much – US per capita GNP in 1991 was higher than that of any other major country in the world, as the table below shows.

If one moves from what America is to what it might be, the factual tally would still be positive. If one takes research excellence as a forward-looking indicator, the US would be on top. It produces more Nobel prizewinners for science and technology than any other country: 159 of the 410 awarded up to 1991, and over half of the 68 prizes awarded during the 1980s. True, the lead might be shortening – witness the rise in Japanese patents; but, broadly speaking, critical mass in research is still with the US. The US would seem to be well-placed in the areas of economic activity which are likely to grow most rapidly, like telecommunications and computer software, financial services, tourism and entertainment, education and health care; and it has relatively little exposure to areas of activity which seem set to stagnate, like mechanical engineering, textiles, and production of most basic consumer durables. Geographically, too, the US has a spread of interests. It has a Pacific zone, linking it psychologically and (though the distances are very long) to some extent physically, with the rapidly-growing countries of East Asia. As the core area of an emerging North American Free Trade Agreement, it has access both to further natural resources in Canada, and to the low labour costs and ready labour supply of Mexico. This gives it a spread of interests which no European

GNP/GDP per capita in 1991[4]

	Actual foreign exchange rates (US$)	PPP* foreign exchange rates (US$)
Luxembourg	23,733	20,834
Germany	25,171	19,797
France	21,011	18,044
Belgium	20,030	17,405
Denmark	25,243	17,305
Italy	19,835	16,739
Netherlands	19,024	16,467
United Kingdom	17,654	16,066
Spain	13,522	12,434
Ireland	12,358	11,184
Portugal	6,465	8,194
Greece	6,778	7,626
TOTAL EC	19,055	16,315
Switzerland	33,222	21,363
Austria	20,951	17,349
Sweden	27,527	17,197
Norway	24,777	16,855
Iceland	24,231	16,565
Finland	25,180	15,985
TOTAL EFTA	26,409	17,870
United States	21,961	21,961
Canada	21,730	19,299
Japan	27,141	19,042
Australia	16,875	15,926
New Zealand	12,426	13,665

*Purchasing power parities

or East Asian nation can match. Its eggs, so to speak, are not all in one basket.

So what is wrong? Part of the problem for the US is that it has made an adjustment out of manufacturing and towards services earlier than most other industrial countries. As in Britain, but not Germany and Japan, US manufacturing industry shrank rapidly as a proportion of GDP during the 1970s and 1980s. The shrinkage was a response to market signals: newly industrialized countries had a comparative advantage over their mature (and higher-waged) competitors, and since manufactured goods are widely traded internationally, these countries gained market share. Some contraction in US manufacturing was inevitable, but the speed at which it took place had negative consequences. One effect was to push the US into a balance of payments deficit during the 1980s and to increase unemployment in regions where manufacturing had been a dominant employer. This almost certainly exacerbated social problems: the lack of jobs for unskilled males was associated with rising numbers of families breaking up and with more crime, though the economic changes were by no means the sole cause of these. However, the US was merely making an adjustment which other mature industrial countries will at some time also have to make. Arguably the process could well have been slowed had US manufacturing been able to move upmarket more quickly, producing higher-value-added products which can more easily absorb high labour costs. But the direction of the change was inevitable, and the advantages of moving early will become clearer in the early years of the next century, as international trade gradually shifts from trade in goods to trade in services.

Already in 1990 services accounted for 36.1 per cent of world trade, having grown during the 1980s at roughly double the rate of merchandise trade.[5] The US generates a larger proportion of its GDP from services – 72 per cent – than any country in the world, and is the largest exporter of services: in 1991 they accounted for 30 per cent of the country's exports.[6] While, as argued later, the scale of some of those service industries may be too large – the law and health care, for example – and reflect inefficiencies in US society, others give the US a genuine comparative advantage in the world economy.

Another part of the explanation for America's relative decline is that its earlier dominance was unsustainable. Some retreat was inevitable. The US position in the industrial world of the 1950s, when it accounted for more than half the industrial world's output, was in large measure a function of the chaos into which Europe and Japan had been plunged by war. The relative positions of North America and western Europe in the 1990s in terms of GNP per head are much the same as they were in the 1890s. Indeed because the US has a larger population relative to western Europe than it had then, it actually has a greater impact on the global economy – quite aside from its intellectual and cultural dominance, discussed below. America's economic position has changed significantly relative to East Asia – and in particular to Japan – since the last part of the last century, but it is just as easy to see this in terms of Asia catching up as in terms of the US falling behind. The concept of catching-up is particularly appropriate in the case of Japan, which had a highly developed pre-industrial society before it was opened to the west after the Meiji restoration in 1868, but which then applied western best practice to its economy and institutions to create a modern industrial state by 1914. Its burst of economic development since 1945 mirrors that earlier achievement.

The final part of the answer lies in the fact that the US does indeed have serious problems; but they are not necessarily those which are usually cited. Nor indeed are the strengths.

The real strengths of North America

The principal strengths of the North American economy are not its natural resources (although thanks to these it is the cheapest food producer in the world), nor its economies of scale (though these help it to be the most efficient manufacturer), but rather two related but slightly different qualities: its culture and its intellect. These are both human resources, rather than physical ones. Most people, thinking of the US, would also admire its scientific skills – scientific advance is certainly brought about by clever and well-educated people. But in economic terms it is the culture of America and the flexibility of thought the US culture encourages which give the country its unique and enviable role in the world.

Visit almost any country in the world and the impact of American culture is immediately obvious: American films, television, videos, popular music, books, newspapers and magazines are ubiquitous. Directly these 'intellectual exports' account for around 3 per cent of total US exports. In absolute terms, this is of course quite small, but they are extremely valuable exports, for they have high added value and low import content. Better still, they are extremely difficult for other countries to develop. The US's largest single export, civil aircraft – around 5 per cent of the total – is being seriously threatened by the European aerospace industry, which had grown from one-third in 1985 to nearly half the size of the US industry by 1990. But US cultural exports are less easily challenged: any country can make films, but only the US has a Hollywood. The cultural dominance of the US also underpins many other exports: the licensing arrangements of Coca-Cola or Walt Disney, or sales of basic products like blue jeans or sneakers where the culture adds the value to something that could be (and is) produced anywhere in the world. The intellectual dominance is the basis of the foreign earnings of drug companies, or software producers; it brings fees of foreign students who attend universities in the US.

The two qualities are different in an important way. Culture cannot be replicated abroad; intellect can. The worlds of both culture and ideas have increasingly become international ones, but when the output of a pop star like Madonna is exported around the world, the receipts (or at least a large part of them) go back to America. (In 1992 she was certainly the entertainment industry's highest paid woman, quite possibly the world's, earning nearly $40 million.[7]) The only way in which other countries can benefit is to buy control of the output. The purchase of the major Hollywood studios by Japanese electronics groups is normally viewed as the hardware companies buying control of the software to push through their equipment, but it could equally well be seen as a country buying the principal thing it cannot replicate: a foreign culture.

Do such foreign purchases matter? Not really. For a generation at least, the US is likely to continue to dominate the industrial world's output of popular culture. But much of the distribution chain for the industry's products will be foreign owned: Japan owns the two largest studios, Columbia and Universal; Australia's News Corporation owns the third, 20th Century-Fox. This might seem alarming to enthusiasts for the US, but it need not be. It is not at all clear that these distribution chains will continue to dominate the output of the entertainment industry, for two reasons. In the first place entry into the business is open: there is nothing to stop new companies being formed, which – while they will not own the film or record libraries of the big groups – might take an increasing share of new production. Second, there is likely to be a change in the balance of power from the distributors to the performers, from the film companies to the writers, actors and producers, from the record companies to the artists. Indeed this is already happening, as the performers become aware that their names, backed by effective public relations, are worth more in sales than the studio or record companies' names, backed by effective distribution: it is the artist that sells. So while some of the industry's earnings may accrue to the new owners of the distribution chain, the lion's share of those earnings will be retained in the US. The US position as an exporter of culture would only be threatened if the world's tastes were to change radically or the culture itself were to lose its vitality. Either could certainly happen, but there is no sign of this yet.

The intellectual vigour of the US is as strong as its cultural vitality, but the country's ability to profit from it is less secure. This is partly a question of the traditionally generous ethic of the education industry: its desire to spread the word. Ideas generated in Harvard, MIT, or Berkeley are published in the scientific literature for others to share, partly because the mission of these institutions is to explain and to teach, partly because the whole process of scientific endeavour involves the sharing of information. Of course there is some protection: the intellectual output of the US is not generated solely in the universities; it is carried on in corporate research laboratories and in defence establishments, where it can be sheltered until it is ready for commercial or military use, and in the scientific field, too, the patent system naturally gives further protection.

There is one area of US technological excellence where it has been possible to reap the commercial rewards of brain-power: military equipment. The US is the world's largest arms exporter and has devoted a very high proportion – some 60 per cent – of its Research and Development to the defence industry. Leaving aside any moral arguments, from a purely commercial point of view this is almost certainly too high: while in total R&D expenditure the US compares quite favourably to Germany or Japan, in R&D for non-military purposes it lags badly. The arms industry has, for most of the period since the Second World War, been a secure and profitable export market, but the commercial benefits to the US of having a large arms industry have diminished with the collapse of the Soviet Union and are likely to shrink further. This is not particularly because the world will become a safer place – in some respects it will become a more dangerous one – but more because potential buyers will find it increasingly hard to find the resources to pay for the ultra-high-technology military equipment that the US produces. They will turn instead to cheaper products from Russia and China.

If there are limits to the degree of protection that can be given to intellectual property in the scientific fields, protection in the non-scientific fields is even harder. Probably the best work on the process and nature of innovation has been done by Henry Ergas at the OECD in Paris. In his view the two most important innovations from the US in recent years have been the personal computer and McDonald's hamburgers. The first put computing power in the hands of ordinary people, on their desks or in their homes, whereas previously it had been available only to large organizations, and then to a handful of specialists. The second applied factory principles of cost management and quality control to a service industry, enabling consistent quality to be delivered in a multiplicity of outlets around the world.[8]

These two innovations have brought many benefits to the US, but the benefits have been shared with the rest of the world. True, the main promoter of the personal computer, IBM, did for a while draw considerable profits from its PCs. True, the two companies which developed the microprocessor, Intel, and the operating software, Microsoft, flourished as a result of their innovations. (In 1993 Microsoft passed IBM in its stock market value.) But the hardware of the PC was quickly imitated by the reverse engineers of East Asia, who found that they could produce PC 'clones' much more cheaply than American factories. In 1992, 90 per cent of the IBM clones were made in Taiwan. The result was that in hardware terms, at least, the US failed to benefit. Indeed since the PC undermined the mainframe business of IBM, its main promoter may even have been a net loser from the project. IBM itself is now no longer convinced that it should be in the hardware business and is looking more closely at software.

McDonald's as a company has benefited greatly from its ability to innovate – in 1992 it had 13,000 outlets in sixty-three countries, and worldwide sales of $21.9 billion, which would put it at number 54 in Fortune magazine's Global 500 ranking of the largest corporations in the world, ahead of Britain's ICI, Japan's Mazda, the US's Xerox, and a host of other major international players. Its influence is such that the UK's respected newspaper *The Economist* even uses the price of a McDonald's 'Big Mac' to demonstrate international purchasing power parities between currencies ('burgernomics'!). But by its very nature, as a franchise operation it has to be open about its management techniques. Like a university it must export its knowledge: it must teach its franchise operators how to run their business. (It is no coincidence that at the headquarters of McDonald's in Oak Brook, Illinois, there is a 'university' to teach the culture of hamburgerdom: this is a knowledge-intensive business.) The basic product is impossible to protect, for it is not difficult to reverse engineer a hamburger. As a result, there are now several fast food chains which apply the same techniques as McDonald's. Yet McDonald's has continued to prosper. Why? It must be thanks in part to general good management: for example, the ability to spot changes in social trends such as the move towards more healthy

eating, and to adjust the products to that trend. But it must also surely
be that McDonald's is protected in part by the American culture. As
with Coke, people buy it because it is the real thing.

The obvious conclusion to be drawn from the experience of IBM is
that while it is possible for the US to maintain a competitive advantage
in fields where the principal asset is brain-power – software in the case
of Microsoft, high technology in the case of Intel – it is very hard to
do so in the mass production of a consumer good, unless there is some
powerful cultural content. The obvious conclusion to be drawn from
McDonald's is that US culture is indeed a marketeer's dream: a unique
selling proposition which no other country can copy.

The United States has many other great economic strengths. Fore-
most among these are the productivity of US industry and commerce
noted above, and the flexibility and capacity of the US financial services
industry. The US financial system is impressive:

- It has the world's largest venture capital industry, helping new
      companies start and small-to-medium-sized ones expand
- It has a substantial occupational pension scheme, covering 92
      per cent of its workforce[9]
- It has relatively low transaction costs
- Its dependence on equity finance, rather than bank loans, makes
      it robust in difficult times
- It is a world leader in its ability to innovate and create new
      financial market products.

This last strength may also be a weakness: there is a popular view that
financial innovation got out of hand during the 1980s boom, and that
manipulating money became more important than generating new
wealth. These criticisms are not unique to the US: Akio Morita, chairman of Sony Corporation, said: 'Only manufacturing can provide
employment opportunities of quality, scope and number . . . The service sector can only survive if there is a productive manufacturing
sector to serve.'[10] In fact, Sony itself bought the Columbia film studios
in Hollywood, and one-fifth of its revenues now come from the film
and music business – another example of 'hardware' producers feeling
the need to diversify into 'software'. Yet there is some truth in the
view that manufacturing may suffer if the service sector grows too fast.
If the best and the brightest in the land go into the financial services
industry, that talent is not available for other industries, including

manufacturing. In a sense this is manufacturing's fault: it should be able to offer good opportunities to able people. A more legitimate criticism is that, for all its advantages, there have also been some structural weaknesses in the US financial system, in particular in the Savings and Loans industry. Losses here during the 1980s are estimated to have cost the taxpayer some $500 billion, as these were guaranteed by the US Federal authorities. But in spite of these problems, the capability of the US financial services industry is still a significant strength.

Finally, at its best, US industry is remarkably responsive to changing consumer demand. Companies pick up signals from the marketplace quickly, and generally are adept at responding with new products or services. The economy as a whole also adapts quickly to changing tastes, changing social circumstances, changing demography – it is very good at creating employment, at finding new ways to supply needs, even if the quality of the jobs created is low. The more rapidly society changes, the greater the pressure will be for all countries to adapt their economies to meet these changes. Americans are quick on their feet compared with Europeans, or even the consensus-driven Japanese.

The real weaknesses

Americans worry about their manufacturing industry, yet it is the most productive in the world. In all areas US productivity is higher than that of Germany, while in many it remains higher than Japan.[11] People in the US worry about some of their service industries on the grounds that these can only be sustained by using low-paid (often immigrant) labour, yet these – insofar as it is possible to measure service industry productivity – are also the most efficient in the world. However, there are competitive weaknesses in both manufacturing and services in the US.

In manufacturing perhaps the most worrying is the extent to which technological progress in electronics has shifted away from the US, in particular towards Japan. This lead is evident even in areas where the US is the dominant producer of the end product. For example, during the Gulf War in early 1991, when the world was dazzled by the technical prowess of US military hardware, Japan pointed out that a high proportion of the weapons used in the war incorporated Japanese electronics patents. However, given the absolute levels of productivity of the US economy, concern about the health of manufacturing industry should be muted.

In services, the most serious weakness would seem to be the slow growth of productivity. This rose at only about 0.5 per cent a year during the 1980s, despite large investment in technology, in particular in telecommunications equipment (especially the fax) and personal computers. This has led to concern that US service industries were not applying new technology efficiently, but it is difficult to take these concerns too seriously, for it is hard to believe that the enormous investment now being made in computers, akin to nineteenth-century investment in railways and sewers, will not pay off.

Given the variety of activities lumped together under 'services', the difficulty of measuring productivity in the service sector, and the high absolute levels achieved by US services, it is difficult to see service industry productivity as a core problem of the US. Indeed, it would seem that productivity did climb sharply in 1991/2, when the pressure of recession and deregulation forced many industries, in particular retailing and financial services, to trim labour costs. It is of profound importance that the US continues to get this area right. A recent study by management consultants McKinsey, comparing productivity in five service industries – banking, restaurants, airlines, retailing and telecommunications – in the US, Japan and Europe, showed that the US was ahead of the field on almost every measure.

So where are the problems? The most serious weaknesses of the US economy are essentially social or cultural. The issues are of three main kinds:

- Problems associated with social disruption of some form or other, particularly crime (these principally affect the poorer socio-economic groups)
- Problems associated with bureaucracy and waste (these affect the richer groups)
- Attitudes towards saving and education (these affect the whole society)

The first group of problems includes the sad litany of crime, drug and alchohol abuse, violence and family breakdown. These are seen principally, and quite properly, as social problems with some economic roots, but viewed in terms of international competitiveness, they are also economic problems. Coping with social problems uses up scarce resources, and thus places the country at a competitive disadvantage *vis-à-vis* countries which do not need to deploy resources in this way.

Crime is the most obvious cost: in 1990 there was one violent crime every 17 seconds, and a crime against property every 2 seconds. Most Americans can expect to face theft three or more times in their lives.[12] The US manages to absorb 1.3 per cent of its GDP in law and order.[13] But this is only part of the bill for crime. The US private police force is now larger than the official one: there are 800,000 security guards, compared to 485,000 official police.[14]. And naturally, since even a combination of public and private police does not guarantee safety, crime levels are reflected in higher insurance rates. So the private sector is having to pay for security in at least three different ways: it has to fund a police force which is proportionately at least as large as that of other industrial nations; it has to pay in addition for private policing; and it has to pay higher insurance premiums.

The costs of private policing can be very high, but they are not normally accounted for separately in national figures – they are absorbed within the normal run of labour costs of the industry concerned. A large proportion of the labour cost of a shopping mall goes on security staff, rather than sales staff, but this is absorbed in the total labour costs of the enterprise. These costs are very high by international standards. Shopping malls are not, by their nature, in the internationally traded sector – the relative costs of security in manufacturing industry are lower, but security costs constitute a growing burden on US industry. Similarly, the costs of private security paid for by individuals, rather than businesses, is also absorbed in other charges. The people who live in gated communities in the US are paying part of the charges for maintenance and upkeep of grounds; but they are also paying for the service which encouraged them to chose to live there – guards on the gate. The total cost of private security was estimated as far back as 1980 to be some $21.7 billion[15] and although there was some evidence that, by the late 1980s, this has been effective in cutting burglary, it had had no apparent effect on levels of violence against the person.[16]

Drug abuse also places a burden on the whole of society. Though the immediate sufferers are disproportionately in the lower socio-economic groups, the cost of coping is paid by all. Whilst the actual costs are unknown, they have been estimated at some $60 billion, half of which represents lost productivity by drug users, a third the costs of drug-related crime, and the remainder expenditure on welfare and health care services.[17] The drug trade is of course also a huge unrecorded industry, financing some Latin American countries and giving 'employment' to young males in inner city areas – but it is a profoundly destructive industry

Another set of costs is imposed by family break-up. In 1960 nine in every thousand marriages ended in divorce, and only 5 per cent of children were born to unmarried women; but by the end of the 1980s this had risen to 21 divorces in a thousand, and some 27 per cent of children.[18] The economic cost of family break-up to the country as a whole is less widely appreciated. Even after adjusting for the greater poverty of one-parent families, it appears that their children are more likely to leave school early and to be unemployed than children from homes with two parents present. The conventional family unit is an efficient mechanism for combining bringing up children and earning a living. It is particularly efficient when both parents work and the grandparents, uncles and aunts pitch in to help run the family – the standard pattern of life in the industrial countries two generations ago, and still the norm in much of the world today. It may be difficult to quantify precisely the economic cost to US society of the breakdown of this pattern, but in both the short and long term the cost will be significant.[19]

It is much easier to identify insurance costs. Roughly half the total insurance business in the world, measured by premium income, is carried out in North America. That reflects the material wealth of the society as much as its tensions – poor societies do not spend much on insurance because there is little of value to insure. It also reflects the US tradition of looking to litigation, rather than the state, for redress. Insurance is the private sector's way of paying for services which, in many countries, would be provided through the tax net, and it gives an easy, if crude, measure of the cost of coping with disorder – a country with a good car accident record will have lower motor insurance premiums than one with a poor record. What the US spends on insurance reflects in part, at least, the costs of coping with what is, by European or East Asian standards, an unusually volatile society.

Insurance also looms large in the second group of inefficiencies, those concerning waste. This is not waste in the usually-understood sense of wasting natural resources but rather in the sense of rising transaction costs: the extent to which wealth is eaten up by what Jonathan Rauch of the *National Journal* calls the 'parasite economy'.[20] In any advanced society some resources have to be devoted to protecting and organizing wealth creation, and not to wealth creation itself. All countries need to spend something on national defence to protect the country from external threats, and they also need to devote resources to public administration, legal services, and regulation of various sorts. Democracies need to devote resources to informing and representing the views of the electorate (and arguably dictatorships need to devote resources to repression!). The issue here is: does the US devote too much resource to these non-wealth-creating activities?

The answer is surely yes. Over the forty years between 1950 and 1990 these so-called 'transaction activities' grew much faster than GDP. As a result Americans were poorer than they should have been given the rise in per capita GNP that took place over this period. Just how much poorer is open to debate, but it has been calculated that growth in these transaction activities accounted for more than one-tenth of the overall growth that appeared to have taken place.[21]

One such activity is the law. Around three-quarters of the world's lawyers live in the US. In 1960 it had 260,000 lawyers; in 1990 there were 756,000. Not only is this an enormous figure by international standards (Japan with half the population of the US manages with less than 15,000 lawyers[22]), but there is some evidence that the number of lawyers in a country is in inverse proportion to its growth rate.[23] Too many lawyers, so it would seem, actually destroy wealth.

Another 'transaction' cost is political lobbying. Here too there has been an astonishing rise. There were 4,900 trade associations in 1956; 23,000 in 1989. The number of political lobbyists registered with the US Senate soared from 365 in 1960 to 40,111 in 1992.

The principal reason for this is the rise in regulation. The more regulation there is, the more worthwhile it is for organizations to devote resources to trying to influence it. One of the themes of US government in the 1980s was deregulation, and this certainly took place in some areas, but nevertheless the overall burden of regulation rose. In 1992 the cost was put at some $400 billion or $4,000 per household, a burden in itself[24] – but worse, in a way, is the impact of regulation on growth. Federal regulation has been calculated to take 0.5 per cent off productivity growth, which in turn is bound to reduce the growth of GDP by a similar amount.

The burden of inappropriate regulation is often discussed in the US, but because the costs are absorbed in the price of products and are therefore hard to identify, there is little political capital to be made by challenging it. Not so in the case of medical costs, which emerged as a big political issue during the 1992 presidential election, and which the Clinton Administration seeks to reduce. Indeed, whichever administration is in power for the next two decades is likely to be preoccupied with trying to curb the cost of the US medical service. The US spends over 13 per cent of its GNP on medical care – double the proportion of UK or Japan (see the table below) and more per capita on a purchasing-power-parity basis than the two together – $2,867 per head compared with $1,043 for the UK and $1,267 for Japan.[25] Yet on what is probably the best general indicator of medical care, infant mortality, its performance is worse that most of the rest of the industrial world. Moreover, despite the enormous resources devoted to medical care, 20 per cent of the US population is uncovered by medical insurance.

Health Expenditure as a percentage of GDP in 1991[26]

	Total	Public
Belgium	7.9	7.0
France	9.1	6.7
Luxembourg	7.2	6.6
Italy	8.3	6.5
Netherlands	8.3	6.1
Germany	8.5	6.1
Ireland	7.3	5.6
United Kingdom	6.6	5.5
Spain	6.7	5.5
Denmark	6.5	5.3
Portugal	6.8	4.1
Greece	5.2	4.1
Japan	6.6	4.7
Canada	10.0	7.2
United States	13.4	5.9

The burden on the American taxpayer is such that in 1992 the US government was spending only marginally more, relative to GDP, than the British, but in Britain this covered over 80 per cent of the cost of the nation's medical care, while in the US it covered only just over 40 per cent.[27] The burden on business is such that in 1989 Lee Iacocca, chairman of Chrysler Motors, estimated that medical insurance for its workforce added $700 to the price of each car the company built, compared with an average of $246 for Japanese car makers.[28] All industrial countries already find it hard to contain medical costs. They will find it harder to do so as their populations age, for this will inevitably increase the demand for medical services. This demographic shift makes it all the more vital that countries take control of their medical costs: this is a key to competitiveness in the next century.

Reforming US health care will be peculiarly hard because the problem is so complex. The burden is carried partly by the taxpayer, but it is also borne by US industry, which has to provide medical cover for its workers. The system has inadequate cost control at many levels; it also has excessive administrative costs, for some 40 per cent of the money spent on medical care is absorbed in insurance and administration charges. Malpractice insurance further increases costs (liability premiums nearly tripled over the period 1982–89), accounting for one-third, or more, of doctors' charges, and it also encourages waste – the profession's fear of malpractice suits encourages it to carry out tests for which there is little medical case, but which, if not carried out, might give rise to litigation. Finally, by world standards US medics are paid too much for their skill levels.

The third set of problems facing the US economy relates to US attitudes to saving and education. Both, in different ways, are about deferred gratification – putting off pleasure today for some greater good in the long term. That is something which saving self-evidently requires, for money saved is money not spent, and it applies just as well in education. Education may or may not require an investment by parents; it may or may not require students to take part-time jobs to see themselves through college; but it invariably requires students to work at their studies instead of either working for money or having more leisure. They will, almost always, get back any income foregone in the form of higher earnings in later life, but in the short-term there is a cost.

The figures for savings show that the US saved less than any other large advanced industrial nation during the second half of the 1980s:

The damage done by low savings is fourfold:

- It tends to reduce investment and so inhibit growth (though a
   qualification should be made here, for low investment may
   be a cause of low savings as well as an effect)
- If savings are lower than investment requires, there is likely to
   be a deficit on the current account of the balance of payments.

This happened in the US during the 1980s, when cumulative current account deficits turned the country from being the world's largest creditor nation to the world's largest debtor in less than ten years

- If people have few savings (including occupational pension schemes) the burden of supporting them in old age will have to be borne by the state, which will have to tax the next generation of workers to provide for the retired
- It exacerbates social problems, for individuals or families with few savings are less able to cope with economic reverses: loss of a job, divorce, illness and so on

Gross saving as a percentage of GDP 1985–89[29]

United States	16.4
Japan	32.7
Germany	24.0
France	20.1
Italy	20.9
United Kingdom	16.8
Canada	19.4

Just why the US should have lower savings than other industrial countries is particularly odd when one considers that it has a less well-developed welfare system than Europe and, in some respects, Japan. The answer is almost certainly cultural. Other Anglo-Saxon societies also show fairly low savings ratios (Britain, though higher than the US, is low by European standards) – the pressure to spend, rather than save, must surely be associated with the emphasis on advertising in Anglo-Saxon societies: advertising in the US is equivalent to 1.36 per cent of GDP, against 0.85 per cent in Germany and 0.89 per cent in Japan.[30] Anglo-Saxon societies also have highly developed credit institutions, giving much easier access to credit than in, say, Germany or Japan, but to say that is not to explain why the US is different: advertising is highly developed because the society wants and values that service; consumer credit is easily available because there is demand for it, for if no-one wanted to borrow there would be no institutions providing the loans. The explanation lies in something deeper. Maybe it is associated with the cultural self-confidence of North American society and a generation's experience of material wealth. Maybe it is a function of Americans' physical sense of security, the fact that the US has not, unlike the whole of continental Europe and most of East Asia, been invaded by a hostile power within living memory. Whatever the reason, the fact that Americans don't save much is a serious competitive disadvantage in the post-industrial world.

So are their attitudes to education. That the best of North American education is the best in the world is hardly in dispute, as the, albeit crude, measure of Nobel prizewinners produced would testify. The US also scores highly in the proportion of school-leavers passing on to higher education as the table shows:

Proportions entering higher education[31]

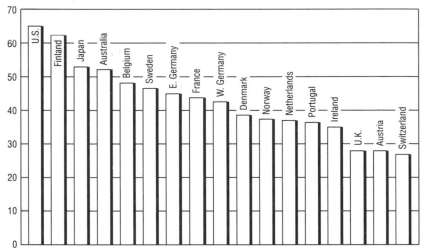

And it spends a lot on education – over 5 per cent of GDP on public education alone. But the educational achievement levels of the majority of students are very poor: considerably worse than Europe, far worse than Japan, Korea or Taiwan (for details, see the table on page 78). Squaring the resources put into education with the quality of output leads to some uncomfortable conclusions.

The first is that the problem is the students, not the educational system itself. Of course the system has serious shortcomings, in particular in the inner cities. The fluidity of the US population, with large-scale immigration from groups where English is not the first language, inevitably gives rise to changes in the ethnic mix of pupils coming into the schools, and makes it difficult for the education system to adapt and cope with different children's special needs. There is probably, also, a resource problem, with cutbacks in the school system of the 1970s and 1980s reducing the quality of education available. But the hard fact remains that Japan, spending far less on education than the US, gets far better results.

Confirmation of this comes from the evidence that foreign students do better in the US educational system than do home students. Much has been made of the fact that Asian students perform better than white Americans, who in turn perform better than Hispanics or Blacks.[32] Less attention has been paid to the fact that 13 per cent of all new PhD scientists entering the US workforce are foreign nationals. In engineering the position is even more extreme: 36 per cent of engineering PhDs are foreign.[33]

The second conclusion is that the educational system is too closely focused on university-level research and not sufficiently on teaching at the primary and secondary levels in schools. The quality of research in most fields in the US is the best in the world; the average level of attainment by pupils leaving school is the worst in the industrial world. The US educational system gives great benefits to the rest of the world in that it is where the majority of the great scientific discoveries are being made, but it does not ideally match US needs by supplying a broadly-skilled, literate, numerate and self-disciplined workforce. The best is wonderful; but the best may be the enemy of the good.

The capacity to change

America's economic strengths are frequently those characteristics which the US either takes for granted or even undervalues: the productiveness of its industry, the willingness to transform the economy away from manufacturing towards services, and the power of its intellect and culture. Its weaknesses are things that people in the US quite often regard as strengths: the individualism, even the freedoms, of ordinary Americans; their 'I want it and I want it now' expectations; even the self-image of the US as Number One nation. The task Americans face is to maintain their nation's vigour while becoming more self-disciplined in the way that vigour is applied to economic affairs.

Most people would see this task as a political issue, and in the sense that the country looks to politicians to guide it, it is. The US system of government certainly has structural deficiencies which make it diffi-

cult for the country to respond to change. Political commentators
identify in particular the relatively limited powers of the president,
and the dominance of Congress by special interest groups. But it is
unrealistic to blame politicians, for the ability of US society to adapt
is at its root an attitudinal issue: politicians usually try to do what
they are asked to do by the people who elect them. The long-term
significance of the Clinton presidency will be as a measure of the
country's ability to adapt.

The best way to gauge the ability of the US to respond to the
changes it needs to make is to identify the areas in which change would
help economic performance. The most important of these are:

- A change in fiscal policies. If ordinary Americans will not save
    enough to fund investment, then the central government will
    have to do it for them. Ideally the US ought to be running
    a large budget surplus, for its deficit exacerbates the problem
    of low personal savings. A set of decisions made in the 1980s
    will ensure that Americans will be relatively highly taxed
    through at least the first decade of the next century, even if the
    deficit reduction programme of President Clinton succeeds
- Reform of medical services. High medical costs will handicap
    the US for a generation, for even if the Clinton reforms
    succeed in curbing the growth of costs, these will remain the
    highest in the world
- Reform of education. Resources need to be switched from
    research to teaching, but more importantly, US students
    will need to show the sort of application that Japanese or
    Chinese students do if the US is to retain its lead in world
    living standards
- A change in the attitude of government in its role as a regulator,
    so that it takes into account the costs of intervention and
    regulation, and the need to balance the gains against these costs
- A reduction in crime. The moral case against crime (or at least
    most crime) is beyond dispute, but the economic case
    frequently escapes notice. The US will in all probability
    continue to have relatively high crime levels for another
    generation, but if crime continues to rise the effect will be
    to impose a grave burden on its international
    competitiveness
- A restoration of 'family values', the toughest issue of all. The

inverted commas are necessary because the phrase has become a coded attack on people who, for whatever reason, choose not to marry and have children. To list this as an economic issue is not to make that attack. The point is simply that the conventional family unit is an efficient mechanism for combining bringing up children and earning a living. One does not need to call for a return to the extended family to acknowledge that single parenthood and divorce make people, and countries, poor.

The prospects for the United States, and hence the whole of North America, turn on the ability of the country to make tough choices. The difficulty it faces is that while some of America's problems – like balancing the Federal budget or reforming health care – can be tackled from the centre, others – like fighting crime, or cutting the divorce rate – can be changed only by altering people's attitudes. Those problems which can be tackled from the centre may or may not respond to whatever measures are taken, but at least it is easy to see where to begin. This is not the case with those problems which stem from people's behaviour and attitudes, particularly when there is no consensus on the desirability of such change. Most people would agree that rising crime is unsatisfactory, but most would also shy away from draconian measures to curb crime, such as gun control or legalizing drugs. Without a consensus, it is very hard to employ the weapon of social pressure against anti-social activities.

A bleak picture of American society was painted by Alistair Cooke, the veteran British-born broadcaster, who has lived in the US for many years. America's problem, he argued, was not one of economic failure, nor even the idea popularized by Paul Kennedy of 'imperial overstretch', but one of moral decay:

> The city crime rates are regularly beyond those of all but the worst previous years, and random street crime at night matches the jottings of eighteenth-century diaries. Drugs are a pestilence afflicting all classes and every age. We have just wakened to the discovery that for a long time, maybe for several decades, public education in America has been setting such easy and dithering standards that, at the least, a large minority, perhaps a majority, of high school graduates are, in common with their European and Asian fellows, semi-literate.[34]

Alistair Cooke noted other symptoms of cultural breakdown: the abuse of liberty, the failure of the courts to define and constrain obscenity, the steep decline in public manners, and, in Gibbon's phrase, 'freakishness masquerading as originality, enthusiasm pretending to vitality'. He concluded that there would be some great historical turning point, some dramatic outcome such as a second American Civil War, the arrival of a populist dictator, or 'an emergency return to the benevolent form of national socialism created by Franklin Roosevelt in the first New Deal'.

One must be very careful not to make a blanket condemnation of American society, even if one recognizes to some extent the symptoms of moral decay sketched by Alistair Cooke. Not only do other countries show many of the same trends; there are in the US counter-forces which are already working in the opposite direction. What one can reasonably say is that the US, with its enormous cultural diversity and its tradition of individualism, will find it hard to rebuild the disciplines which it needs if it is not to be at a serious competitive disadvantage in the world.

Yet there is a paradox here. Many of the qualities which make the US economy successful, and which will become even more important in the coming decades, require a climate not just of intellectual freedom but of licence. The intellectual freedom produces a computer operating system like Microsoft's Windows. The licence, sometimes the licence to shock, produces the singer Madonna. Part of her massive earnings in 1992 came from her book, a book with a series of brilliantly-produced photographs of her, but one which would probably have been declared illegal thirty years earlier.[35] The naughtiness is an essential part of the appeal, an essential part of this product that the US is exporting to the world. Without a climate which accepts the naughtiness, America would be unable to generate much of the culture which it exports to the world, but it is not a climate which encourages, for example, stable marriages or even stable relationships.

Many Americans would be disturbed to have Madonna cited as an important cultural export – she is a long way from the Chicago Philharmonic – but cultural exports take many forms. US exports of records are larger than its exports of wheat; add in films, videos and books and together these cultural exports approach the value of exports of civil aircraft, the one industry in which the US is still world leader. The point about Hollywood is that the vision of American culture it exports so successfully is one which has been, from the perspective of the early

1990s, setting a bad example for American society. Most people do not spend their days machine-gunning scores of other human beings, as Rambo does. But some boys in the ghettos do.

The US needs to rebalance its priorities. It needs to retain its intellectual and cultural creativity and yet instill in its people a greater degree of self-discipline. It must do this if it is not to find itself playing a smaller and smaller role in the world in the next century. It may remain the only superpower for another generation, but unless it can make a serious attack on the problems noted above, relative decline will continue. That need not lead to a catastrophe on the lines predicted by Alistair Cooke, but it would mean that the bout of soul-searching from the early 1990s would continue for another generation at least, as Americans came to terms with their reduced influence in the world.

Its culture, however, is set fair for at least a generation to come. In the past, civilizations in economic decline have sometimes become the main exporters of cultural values, as Greece gave its culture to Rome. As nations quickly copy the class leaders in industrial techniques, so culture, the driving force behind many of its service industry exports, becomes relatively more important. If this is right, there is an enormous opportunity for the United States to profit from the boom in international trade in services. If it can do so, it need not be condemned to continue the slow relative decline of the post-Second World War years.

THREE

EUROPE: THE BABBLE OF MANY TONGUES

Diversity or division?

IF THE UNITED STATES has a diversified economy unified by a common culture, Europe, certainly western Europe, is rapidly developing a common economy separated by diverse cultures. Naturally the process of economic integration has gone furthest in the original six countries of the European Community: the Netherlands, for example, had exports in 1991 equivalent to 47 per cent of its GDP, of which the vast majority went to other EC countries. All western European economies live by trade. In 1991 Germany exported 25 per cent of its output, France and Britain 18 per cent, and Italy 15 per cent. By contrast the United States exported only 7 per cent and Japan, despite its fearsome reputation as an exporter, sold only 9 per cent of its output abroad. Even European countries outside the EU have economies which are closely integrated with it. Switzerland, Austria, Norway and Sweden have all been part of a western European economic system since the 1950s, even though they are not yet EU members. Switzerland looks unlikely to join for a generation at least, yet it manages to export proportionately even more than Germany: 27 per cent of GDP.

Part and parcel of this integration is intense specialization. European nations export a lot, but they import a lot too. They have to import because in many cases the products are simply not made in the country concerned. Norway, Denmark and Switzerland, three of the richest countries not just in Europe but in the world, do not make any cars, the most important consumer product of all. In any European supermarket a large proportion of the household goods will have come from other countries, as a glance at the labels printed in half a dozen languages would reveal. In the US or Japan only the luxury items tend to be imported and it would be surprising to have labels printed in more than one language. So the European economies are glued together by mutual self-interest: unlike the US or even, to some extent, Japan, European countries have to trade with each other to supply their daily needs.

Specialization has led to wealth. Western Europe is rich by any standards: on the economist's measure of GDP per head at market exchange rates it is, on balance, richer than North America; on the more realistic basis of purchasing power parity exchange rates it is on average about 80 per cent of North American levels. It is also rich in terms of quality of life, the range of public services, the availability of leisure and the variety of ways of using that leisure. It has managed to create a lifestyle, or rather, since there are large cultural differences across the Continent, a variety of lifestyles, which the rest of the world finds deeply enviable. Out of the five largest tourist destinations, three are in western Europe: France, Spain and Italy. Between them these three countries attract more foreign visitors than the whole of North America.[1]

The renaissance of western Europe after the devastation of war has been widely attributed to the spur of economic integration provided first by the EEC (the 'Common Market'), and then by the European Community when the EEC sought a wider remit following the Single European Act in 1986. Naturally the development of a free trade area will have stimulated cross-border trade and hence, to some extent, economic growth. But countries outside the EC (which became the European Union in 1994) like Sweden, Austria and Switzerland managed to grow just as rapidly as their neighbours inside it. In fact the countries of the European Free Trade Area, in practice non-EU western Europe, have a higher average GDP per head than the members of the EU. The EU is certainly a part of Europe's success story, but it is only a part, and maybe not the most important one.

The political division of Europe after the Second World War meant that the countries of the Soviet bloc failed to share in the economic growth of the west. In 1989, when the Berlin Wall came down, even the more developed central and eastern European countries like East Germany, Hungary and Czechoslovakia had living standards little higher than those of Britain and France on the eve of war in 1939. Central and eastern Europe will rejoin the west, forming a common European economic area, but the process of integration will be slow. The experience of the rapid 'force-fed' integration of East Germany shows that even with enormous financial transfers from the west it is simply not possible to develop an efficient market economy quickly.

Seen from the perspective of the early 1990s this issue of the integration of east and west is one of the two great political questions which Europe must confront; the other is the pace and extent of integration within western Europe itself. The way these two issues are tackled will have a material effect on the political map of Europe in the next century. But there are a string of economic issues which are at least as important as either of these:

- Will the various European economies continue to be as innovative in the first part of the next century as they have been in the second half of the present one?
- How far should economic specialization go when countries remain separate sovereign states?
- Is the European way of providing social services, in particular health care (financed largely out of taxation, and sometimes provided by state enterprises), more or less effective than the North American or East Asian models?
- Can the 'peace dividend', the resources released by the reduction in armed forces in what was for forty years the most militarized region in the world, be used positively to improve the welfare of Europe's population?
- Perhaps most important, is the cultural, attitudinal and linguistic diversity of Europe a strength or a weakness in economic life? It is self-evidently a political weakness, for even members of the EU find it difficult to agree, but nevertheless may also be a source of economic strength.

The next sections of this chapter seek to identify both the real economic strengths of Europe, and the weaknesses. But first, consider a curious paradox: the most 'European' companies in Europe are generally not European at all, but the subsidiaries of American multinationals. In the motor manufacturing sector, the native companies of various EU members still largely make their cars in the home country: Peugeot-Citröen makes most of its cars in France; Volkswagen, Mercedes and BMW in Germany; Fiat in Italy; but the true pan-European companies are Ford and General Motors, which manufacture in several countries. Similarly, in banking, the widest range of branch banks belong to American banks such as Citibank and Bank of America, not to any German, French or British group; the widest range of pan-European investment banking services come from Goldman Sachs and Salomon Brothers, not from any London merchant bank or its equivalents in France or Germany. European countries can co-operate in industrial activities: witness the success of the Airbus consortium. But frequently they seem to need an external force, such as the Americans, to push them together.

Diversity as a strength

Europe, seen as a purely economic entity, has its eggs in many different baskets. Name an economic activity, and a country somewhere in Europe will be good at it. Almost every industry has a significant European presence. In consumer electronics, Philips provides the main competition to Japan. In civil aviation, the Airbus consortium is the only competitor to Boeing and McDonnell Douglas in airframes, while in engines Rolls-Royce shares the world market with Pratt & Whitney and General Electric. (In 1985, the EU aerospace industry was one-third the size of the US industry, but this proportion had risen to a half by 1990.[2]) The three largest chemical companies in the world, Hoechst, BASF and Bayer, are German, and the fourth, ICI, is British. Two of the five largest oil companies, Shell and BP, are Anglo-Dutch and British. Europe has the technology to build nuclear power stations (and of course nuclear weapons); France and Britain are the two main exporters of conventional arms after the US and Russia; Europe can launch satellites; it can discover new drugs – out of the top ten pharmaceutical companies in the world, seven are European, led by the UK's Glaxo (and of the seven, three are Swiss: Ciba-Geigy, Sandoz and Roche).[3] Europe also has the largest motor industry in the world, producing in 1990 more than 13 million cars, against 10 million in Japan and 7 million in the US and Canada.

If one turns away from manufacturing, the 'hard' industries, and looks at the 'soft' ones, there is a similarly wide spread of competence: fashion and design from Italy; a vast array of luxury products, from perfume to *haute couture* to champagne, from France; whisky and woollens from Scotland; modern consumer products from Scandinavia; watches from Switzerland, and so on. The best brand names for luxury items are all European: the rich the world over want to spend their money on goodies that only Europe can supply.

Move further on to the range of services, and the breadth of Europe's expertise is even greater, particularly in the public sector, for the region has developed the most comprehensive network of state support in education, health care and social security that exists. Provision varies from country to country, but even people in the poorer parts of western Europe have a vastly better system of welfare care than exists anywhere else in the world, with the possible exception of Japan. To have developed this in the space of little more than a generation is an extraordinary achievement: the social welfare revolution of western Europe in the last half of this century is analogous to the industrial revolution in the first half of the last in the scale of the change it has meant to the people involved.

In part, Europe's social welfare system represents the consumption of the wealth generated by other economic activities. Pensions for the elderly and social security payments for the unemployed are just that. Certainly neither is an exportable service. Health care, too, can be seen as one way a rich society decides to consume part of its wealth. But health care, and even more so education, should also been seen as productive industries. These services are not yet, in the early 1990s, traded internationally to any great extent. A few patients, particularly from the Middle East, come to London or Switzerland for their operations; many students study abroad (though the US is a more important exporter of educational services than Europe); but in neither industry is this 'export' turnover large in relation to the total. Education and health care are, for the time being, mainly domestic businesses and for the foreseeable future they will remain so: most people will continue to want their children educated near home and, if they are ill, to be treated near home too.

However, both education and health care can be seen as part of Europe's economic resource base, not just because these two industries make life more pleasant for Europe's citizens, but also because they enhance Europe's competitiveness in the world. A healthy and well-educated population will be better at generating wealth than a sickly and poorly-educated one. And, as gradually the proportion of international trade in these services increases, they will become export industries, earning foreign revenues too. Whereas pensions and unemployment benefit are just financial transfers, taking money from one group of people and giving it to another, health and education are wealth-generating services and should be seen as an economic resource.

Added to all this there is a solid range of private sector services in which European countries are very large exporters. These include financial services (where London is the world's largest exporter); insurance (where both the UK and Switzerland are world leaders); television and popular music (where Britain is a very strong exporter); legal services (ditto); and tourism (France, Spain and Italy are the most visited countries in the world – taken as a region, Europe receives far more tourist revenues than the rest of the world put together).[4]

Finally, agriculture: those who quite correctly observe that Europe does not have much comparative advantage in food production should note that the European Union is both the largest exporter of food in the world, accounting for 16 per cent of world exports, and by far the largest food importer, with 21 per cent of world food imports.[5]

The development of the European economy has not, with two important exceptions, been the result of any central political policy. It has happened naturally as a result of the process of competition between nation states. The specialization which has taken place has been partly a function of different climatic and historical accidents – Spain attracts tourists because of its weather, Italy because of its historical riches such as Pompeii and Florence. The industrial revolution first happened in Britain for complex socio-political reasons, but it is also the result of the cultural diversity of the European people. The different nationalities are clearly good at different things.

The two exceptions are important, for they are not unqualified successes. One is agriculture, where the Common Agricultural Policy of the EU has encouraged Europe to become self-sufficient in all temperate agricultural products. The other is civil aircraft, where, in the Airbus consortium, Europe provides the only significant competition to the United States.

As far as agriculture is concerned, Europe has demonstrated that it is perfectly possible to grow a lot of food in a crowded region given sufficient financial incentives to do so. Many products are still imported either because they cannot easily be grown in Europe, or because they would otherwise only be available in certain seasons. But whether it is really sensible for Europe to attempt to export agricultural products is questionable, for this requires enormous subsidies to producers to bring down the cost to world levels. Europe is a very expensive producer of food. Sometimes, even with export subsidies, it can't clear its stocks. The generation of wheat and sugar mountains, not to mention wine and milk lakes, is clearly absurd. As for civil aviation, although by pooling Europe's technical skills and gaining substantial state funding it has become possible to challenge US domination of the production of large civil aircraft, and although Airbus seems currently to be viable, it is not clear whether it makes commercial sense in the long-term.

Europe also co-operates on some technical research, for example at the CERN laboratories (Conseil Européen pour la Recherche Nucléaire) in Geneva, and this research is supported by national governments.[6] But the main process of economic integration is essentially market-driven. European companies do not link up because they are told to by the EU bureaucracy; they do so because they expect to make more money that way. Countries do not specialize because of some Europewide industrial policy; they do so because they appear to be more successful in some areas than in others. The EC Commission intervenes in competition policy, and on occasion it helps to organize the orderly run-down of declining industries – steel, for example. But there is no real co-operation between the EU members and the other western European countries even in sharing the pain of cutbacks. In the rapidly-growing parts of the European economy the market rules. Individual governments might attempt to maintain an industrial policy, but the region has no plan, no vision of the areas into which it should head, no detailed assessment of its strengths and weaknesses in the world economy.

This lack of an overarching plan is an important strength. Europe has become an economic giant because it has allowed the different countries to sort out among themselves the areas at which each seems to excel. It has, certainly in manufacturing, managed to make a virtue out of a lack of a strong central political voice by allowing market signals to determine industrial structure. It has, however, hardly begun to allow the same process of specialization to take place in services, one of the potential weaknesses which the next section examines.

Diversity as a weakness

Europe's weaknesses are the mirror-image of its strengths. Its industries, while broad and diversified, have failed to achieve, on average, the productivity levels of their counterparts in the United States; its

service sector is uneven, with parts that are world class in their performance and their productivity, but other parts that are far below standard
US practice and below best East Asian practice too. Perhaps more
serious, the social security network created by European governments
has become extremely expensive to operate, and will become more so
as the European population gets older and a diminishing proportion of
people of working age have to support a larger number of dependants.
Viewed strategically, the European welfare system, while impressive
in its range and scope, may have begun to put the European economy
at a serious competitive disadvantage *vis-à-vis* the rest of the world. If
the United States has over-expensive health care, Europe's equivalent
burden is over-elaborate social security.

In industry, Germany's problem is Europe's problem writ large.
Thanks to its dominance of manufacturing, Germany is the world's
largest exporter. Not only is the industrial sector in Germany proportionately bigger than in any of the other large European economies
– France, Italy, Britain or Spain – but it also tends to rely on home-
grown technology, in terms both of product development and factory
organization. That technology has been shown to be excellent in the
past, and Germany's export success is testimony to that; but there are
a number of reasons for suspecting that Germany's run of industrial
success is drawing to a close. These include:

– High direct and indirect labour costs (it has the highest labour
     costs in the world and among the shortest working hours
     of any large industrial nation)
– The imbalance in the structure of German industry, with heavy
     dependence on electro-mechanical manufacturing, and a
     relatively weak electronics sector
– Inflexible manufacturing technology and organization
– The burden of integrating the former East Germany's industry
     into the west

High labour costs are really a result of success. German workers are
highly paid because they are productive, and because the country's
design skills have enabled industry to charge a premium price for its
products. If their performance can be maintained, then their wage
rates can continue to be justified. If not, German companies will have
to shift part of their production to lower-wage countries. There is
evidence that this is already happening.

More intractable is the problem of the structure of industry itself, with its dependence on capital goods, on mechanical engineering products (in particular cars and commercial vehicles) and on basic industrial commodities like chemicals. German industry is very good at adding value to these sorts of products, and at being sensitive to shifts in market demand. It is, for example, strong in high quality consumer durables, and is the world leader in anti-pollution and medical equipment. Strong demand for these last two types of product is assured for at least a generation, but the same cannot be said for cars and consumer durables. Demand here will slacken as saturation point is reached in these markets, at least in the developed world. Unless some radical new products are developed, Germany may find its product mix is unsuitable for the next century. Since, as argued later, such developments look more likely to be in electronics than in mechanical engineering, Germany will tend to lose its comparative advantage.

Further, there is some evidence that even in the segments where Germany is strong, she has failed to keep up with best practice abroad. The best example of this failure is in the automotive business, where German car companies were slow to adopt the 'lean manufacturing' techniques developed by Japanese producers, in particular Toyota. Toyota demonstrated that it was possible to achieve similar production quality (and, with the Lexus car, similar design standards to BMW or Mercedes Benz) to the best German practice with significantly lower production costs. Japan does have production facilities in Europe, mainly in the UK, and is starting there to teach others its methods. But Germany is finding it hard to acknowledge that it needs to reform many of its basic ideas as to how manufacturing production should be organized.

Finally, the problem of East Germany hangs over the whole economy. Reunification has damaged German performance in a number of ways. Some costs are direct: the burden of transferring cash to the east has reduced living standards in the west and pushed up inflation. It is the indirect costs that are more worrying, for German industry's preoccupation with problems to the east has meant the neglect of problems to the west, in particular the slowdown in world economic growth in the late 1980s. This was partly because the former East Germany created a new source of demand for the west's products just as the rest of the world economy turned down, but it was also a result of the psychology of success: because German industry had managed to overcome difficulties in the past, in particular to adjust to the rise in the external value of the mark, it assumed that it would be able to succeed again. Given time it will. The recession of 1992/93 forced German companies to make a start on the process of adjustment. Germany needs to transform itself from being a beautifully organized 1970s industrial economy to one more appropriate to the next century.

The rest of European industry faces problems too, but because in other countries industry is less important relative to services, the scale of the structural change needed is more limited. Besides, some of that adjustment has already been made. In Britain, for example, three main changes took place during the 1980s:

- The size of the industrial sector, relative to services, was scaled down
- Deregulation and privatization vastly improved the productivity and quality performance of much of what remained
- Japanese investment materially improved the quality of the motor industry (with a knock-on effect on the suppliers), and rebuilt parts of the consumer electronics industry.

France also restructured its industries during the 1980s, though it used centrally-driven political decisions as the spur, rather than privatization and foreign investment. Some privatizations took place, and there was some inward investment, but the balance of policy was different: for example, instead of selling Renault, it reformed its management; instead of encouraging Japanese electronics firms to base themselves in France, it supported domestic electronics producers such as Thomson. The result has been a less dramatic transformation of industrial structure than in the UK, but the direction has been similar. France has also made considerable strides in improving industrial productivity, which is on average higher than that of the UK and close to that of Germany.

Italy had, by the end of the 1980s, embarked on a restructuring programme akin to that of the UK, though at a slower pace. Much state-owned industry was gradually privatized, though the positive results are not yet evident.

What happens to industry in Britain, France and Italy – or indeed in Spain, Sweden, or Poland – will not have a material effect on the future prosperity of Europe as a whole. At the margin, it will make these countries a little more prosperous, or a little less, than they would otherwise have been. But what happens in Germany will heavily influence Europe's industrial future simply because German industry is such a big part of it. If Germany is able to redirect successfully, this will pull the rest of European industry along behind. If it cannot, then the other smaller countries will have to hope that their specializations are strong enough to enable them to carve out niches for themselves in world markets.

European industry as a whole will perform best when it can go back to its craft-based roots, where skilled labour can create excellence: in fashion clothing, in some forms of specialized manufacturing, in high technology bespoke projects. Europe has to try to make a virtue of its high cost base – Europeans are the highest paid workers in the world and have the highest fringe benefits – but this will be tough. Given the costs of making things in Europe, though, Europe's industries will have to be very clever even to stay still; some retreat is much more likely, leaving services to fill the gap in jobs.

In services, Europe's position is most uneven both between and within countries, making it dangerous to generalize about its competitive position as a whole. At the top end of the market, Europe excels at providing services for the rich. You cannot eat in better restaurants, listen to better opera, see better plays, shop in more glamorous stores anywhere in the world: Europe is a good place to spend money. But middle-market services show a number of weaknesses, both in quality and efficiency. In the private sector, for example:

– Banking services in much of continental Europe are more primitive and costly than in North America or the most advanced parts of East Asia, such as Hong Kong
– Retailing margins are typically higher than in North America
– Transport remains highly regulated and costly, with airlines in particular significantly less efficient than in North America. Management consultants McKinsey have estimated that European airlines' overall productivity is only 72 per cent that of US airlines, and in some areas, such as ticketing and sales, and maintenance, it is little above half.[7]
– The quality of fast food is frequently poor
– Telecommunications services, while adequate, are less developed than in North America or parts of East Asia

In theory the process of European integration should help improve service industry performance. Why should it not do for services what it did for manufacturing? Most services, however, are very difficult to sell across cultural and linguistic boundaries. It is hard enough to export professional services (for example, the law, medicine or education) to culturally similar countries that use the same language (Britain is, in fact, highly successful in exporting legal services – her lawyers are paid more than their US counterparts – but does not, in contrast, export much education to Australia). It is even harder to market such services abroad when there is a language barrier and no common cultural ground. Furthermore, in commercial services like retailing, it is very difficult to deliver consistent quality of service at a multiplicity of outlets. In theory the different European nations ought to be able to use each other as testing grounds as the European market develops from free trade in goods towards free trade in services, but in practice, it is not easy to do so. The English pub does not export comfortably across the Channel, nor the German beer tent easily to Britain.

At least the issue in private sector services is easy to see. Can Europe learn how to attain North American productivity levels or better, yet still maintain the variety of services which its diverse nations want to buy? It is difficult enough to deliver a uniform 'mass-produced' service like a McDonald's hamburger across the world. It is harder still to deliver consistently high standards in a more varied service, such as the English pub. European nations probably face a choice: either they accept greater standardization of service, or their services will remain relatively more expensive than those of North America, and hence Europeans will feel poorer in this area of their lives than North Americans.

In public sector services, performance is also uneven. In the case of education, there are sharp divides between the various nations' performance. Thus in Britain, while the best secondary education is of outstanding quality, and the university system is a world leader in producing quality graduates with great efficiency, the average levels of educational attainment are poor, and non-academic students are not given the rigorous technical training which is available in Germany. Business managers in particular are poorly educated: according to one study, only 24 per cent of senior British managers have degrees, against 85 per cent in both the US and Japan, 62 per cent in West Germany and 65 per cent in France.[8] Britain does, however, have a high proportion of accountants and these supply much of the management talent – although whether this is an appropriate training for business leadership is unclear. Either way, accountancy training is an example of the private sector filling the gap in state-provided education.

There are two kind things that can be said about the way in which Britain educates the mass of its people (though not its elite). The first is that the informality of education may foster creativity, and could therefore be associated with Britain's success in the arts and entertainment world. The other is rather different: it is that at least the country is aware that there is a problem, and that efforts are being made to solve it. The first step to reform is to admit that something is wrong.

In Germany the problems with the education system are quite different. The average level of attainment is high, but is achieved at great cost. The university system is extremely inefficient: the drop-out rate is high, and it can take up to seven years to teach what the UK universities typically do in four.[9] In addition, in certain subject areas (such as Business Studies) up to 40 per cent of first degree students go on to study for doctorates (again taking up to five years), with the result that many of Germany's best brains do not enter the labour market until their late twenties or early thirties. This is a double handicap: people are being taught for longer than necessary, which is a burden on the rest of society (university education is paid for by the taxpayer); and Germany's dwindling supply of young people is not available to employers. German technical education is more impressive, turning out a competent and numerate workforce for industry. The only potential problem is that Germany may be training people for the jobs of the past, not the jobs of the future.

At French and Italian universities, it can also take an inefficient six years to obtain a first degree. When the number of students expanded explosively in the 1960s, not enough resources were put into the universities to make sure that they were adequately taught. The legacy of that period remains. Arguably, there is no world-class university, ranking alongside the top US or UK universities, in the whole of Continental Europe. That is certainly the view of the distinguished German economist and former EC Commissioner, Professor Lord Dahrendorf.[10]

Finally, Europe's educational system as a whole turns out half as many technology students as either the US or Japan – relative to the total number of graduates – and tends to separate science, technology and the humanities. The result tends to be that scientists and technologists cannot explain their ideas in language which other people can

understand, and arts graduates make mistakes when applying technology because they are unaware of its potential.

The picture which emerges of European education, then, is a mixed
one. Some aspects clearly work well. But, with the exception of the
UK, it lacks the peaks of excellence of the best of the US system, and
it fails to deliver the consistently high average quality of the Japanese
or Korean systems. It is typical of Europe: if only the best aspects
could be more universally applied, European performance would be
as good as or better than anywhere else in the world. But European
countries find it difficult to learn from each other.

Much the same conclusions emerge in health care. Again the different countries have chosen very different approaches. Britain is particularly unusual in Europe in supplying some 90 per cent of its health
care through a single state monopoly, the National Health Service, at
no charge to the consumer. In the rest of Europe health care is also
free, or virtually free, and everywhere revenues to pay for the service
are raised either through general taxation or by social security payments, but in most countries other than Britain the actual service is
supplied by a mixture of private and public sector agencies, with the state
as a compulsory insurer. In terms of the input, costs range from 9.1 per
cent of GDP in the case of France to 5.2 per cent in Greece. The UK is
6.6 per cent, towards the bottom of the range, and the same, incidentally,
as Japan.[11] In terms of output, Iceland delivers the second lowest infant
mortality in the world, and on this measure, at least, has the best in
European health care – with expenditure similarly near the top of the
European range. (Turkey's health-care expenditure is only 4 per cent of
GDP, but only 35 per cent of this is state-funded; and it has the worst
infant mortality in the OECD, ten times that of Iceland.)

When measuring the effectiveness of health care it is always hard
to distinguish between the effects of poor medical care, and those of,
say, unsuitable diet, high levels of alcohol abuse or high consumption
of tobacco. Nevertheless, European systems in general, while avoiding
the cost explosion of the US, do not seem to provide general care
which is as good, on average, as the medical service of Japan. Japan
has a centrally-funded system (as in Britain) which gives access to
health care to all, at a cost of 6.6 per cent of GDP. With this, it
delivers the lowest infant mortality and the longest life expectancy of
any country in the world. Given the Japanese example, the cost-
effectiveness of European medical care on much of the continent leaves
considerable room for improvement.

The fact that education and health in Europe are principally financed by the state, and will continue to be so for the foreseeable future, places a great and growing burden on European tax levels. Already European countries have a high proportion of government spending relative to GDP; as the European population ages, health care for the old will place a still greater burden on the smaller cohort of people of working age. To this should be added the cost of state pensions. With the exception of Britain, the Netherlands and to some extent Germany, European countries do not have substantial funded pension schemes, where each generation of workers saves for its own pension. Instead these countries rely on the next generation of taxpayers to pay for the pensions of the previous one. As the ratio of worker to dependant deteriorates, all European countries will find their government budgets or social security funds under increasing pressure.

In the long term, pensions are a more serious problem than the burden of unemployment benefit, but during the 1980s and early 1990s unemployment benefit became an increasing cost throughout Europe, in contrast to North America and, particularly, Japan. In the US in the 1950s and 1960s, unemployment levels were consistently higher than those in western Europe; in the 1980s and 1990s they were consistently lower, and in Japan unemployment has been low since the mid-1950s. The experience of the 1980s and 1990s at least raises the possibility that high social security payments to the unemployed has contributed to Europe's high unemployment rates. In its efforts to create a good, humane system to support those who are unemployed, Europe may have unwittingly created a 'poverty trap': were social security payments lower (as in the apparently more brutal, but possibly more effective US system), some of the unemployed would move back into work. Of course, some may be in work already in the black economy, though there is no general agreement as to how many.[12]

In short, Europe's system of social welfare, while excellent in many ways, has serious problems of efficiency and direction. It is hard to measure the performance of different government services on an internationally comparable basis. But while it is not clear whether Europe's public sector is better or worse than that of the US or Japan, it is indisputably bigger. On balance that must rank as a competitive disadvantage.

Miracles, sclerosis, renaissance, and the reunification of Europe

For most of the post-war period the central issue on the frontier between economics and politics was the development of the European Union. But as argued earlier, economic integration took place between the different countries irrespective of whether they were members of the EC or not. By the early 1990s it was quite clear that the western European nations which were not already members of the EC would be able either to join, or to negotiate a free trade area with the EC.

How the EU develops may be of considerable political importance, but in economic terms it is no longer a vital issue. As long as western Europe is a free trade area, it can continue to make economic progress. The relationship between western Europe and the former members of the Comecon, the economic community of central and eastern Europe, is another matter. These countries can progress only if they are brought into western Europe's economic space. This raises a vital question: are the former Soviet bloc countries, including Russia, a source of strength or of weakness to the west?

The post-war economic history of western Europe falls into four main periods: the reconstruction of the shattered economies of the 1940s; the economic miracles of the 1950s and 1960s; a period of slow growth, dubbed 'Eurosclerosis', from the first oil shock of 1973/4 to the middle 1980s; and then a burst of growth associated with moves towards the EC's single market of 1992. The countries of western Europe moved at different speeds during this period. Both Germany and Italy experienced miracles of economic advance, while growth in France, and to a greater extent in the UK, merely plodded. The Nordic nations, in particular Sweden, seemed to be performing even better than the large countries of the EC; by contrast, the southern fringe of Europe – Spain, Portugal, Greece and southern Italy – lagged behind. But even the poorer performers shared in the broad fortunes of the region: while for most the 1970s were difficult, the 1980s saw a boom.

However, while this was happening in the market economies of western Europe, one-third of the continent's population was excluded. Here an alternative and apparently successful economic system was being developed. True, this system did not deliver the wealth of consumer durables that the west enjoyed, but it seemed to deliver other benefits: security of employment, child care, equal treatment of the men and women, and low crime. It also won a lot of gold medals at the Olympics. It is quite hard, writing in the early 1990s, to recall the admiration that many people in the west felt, until as late as the mid-1980s, for the achievements of the eastern European economies.

The collapse of Communism at the end of the 1980s and the triumph of the western liberal democracies has led to a reassessment of the political history of the whole post-war period; it is the great issue of global politics of our age. From an economic point of view, it is principally an issue for Europe. Of course the introduction of market reforms elsewhere in the world is having a dramatic impact on economic performance. In China, as will be argued in the next chapter, economic reform has preceded political reform; in South America economic reforms and political reforms have been travelling along different tracks, heading broadly in the same direction but only occasionally converging. But while whatever happens in China or Latin America will have a profound effect principally on the region where the change is taking place, what happens in eastern Europe will have a profound effect on western Europe. Europe has the opportunity to recreate an integrated economy, such as it had both before the First World War and again between the wars. Europe is going back to its roots.

The economic integration of east and west is a painful process. Paying for the transformation of East Germany from a command to a market economy eliminated West Germany's current account surplus and cost more than $100 billion in public sector payments alone in 1992. The consequent high interest rates in Germany were in turn passed to the countries linked to the Deutschmark. Europe's recession of the early 1990s and the collapse of the European Monetary System were in part the result of the costs of German unification. The pain of adjustment has been felt more directly by the citizens of central and eastern Europe which have received no similar transfer payments, with sharp rises in unemployment, falls in GDP, and soaring inflation. Transformation of a command economy into a market one takes time – anyone who recalls the state of the western European economies in 1950 will appreciate that. Most central European economies are still, in the early 1990s, in the equivalent stage of post-war reconstruction. Some, like Bulgaria and Romania, are not yet at the point most of western Europe had reached by the late 1940s; for them the economic miracles of the 1950s and 1960s are still some way off.

The cost of transforming the East German economy and the fact that the other former centrally-planned economies do not have access to large sources of external finance has led to scepticism about the pace at which the former Comecon countries can transform themselves. But anyone who doubts the potential should look at the past. In the middle of the nineteenth century, central and eastern Europe were still agrarian societies, but in the second half of the century they achieved economic take-off. One has only to look at the turn-of-the-century splendour of Budapest to see how wealthy central Europe once was: on the eve of the First World War Austria-Hungary was almost as rich as Italy, and richer than Norway;[13] it had a high-technology electrical industry which was competing successfully against Germany. Between 1900 and 1914, Russia was the world's fastest growing economy financing its development with a flood of Tsarist bonds which were eagerly bought by investors in France and Britain, anxious to benefit from the east European boom. To achieve another similar boom requires only a modicum of political stability and reasonable access to world markets. The problem is the 'only'.

In the long term, having central and eastern Europe operating the market system must strengthen the whole European economy. These countries bring not only cheaper, highly educated labour; they bring space which can be developed for leisure purposes; they bring a wealth of cultural skills; some, like Poland and Hungary, can draw on their expatriate communities in western Europe and North America; others, in particular Russia itself, bring the natural resources which western Europe lacks. Politically the region has become a patchwork and it will remain so. But that does not matter in economic terms providing the patchwork is a stable one, as western Europe has shown, and as long as trade relations can be developed. Gradually the region will become integrated into the west and be a source of strength to it.

But that is the long term. Meanwhile, western Europe has very little influence on the political development of the countries to the east. Its most important decision is at what pace to allow economic integration between east and west to take place. In particular it has to decide how open its markets should be to eastern European goods and what scale of investment it is prepared to make to assist the region's economic development. Its early record has not been good on either score. It is curious that the EU welcomes electronic products from countries in East Asia with which it has large trade deficits, yet baulks at much smaller quantities of imports of food products from countries which are much closer to it and which share its cultural traditions. As far as finance is concerned, while it has created a banking institution to funnel money eastwards – the European Bank for Reconstruction and Development – private sector companies have been, in general, slow to respond. Political upheaval in what was Yugoslavia and Czechoslovakia, and in Russia itself, has certainly underlined the commercial case for caution.

Nevertheless, the economic logic of pressing towards an integrated European economic space is so overwhelming that it will take place. The only issue is the timescale over which this happens. Just how quickly Europe will unify, and the extent to which it can unify, will turn on its more general ability to adapt to change.

Will Europe look inwards or outwards?

Europe's competitive future depends on whether it looks inwards, particularly within the EU, or outwards to the rest of the world. The GATT (General Agreement on Tariffs and Trade) system of reducing international trade barriers has enabled the world to enjoy the longest period of sustained growth it has ever attained. Europe's own post-war experience supports this liberal view of the world – it is by dropping internal barriers and boosting cross-border trade that Europe has managed to make the extraordinary progress that it has. But there is a problem. Europe, and particularly the EU, may be reaching the limits of the benefits of economic integration.

Of course there are still things to be done which could improve the economic efficiency of the region: cross-border trade within the EU is in theory completely free, but in practice is not always so, and trade in services still has a long way to go before it is fully liberalized. The physical infrastructure of the continent is still poor by comparison with the US, with road transport times and air travel costs significantly higher for similar distances, and until the EFTA (European Free Trade Association) countries complete their trade agreement with the EU, there are still some inefficiencies which have yet to be attacked. Taken together, these restrictions are surely more damaging to the growth of cross-border trade than the fact that the EU countries still operate their own currencies. After all, paying the foreign exchange trading margins has not stopped the nations of East Asia from being immensely successful exporters.

But there may soon be diminishing returns to economic specialization. There are both political and economic limits: politically it becomes hard to justify to voters the wisdom of moving out of whole areas of economic activity; and the economic benefit, beyond a certain point, may not be worth it. To see why, compare the Midwest of the US with Germany, the country in Europe which in terms of industrial structure it most closely resembles.[14] Like the Midwest, Germany's industrial base is built round the motor industry, but whereas in 1991 the Midwest made 66 per cent of US cars, Germany made only 43 per cent of Europe's. The Midwest, however, has almost entirely moved out of textiles, while Germany still has a textile industry of roughly half the size (proportionate to GDP) of the European leader, Italy. If European specialization were to move to US levels, Italy would close down its motor industry and Germany its textiles. But not only would that be extraordinarily difficult to envisage for political reasons, the levels of human disruption created by such a change would be enormous – the adjustment would require vast shifts both of capital and labour between the various European nations. While in theory, within the EU at least, such movements are free to occur, in practice they don't. Capital movements within Europe are no more likely to take place than capital movements between European countries and the US or Japan. Large labour movements within Europe have not as yet happened: within the EU only Portugal and Ireland have more than 10 per cent of their nationals living in another EU member state.

Besides, even if countries could make these structural adjustments there is little reason to suppose that it would be economically beneficial. This is partly because Europe is culturally more diverse than the US. Tastes in both clothes and cars vary between Germany and Italy in a way they do not between the Midwest and the South of the US. People in Italy buy different cars – smaller and with lower specification – than people in Germany, while any European would recognize that a German dresses differently from an Italian. These tastes are shaped by a variety of different forces, from fuel prices to fashion, which simply do not apply in the US. It is not, however, just culture which restricts further specialization. As discussed in Chapter 8, changes are taking place in manufacturing which will make it less necessary to go for size. In many fields the optimum size of a factory is diminishing; economies of scale are coming to matter less than nearness (both physically and culturally) to the market; electronic management of production, where goods are tailored to the demand signalled by data transmitted from cash registers in retail outlets, means that it is more important to have a factory which is nimble in switching product lines than one which can churn out identical items at the lowest cost. Italy's highly successful fashion knitwear retailer, Benetton, by making up all its garments in grey and dyeing to order, is able, using up-to-the minute sales data, to re-stock its shops with the most popular colours in a matter of days.

Europe has, in all probability, not yet reached an optimal degree of specialization; there is still some way to go, particularly in service industries. But the gains are now going to be much harder to win than they were a generation ago. It is hard to avoid the general conclusion that the various countries have become so specialized, and international trade such a large part of their GDP, that it will become very difficult for them to get richer simply by boosting still further their trade with western European partners. To progress, Europe has to find ways of increasing its trade with the rest of the world.

This suggests that a change of direction is needed: the policies which have worked extraordinarily well since the Second World War are close to reaching their natural conclusion. Europe can now go in one of two directions. It can build out from economic union to political union. Or it can put political union on hold and build more open relations with the rest of the world. The first, if it could be achieved, would increase Europe's political clout, at least in the short term. The second would increase its economic wealth relative to the rest of the world, and might, in the very long term, even give it a larger political voice too.

This whole debate has taken on a hard political edge which may itself become destructive. Many people in Britain see the European Union as a malign bureaucracy, determined to make the whole of Europe and particularly Britain less able to compete in the world. Many people in continental Europe see Britain as an irrelevance and a nuisance: a country which still looks to other parts of the world, rather than to its natural neighbours, for its future. The difference was encapsulated by Helmut Schmidt, former chancellor of Germany, when he noted the way in which Italy has passed the UK in GDP per head. 'One important reason,' he argued, 'is that Italian entrepreneurs have, since the late 1950s, successfully made use of the enormous opportunities of the common market, while British entrepreneurs even today prefer to look to Hong Kong.'[15]

The comment is interesting both in its perception of Britain as a country looking in the wrong direction, and as a perception of Europe as a region which should look to its internal opportunities rather than to its external ones. Objectively, for the past forty years the countries which have concentrated on internal European markets have done better than those which, for historical or other reasons, have looked to the rest of the world. In that sense Helmut Schmidt is quite right. Maybe if the world does split into antagonistic regional trading blocs he will continue to be right. But equally objectively, provided international trade continues to grow, Europe's best future opportunities will come from the rest of the world. Thus Hong Kong, when it becomes the financial capital of mainland China, must potentially be a more important market than any European nation could ever be. China also is not only a far bigger market, but is growing much faster. So the comment catches Europe's dilemma: viewed from Germany the European continent is more important than the rest of the world, but viewed from Britain the rest of the world matters more.

Finally, a word about Britain's position in Europe. If it is right that European economic specialization is beginning to reach a plateau, countries which have gained most from the process in the past have least to gain in the future. In relative terms, this ought to benefit Britain: she should move up the pecking order of Europe. In absolute terms, too, there are reasons to be encouraged. Britain has been much criticized for allowing her industries to run down rather faster than those of most European nations. Yet in a way she has simply specialized rather more aggressively than Germany, France or Italy, making a number of adjustments earlier than they have done. This was not necessarily a conscious policy – the decline of much of her industry happened by default – but it may turn out to have been the right thing to do.[16] It was argued at the start of this chapter that what distinguishes European nations is their economic diversity, the fact that outwardly similar countries with not so very different levels of wealth are actually good at rather different things. The interesting question for Britain is whether the things at which she happens to be really good – service industries such as entertainment and financial services, products with a high 'craft' input – will come to be valued relatively more highly in the world marketplace than the things – largely mass manufacturing – at which she has been mediocre or worse.

Europe, as a region, may fail to look outward and accordingly find itself facing a period of economic stagnation. If this were to happen, it may turn out that the individual countries in Europe which have a tradition of looking outwards, and whose economies produce the goods and, more importantly, the services which other parts of the world cannot produce, fare better than the perceived industrial powerhouse centred on Germany. Much of the conventional wisdom about Europe's future would hold that one of its key problems is that the core has drawn ahead of the periphery: that industry has become more concentrated in the centre, leaving the distant parts of the community – Ireland, Denmark, Scotland and northern England, western France and western Spain, Portugal, southern Italy and Greece – out in the cold. But if Europe in general starts to reach the limits of specialization, then the magnet of the centre will become less strong. Not all the peripheral regions will benefit, for many have structural problems which will take at least a generation to correct. But it is possible that being on the fringe of Europe, both physically and intellectually, may be a warmer place than being at the core.

FOUR

EAST ASIA: THE FRAGILE BOOM CONTINUES

The world's greatest growth area

IT IS EASY TO BE dazzled by East Asia, the region which Britons call the Far East, and which, when linked with Australia and New Zealand, has come to be dubbed the Asia/Pacific region. The countries within it lie along a great arc that stretches from Russia's Sakhalin, through Japan and the Koreas to Taiwan, Hong Kong and the coastal regions of mainland China. It runs down through to the Vietnam peninsula, to Malaysia and Singapore, and across to the giant of Indonesia. It would contain, if one were to include the whole of China, more than two billion people, though the area of potential economic dynamism for the next generation is rather smaller: more like half a billion.

This chapter does not cover what is generally known as South Asia, the Indian sub-continent. This is a deliberate omission, not because these countries are unimportant or lack economic potential – India is, of course, second only to China in terms of population, and there are pockets of economic take-off in the region, where high-technology industries thrive – but because they are not an integrated part of the East Asian economy. They seem to be qualitatively different in their approach to commercial and industrial activity. Parts of the region may well make a greater contribution to world prosperity over the next three decades, but it will be marginal when set against the potential of East Asia.

It not just the economic growth of East Asia that impresses, extraordinary though that growth has been. It is more the sense of order and purpose which has generated that growth: the commitment to education, the high savings, the attention to detail in a variety of different types of economic activity, the evident discipline and industriousness of the region's people. Catching common themes from the region is vital to understanding its potential, for it is a much less cohesive region than North America, or even than Europe. It is racially and culturally diverse, and includes the full range of different political systems, from a fair approximation of a western parliamentary democracy to hard-line Communist dictatorships. And it includes not only one of the richest nations in the world, Japan, but also several of the poorest.

As this chapter will argue, economic development, uneven at present, will not envelop the entire region. But the region as a whole will benefit from three resources on its periphery:

- The availability of cheap labour, particularly from the interior of China
- The vast natural resources of Siberia, principally oil, gas and strategic minerals
- The natural resources and human skills of the two 'Anglo' societies of the eastern Pacific, Australia and New Zealand.

Easy though it is to be dazzled by East Asia, it is important not to be. What has happened is certainly extraordinary: a whole cluster of countries doing in one or two generations what took Europe or America (or, for that matter, Australia and New Zealand) three or four. But this explosion of economic growth is quite thinly based. It has happened thanks to a set of favourable conditions which will probably be sustained for another generation, but which may not be. East Asia is more vulnerable to setbacks than either Europe or North America because it has fewer natural resources, a less developed infrastructure, narrower product ranges, less robust political institutions, and it depends overwhelmingly on western technology for its products, and western markets for its exports. Large parts of the region, in addition, depend on US military protection for their security.

The economic balance of the world in the first half of the next century will be determined, more than anything else, by what happens in East Asia. The North American economy will remain enormously strong, though it may in relative terms decline somewhat. Europe, currently the region with the largest total output, will inevitably have enormous weight too, whatever difficulties it may encounter. But the overall balance depends on whether the fast-growing countries of East Asia can continue their helter-skelter growth. Can the leaders sustain that pace, or, as is much more likely, will they find that once they have achieved full developed country status, growth slows to the sorts of rates ruling in North America and western Europe? Can the middle-income group catch up the leaders? And how many of the countries which have yet to make a start will succeed?

In the early 1990s, the output of the Asia/Pacific region, despite the explosive growth of the 1980s, and including the 1.2 billion Chinese, was still somewhat smaller than that of North America or Europe. If growth is sustained for another generation, East Asia's output will almost certainly overtake them both. Because the region is by its nature more diverse, it is unlikely to become as important a political entity – indeed it will not be a single political entity at all — but if the economic balance of power continues to shift to the Pacific, then this will have profound political consequences for its trading partners of the west.

What makes East Asia so good?

It is best to start with a harsh truth.

The explosive growth of East Asia has been based on taking goods which the west has developed and making them initially more cheaply and ultimately to higher quality. In the 1950s people used to joke about cheap Japanese imitations – goods made in Japan which were exact copies of products of the west. Japan has long since ceased to need to copy in such a blatant way, but elsewhere that process continues. Go to the shopping area of a city like Bangkok or Seoul, and it will be full of rip-offs of western brand names: there will be fake Rolex watches, fake Dunhill lighters, fake Cartier handbags, even fake Oxford English Dictionaries. Anyone brought up in the west with the notion that cheating at exams is wrong will view this with a mixture of irritation and contempt. But the ability to copy is not much different from the ability to learn from others. In reality, it is a strength rather than a weakness – certainly for nations seeking to catch up rivals in the west. Reverse engineering, taking something to bits and making a copy of it, has enabled Taiwan to become the world's largest producer of system boards for personal computers.[1] In Japan the fact that any new product is immediately taken to bits by rivals has generated intense internal competition in product development. This in turn has encouraged companies to shorten development times, to listen hard to customers' perceived desires, and to develop manufacturing techniques which are flexible enough to meet these.

So the ability to imitate is actually much more than the simple copying of someone else's product: it leads to a process of manufacturing which itself facilitates product development. Add an education system, or rather an attitude to education, which insists on precision and attention to detail; add, in the early stages of a country's development, low wages; add universally high savings, which make capital for expansion readily available, and it is not hard to see why in general terms East Asia is such an effective competitor against the west. But it is much harder to identify the specifics. It is easier to say that educational performance is better than in the west than to explain why this should be. Japan spends no more than Britain on public education, yet apparently achieves higher standards; Japanese savers are no better rewarded than British (actually they have over the years usually been worse rewarded) yet save much more.

To explain the economic success of such political and cultural diversity, the obvious thing to look for is features which are common to the region but are not so evident elsewhere in the world. There are at least five:

- Industrial flexibility, with great ability to shift from one product
     to another
- Rapid product development (or imitation)
- High savings
- Respect for educational achievement
- The work ethic

The nimble nature of East Asian industry is perhaps its greatest strength. Japan has given the best demonstration of the way in which a country can move in and out of different industrial sectors. Much of its initial economic growth after the Second World War came from textiles, which is generally one of the first manufactured products to be exported as a country develops. After textiles came steel, shipbuilding and motorcycles. Demand for these fell off in the late 1970s, but by then the motor manufacturers had started to export on a large scale. In the 1980s, the focus of exports shifted to consumer electronics, in particular TVs and video recorders.

In Japan these shifts were partly the result of government policy, with companies guided by the Ministry of Trade and Industry, but the influence of MITI has often been over-stated. Some of the large companies individually targeted particular export sectors, and because companies in any particular industry tended to follow each other, this gave the appearance of co-ordinated action.

Elsewhere, the involvement of government varied. In Korea it clearly did play a large part in industrial strategy, selecting particular industries (and companies) for export promotion, and raising much of the external capital needed to finance the expansion. In Singapore, the government actively promoted the region as a financial centre, 'inventing' the Asiadollar market as a competitor to the Eurodollar market, and developing the country's port and airport facilities. The result has been remarkable: Singapore is the largest port in the world, and its Changi airport, opened only in 1981, is now the largest airport in the east, and is in the world top ten in terms of both international passenger traffic and freight.[2]

In many other countries the role of government has been minimal. In Taiwan, the mass of small and medium-sized companies, often family-owned, would not respond to this sort of central direction of economic activity. In Hong Kong – the most completely *laissez-faire* economy on earth – there is in effect no government influence at all. Yet Hong Kong has managed to make a series of radical shifts in its economic structure. After the Second World War it moved from being a small trading centre to a sizeable manufacturing one, first in textiles and then in electronic goods. In the 1980s, with the opening up of China, it became the communications and trading centre through which the mainland sold its exports to the world.

Not only do governments have varying influence on industrial policy, but company structure throughout the region varies widely, too. In Korea development has been pushed by large industrial conglomerates, in Hong Kong and Taiwan by small and medium-sized family firms.

The common theme throughout East Asia is a willingness to adapt, in contrast to the resistance to change evident in North America and Europe. This cannot be explained by industrial policies or an industrial structure which are common to the whole region since they simply do not exist. It is something much more subtle, much harder to identify: factors like culture and education. Culturally there is not just a capacity for hard work but a lack of sentimentality. It may partly be that East Asia has been subjected to so many changes during the last half century that there has not been time to build up the sentimental attachment to, say, coal-mining, that exists in the UK – industries have been created so recently that there has been no time to build up myths about them. But there is surely something more to it than this. There must be an attitude among both managers and workers which facilitates change.

One famous comment on attitudes in Japanese industry comes from Konosuke Matsushita, head of Japan's largest electronics group, in a speech to visiting foreign managers.[3] It is worth quoting at length:

> We are going to win and the industrial west is going to lose; there is nothing much you can do about it because the reasons for your failure are within yourselves. With bosses doing the thinking, while the workers wield the screwdrivers, you are convinced deep down that this is the right way to run a business. For you, the essence of management is getting ideas out of the heads of bosses into the hands of labour . . . For us, the core of management is [the] art of mobilizing and putting together the intellectual resources of all employees in the service of the firm. Because we have measured better than you the scope of the new technological and economic challenges, we know that the intelligence of a handful of technocrats, however brilliant and smart they may be, is no longer enough for a real chance of success.

This is interesting both in its analysis and its arrogance. 'Putting together the intellectual resources of all employees' is a good way of describing the team approach to manufacturing production in Japan, which has proved the most efficient method of making things yet developed anywhere in the world. But the assumption that other countries cannot learn this process is belied by the success of overseas Japanese plants and in particular their local suppliers. This ability of Japanese firms to teach their methods to foreign workers has had an important effect on the Asia/Pacific region. While in the 1970s and early 1980s most Japanese overseas investment was in North America and Europe, in the second half of the 1980s it shifted to Asia, and will help secure the economic take-off in the region. Meanwhile, it is hard not to acknowledge that Mr Matsushita is describing a culture which is more likely to facilitate change. A 'bottom-up' approach to decision-taking is likely to generate less resistance than a 'top-down' one.

Rapid product development flows from this attitude of welcoming change. Product development takes different forms. In parts of East

Asia, factories are making products designed in North America or Europe: this particularly applies to household consumer durables, sports goods and footwear, where European and North American design and brand image are stronger than Asian. Elsewhere, the products are clones of goods developed elsewhere: this particularly applies to PCs and other 'commodity' computer equipment. Japan is now an exporter not just of manufacturing technology, but of product design. In particular it is clearly the world's leading designer of a large range of electronic equipment, and arguably the most innovative designer of cars. This is reflected in the very high proportion of exports in relation to total production in some such goods. In 1991 Japan exported 88 per cent of the cash registers it made, 87 per cent of the video recorders, and 72 per cent of its watches. Even in more basic products like colour TVs, 47 per cent of output is exported, while in the other great export sector, cars, Japan exported 49 per cent of its output. In areas where Japan has not produced particularly innovative design, for example in washing machines, exports were only 16 per cent of output.[4]

Whether product development is merely grabbing the latest design from elsewhere and copying it, simply making goods designed abroad swiftly, or developing whole new lines of technology, Asian industry is remarkably flexible: it does not suffer at all from the Not Invented Here syndrome of North American and Europe.

Another enormous advantage of East Asia is that the people save. Throughout the entire region there are very high personal savings ratios – typically between 30 and 40 per cent of GDP. These high savings are mirrored in high investment ratios. In 1990 Japan invested 32 per cent of its GNP, Singapore 38 per cent. The comparable figure for the US is 17 per cent, for Britain 19 per cent and for France and Germany 21 per cent. These high savings have frequently been seen as a reason for the rapid growth that the East Asian countries have achieved – in other words, the high investment itself causes the rapid growth to take place. That is far too simple. To some extent the relationship is the other way round: the rapid growth of the economies requires high levels of investment to support it. Certainly high investment does not guarantee rapid growth: when, during the 1980s, Japan continued to invest at the high levels of the 1960s and 1970s, its additional investment became less productive. Japan actually over-invested for the growth rate that it was able to sustain, with the result that much of the investment was wasted, and many of the borrowers were unable to service the debt they had incurred.

But high savings do give at least three substantial advantages to the countries which achieve them. First, economic expansion can be largely, maybe entirely, financed without foreign borrowings which will have to be repaid. The reliance on domestic capital, rather than overseas funds, was an important factor distinguishing the majority of East Asian countries from those in Latin America during the 1970s and 1980s. Second, funds will tend to be both available for worthwhile investment projects, and probably relatively cheap compared with external capital. Third, and this is a more general point, societies which save and invest for their own future have a commitment to their future prosperity. Contrast the response of Latin American countries to their debt problems of the 1980s, where they sought to paint foreign banks as the villains, with the attitude of East Asian countries in respecting the need for investment projects to make a proper return on capital. The result has not only been better quality investment: whole societies are united in responsibility for the success of the economy.

The emphasis on educational achievement is similarly impressive. As the graph on page 41 shows, the proportion of those going on to higher education in the most developed East Asian societies is not particularly out of line with North America or western Europe. Some 53 per cent of students were going into higher education in Japan in the early 1990s, less than the 65 per cent in the US or the 63 per cent in Finland, but more than the 44 per cent in France or the 28 per cent in the UK. What stands out is the commitment of students throughout the region to educational attainment. In Japan, over 93 per cent of pupils continue into upper secondary schooling – all the more remarkable considering that the schools charge fees and courses are broad and academic – and nearly all will graduate successfully at eighteen. Contrast western Europe, where 68 per cent of German eighteen-year-olds, 48 per cent of French and only 29 per cent of English youngsters obtain a comparable upper secondary school qualification.[5]

In other parts of East Asia performance is equally high: compared in mathematics and science tests (the easiest areas in which international comparisons are possible) with thirteen-year-olds in twenty countries around the world, Korean and Taiwanese youngsters come out in the top three in both areas, with China beating them both on maths. These achievements seem to be unaffected by differences in the types of teaching materials or methods used, teacher training, or class size – Korea's typical class size is 49 pupils, all of mixed ability, compared with 23 in the US. The only factor which systematically correlates with national educational outcomes appears to be the amount of time children spend studying, as the table below shows.

Proficiency Test Scores in Mathematics and Science for 13-year-old pupils in 20 countries, 1991[6]

Country	Average days' instruction per year	Mathematics Rank %correct	Science Rank %correct
China*	251	1 80	14 = 67
Korea	222	2 = 73	1 78
Taiwan	222	2 = 73	2 76
Switzerland	207	4 71	3 74
former USSR	198	5 70	5 71
Hungary	177	6 68	4 73
France	174	7 = 64	9 = 69
Italy (a)	204	7 = 64	6 = 70
Israel	215	9 63	6 = 70
Canada	188	10 62	9 = 69
Scotland	191	11 = 61	12 = 68
Ireland	173	11 = 61	16 = 63
England*	192	11 = 61	9 = 69
Slovenia	190	14 57	6 = 70
Spain	188	15 = 55	12 = 68
United States	178	15 = 55	14 = 67
Portugal*	172	17 48	16 = 63
Jordan	191	18 40	18 57
Brazil* (b)	181	19 37	19 53
Brazil* (c)	183	20 32	20 46
Mozambique*	193	21 28	n/a n/a

*low participation or restricted grades
(a) Province of Emilia-Romagna only
(b) Sau Paulo only
(c) Fortaleza only

This commitment to education is best shown by the growth of *juku*, private cram schools which children attend in the afternoon and evening after their regular school is finished. These are a Japanese invention, but have subsequently spread to South Korea (whose education system was set up under Japanese military occupation between 1910 and 1945), and, most recently, mainland China. At least half Japanese children attend *juku*, and up to 80 per cent go in their final year before university entry.[7] The specific aim of such schools is to get better exam results – such a national preoccupation in Japan that, during the examination season every February, newspapers publish the university and high school entrance papers, analyse them and tell their readers what the model answers should be.

The main force behind this exam fever is what in the west would be called pushy parents: there is no real evidence that Japanese (or Korean or Chinese) children are any more eager to spend three hours a day in additional study than their European or American counterparts. The schools, for their part, are ambivalent about the influence of *juku*, for while attendance shows respect for education, it also suggests that schoolteachers are not doing a proper job. But the overall effect is to create a climate where educational attainment is greatly valued.

Sometimes the actual achievements are less impressive than the figures suggest, as will be discussed in the next section. But a competent general education is reinforced by emphasis on worker training. Mr Matsushita again: 'Our large companies give their employees three to four times more training than yours ... and they demand from the educational system increasing numbers of graduates as well as bright and well-educated generalists ...' Japanese managers are certainly far better educated than their peers in the UK. As noted in Chapter 3, Some 85 per cent of top managers in Japan have degrees, the same as in the US, compared with 65 per cent in France, 62 per cent in Germany, and only 24 per cent in Britain.[8]

China has made a special effort to catch up with the market economies in both its general educational levels and its management education. It is something of a special case, because, having chosen to retain its ideological commitment to Communism, it had to find a way of linking this to management reform. In the 1980s it set up a series of programmes designed to teach managers to respond to market signals, and although China is still short of people who understand the industrial world's management techniques, it has developed in the space of ten years at least a core of trained top executives.[9,10]

Not only are people in East Asia well-educated: they work hard. All the evidence suggests that East Asia works longer hours than North America or Europe, generally for lower wages. Some convergence is starting to take place, with hours worked in Japan in particular falling towards the levels of the more industrious nations of the west. Indeed, UK factory workers now appear to work as long as Japanese, but holidays outside Japan are almost invariably longer, even were Japanese workers to take their entitlement. Much of the rest of the region is still working similar hours to Japan in the 1960s and 1970s.

Average weekly hours of work, selected countries, 1991 (male and female workers)[11]

Country	Non-agricultural activities	Manufacturing
United States	34.3	40.7
Canada	31.0	37.8
Japan	45.4 (38.8 salaried)	45.0
Korea	47.9	49.3
Belgium	33.7 (a)	33.4 (a)
Spain	48.7 (e,f)	48.9 (a,e,f)
France	39.0 (f)	38.7
Germany	39.3	39.2
Luxembourg	40.5	40.3 (b)
Netherlands	40.1	39.9
Norway	35.0	36.8
Switzerland	42.4 (c)	42.4 (d)
Sweden	37.5 (a)	n/a
United Kingdom	42.9 (a)	41.6 (a)
Greece	n/a	41.1
Hungary	n/a	47.1 (e)
Ireland	n/a	40.7
Australia	35.4 (a)	38.2 (a)
New Zealand	38.5 (a)	40.4 (a)

(a) 1990
(b) 1989
(c) 1988
(d) 1987
(e) average weekly hours per quarter divided by three
(f) average of blue- and white-collar workers

Why do East Asian workers put in such long hours? One answer is peer pressure, but that is an intermediate explanation, for why should there be peer pressure in the first place? Another answer is that a generation ago living standards in the region were much lower and so workers see hard work as a way to escape poverty (as may also be the case in Spain and Hungary, the two European countries that have the longest working hours). Inter-regional competition, too, must act as a spur: all the region's countries can look to Japan as an example of economic achievement, while China has the example of Chinese communities overseas. Some people try to see the work ethic in religious terms – Japan's brand of Buddhism, for example, celebrates work as divine: 'Unlike Christian societies, where work is a necessary evil, we believe labour is an act of God, that working allows us to become closer to God'[12] – and the influence of Confucian philosophy, which stresses discipline and hard work, is apparent throughout East Asia. But none of this completely explains Asia's work ethic.

Perhaps the best answer lies in the fundamental insecurity of the region. Mr Goh Chok Tong, prime minister of Singapore, puts it this way: 'We've got to worry all the time. If we lose our competitive edge, I think the whole house may collapse. To give an example, if we are not competitive, say, with China, we'll find that China will suck in our investments very quickly ... This anxiety is something we've got to live with.'[13] If the prime minister of the most successful of the East Asian 'tigers'[14] feels this, how much more strongly must less successful people in less successful countries feel this too? The layer of prosperity is so recently acquired, and feels so thin, that people believe they must work doubly hard to preserve it.

What could go wrong?

The triumph of East Asia may be dazzling, but its foundations could easily be swept away. It is based on the continuing willingness of western Europe and North America to provide a reasonably open market for exports from the region, the continued importance of consumer electronics (and to some extent motor vehicles) in international trade, and a continued guarantee of external security from the US.

All three conditions may well be sustained; indeed the sensible working assumption must surely be that they will. But even if they are, the East Asian economies have structural weaknesses which need to be acknowledged. Chief among these are:

– The narrow product range of East Asian exports
– Heavy dependence on the North American market
– Weak infrastructure
– Dependence on imported raw materials, including energy

- Failure of the education system to generate original research
- Failure to develop service exports

If the engine of economic growth for the entire region has been exporting to North America and Europe, the triumph of East Asian exporters is all the more remarkable for the narrow range of goods which are exported. Japan, for example, is really a successful exporter in only two main areas, consumer electronics and motor vehicles. These happen to be very important areas, and through its success Japan has become known to the world by a series of brand names like Toyota, Nissan, Panasonic and Sony. But if one remembers that per head of population Japanese exports are relatively small, one is faced with a puzzle. Why is it that everyone fears Japanese competition, when countries like Germany, France or Britain export a much higher proportion of their output? The answer is that the exports of these European countries are spread across a much wider range of products. Outside of the two categories noted above, Japan exports relatively little.

Much the same pattern holds for the other East Asian nations: countries further down the hierarchy export less sophisticated products, but the weight is still overwhelmingly in consumer electronics. One can say that this is simply because it has been in consumer electronics that the recent growth of world trade has been focused, and that these countries have gone into this area precisely because that is where they found the demand. There is something in this. But when observing what the region does export, it is also worth noting what it does not export in any significant quantities: food, aircraft, medical drugs, oil, armaments. To be cruel, East Asia exports the gadgets, the adult toys that the west loves, but not the necessities of life. With the exception of some Japanese high-technology equipment, the world could get along without this output if it had to. But many of these countries need to export simply to feed themselves.

This leaves East Asia vulnerable. It is obviously vulnerable to protectionism, but perhaps more importantly to shifts in taste in the west, and to any of the technical developments which could cut the price at which these products will sell. The vast majority of the region's exports are middle-technology products. Although they are often made in high-technology factories, they are not necessarily difficult to produce. Attempts to add value by making the products more complicated may be frustrated by the fact that consumers do not want more complex products, if only because they are unable to work out how to use them.

Besides, as market penetration of consumer durables reaches a plateau, the demand will come only from the replacement market. Meanwhile, the entire consumer durable industry is liable to find itself undercut in price. The countries at the top of the economic scale – Japan, Singapore, Hong Kong and Taiwan – must all fear that mainland China can manage to make the same goods far more cheaply. Mr Goh is right to be worried.

If the product lines are narrow, so too are the markets. East Asian prosperity depends on the willingness of North America to accept its products. One-third of Japan's exports go to the US. No other major industrial country has anything like that degree of dependence on one market: Britain's largest market, Germany, takes only 14 per cent of British exports, while only 13 per cent of Germany's exports go to its largest market, France. Hong Kong is almost as specialized as Japan, and the US is its largest export market too, taking 23 per cent of its exports. As long as the US is prepared to buy consumer goods from the rest of the world, East Asian exporters are probably sensible to focus on the North American market. In fact, focusing on the US market brings hidden benefits. Quite aside from the number and wealth of its consumers, there is the sophistication of those consumers. Create a product which will sell in the US and the manufacturer has one which will sell to any developed country. East Asia needs North American consumers.

One might expect, given this, that countries like Japan and China would place trade relations with the US at the very top of their priorities. It is hard to believe, from the available evidence, that they have. Japan has allowed the growth of enormous trade surpluses with the US, inevitably creating tensions between the two countries. If it had deliberately set out to try to offend the US, it could hardly have chosen more effective ways of so doing than declaring that it could not import more foreign beef because Japanese people had different intestines from foreigners, or that it should not import US ski-ing equipment because Japanese snow conditions were different from those in the rest of the world. It is curious that Japan should risk offending its main export market by advancing such arguments.

China is also in danger of mismanaging its trade relationships with the US, though more as a by-product of its own internal political difficulties (and in particular its attitude to human rights) than by deliberate obstruction of imports. Nevertheless, its trade relationship with the rest of the world looks particularly fragile. The US has been prepared to maintain open markets for Japan partly because post-war

Japan has been its protégé, partly because Japan has been its barrier against Communism, partly perhaps because Americans feel guilt for dropping the atom bombs. It is a tribute to the US generosity of spirit that it should have helped Japan to the extent to which it has. There is no such special relationship with China, no obvious open market for its products, no desire to support its political system. Europe owes China no favours, either. Besides, given the relative size of China and, say, Taiwan, North America and Europe clearly cannot offer mainland China the open markets that they have offered to the newly industrialized countries, commonly known as NICs. No-one minds too much if three million Singaporeans or twenty million Taiwanese export furiously to the west. But the same liberal attitude is unlikely to be extended to the 200 million Chinese of the new coastal economic zones, let alone China's 1.2 billion total population. So economic expansion on the back of an export drive in western markets – the path followed by the 'tigers' – is not open to China.

East Asia is also weak in both its infrastructure and its dependence on imported raw materials. As far as the former is concerned, it is inevitable that Asia's infrastructure should be relatively poor when compared with that of older industrial countries. It is particularly short of oil refining capacity. Housing quality is frequently poor. Asia will, over the years, invest in transport, power, sewage and other facilities. While the building of the infrastructure will of itself be an important component of the region's economic growth, it will also be a restraint on growth, as resources will have to be diverted from export-orientated industries to invest in building airports, roads and railways.

As for raw materials: do they matter? Part of the thesis of this book is that they matter very much less than they used to, but of all the regions in the world, East Asia is most vulnerable to interruptions of supply. Most countries in the region lack energy supplies, find it hard to feed themselves, and have to import most of the raw materials needed to fabricate the products which they export. Two vast sources of natural resource are on East Asia's periphery: Siberian Russia, and Australia and New Zealand. If the world price of natural resources remains relatively low over the next generation, and trade lines remain open, then paucity of resource may prove a strength, because if things are scarce, countries learn to use them more wisely. Certainly Japan's experience in developing energy-saving technologies after the first oil shock in 1973/4 shows how a potential weakness can be turned to advantage. But lack of natural resources is and will remain a concern for the entire region. In 1991 Japan imported 53 per cent of its food, measured by calorific intake, up from 21 per cent in 1960.[15] China will also have to increase its imports of food over the next generation; it has memories of millions dying of famine. Countries which cannot feed themselves are liable to feel vulnerable, and rightly so.

There can hardly be anything more fundamental than food or energy, yet there is another weakness of the region which may matter even more: the extent to which it is an importer of ideas. This is associated with its otherwise excellent educational systems, discussed earlier. Ideas are not yet a large element in international trade, at least as conventionally measured, though the US, as the world's largest exporter of technology, earned a net $12.6 billion on its technological balance of payments in 1990.[16] But trade in ideas may well become more significant, as the west is likely to become less relaxed about giving its ideas to the rest of the world for free.

The list of things East Asia does well is shorter than the list of things it does badly or not at all, and this is linked to its need to import knowledge. The region has never discovered any oil; it has not, at least up to now, discovered many new drugs or new chemicals; its record on financial services is uneven; it has few centres of excellence in its universities; it is weak on computer software. All these are areas of activity where excellence cannot be developed by learning by rote. Japanese students are taught to memorize facts and judged by their ability to do this, but people taught to pass exams by picking the correct answers to a series of multiple-choice questions are not people who are being encouraged to think creatively. The system may not even add useful practical skills: students in Japan may study English for perhaps ten years, pass their exam, and yet hardly be able to speak a word of the language.

The Japanese inability to learn foreign languages is an extreme example of a fundamental weakness in educational attitudes. Certainly, the depth of the commitment to education in East Asian countries is and will continue to be a source of great strength. The teaching techniques, however, may be more problematic. Education systems vary vastly over the region and it is unfair to generalize. Much more data is available about Japan in this area than any other country in East Asia, but the emergence of *juku* in mainland China as well as South Korea may be one indicator of how far Japanese educational ideas are shared elsewhere in the region. What evidence there is suggests a common emphasis on attainment, often quite narrowly defined, which has led to a learning-by-rote approach to education which will in the long-run damage the region's growth potential. The Japanese experience is fascinating, for while the education system has produced excellent line-workers and talented middle-managers, it has not produced the original thinkers that the best of US universities have. The result is that while Japanese companies are excellent at incremental advance, and in particular the development of inventions made abroad, they have made few great leaps forward. This deficiency matters little for countries which are still in the process of catching up the west, but it makes it very difficult for countries to advance beyond what has been achieved elsewhere. Japan is well aware of the problem and is seeking to encourage creativity in schools, and putting more resources into post-graduate work. But success is not yet evident.

The paucity of Asia's contribution to world knowledge is clear from the distribution of Nobel prizes for natural sciences. Up to 1991 there were 410 prizes awarded. Out of these 159 (or 39 per cent) went to researchers in the US, followed by 65 to the UK, 60 to Germany, and 23 to France. Only five prizes went to Japan, and even fewer to any other Asian nations. Even making some allowance for the tendency of a Swedish foundation to favour European scientists, and the relatively recent climb of East Asia up the ladder of economic progress, the imbalance is startling. Eventually this may change. The closer one comes to developing actual products, rather than generating 'blue sky' abstract or semi-abstract ideas, the greater the progress in research – Japan now registers more patents than any other country in the world. But these patents are churned out by the Japanese industrial machine, not by universities. They are really by-products of the frenzied product-development of Japanese industry. Some must represent excellence of a sort; but it is excellence in areas of known economic strength. The addition to world knowledge is narrowly focused.

If East Asian educational systems fail to develop individual creativity, the region will fail to make progress in the new information-driven, and, as we have seen, culture-based service industries. This is already showing up in the entertainment business. No East Asian country has established a significant export industry in film-making – imports dominate local attendances. In Japan in 1991, the four top-earning films, and almost half of the total films shown, were US-made. Of course there are aspects of Japanese culture that have proved attractive to the west: its martial arts, sushi, and – more successfully – karaoke. Even here, however, while the hardware associated with karaoke is

Japanese, the software – the songs – associated with it are almost exclusively western, even in Japan itself. The world regards it as normal for western and in particular American culture to dominate Asia, and for very little to come back.

Nor has the region been successful in developing other service exports. With the exception of tourism, developed unevenly (few tourists go to Japan, but lots to Thailand), exports of services are limited. Singapore and Hong Kong have succeeded as entrepôt financial centres, but Tokyo's international financial services business is surprisingly limited, given the scale of Japanese savings. The region has not shown great sophistication in the use of its external assets – Taiwan has used these largely to build up official reserves, and Japan has invested, often unwisely, in US property and securities. Service exports will eventually develop, but the process seems to be slow.

Finally, it may not be just creativity which the education systems are failing to deliver; it may also be judgement. If so, that is deeply worrying for the entire region. If the region is indeed going to become economically more important, it will inevitably come to play a larger political role, for which good judgement will be vital. But even in terms of economic management the recent record of the two most important regional powers is discouraging. Despite all Japan's wonderful economic progress it mismanaged the bubble economy of the late 1980s; it has become excessively reliant on exports to sustain demand; it has wasted much of the current account surplus accumulated during the 1980s by poor overseas investment; and its exports are in a narrow range of goods. As for China, it is worth remembering that its extraordinary growth spurt only started in the 1980s – the thirty years of Maoist economic policies which preceded it were a catastrophe. Looking ahead, it is not clear how China will handle the takeover of Hong Kong. It could become its greatest asset, but it might also become a profoundly destabilizing force if the takeover goes wrong.

These minuses do not outweigh the pluses; far from it. The economic balance of the world will shift towards the Asia/Pacific region, for rapid economic growth will continue. But predictions that the west will be dominated by the east within a generation are surely wrong. East Asia's structural weaknesses, which are not easy to correct, will act as a brake for many years to come.

Australia and New Zealand's place in East Asia

The two 'Anglo' societies of the Asia/Pacific region potentially link East Asia into the rest of the world. They have in abundance some of the resources most clearly lacking in the rest of the region: their natural resources and their space. Their most important asset, though, may be their people – including their new immigrants from non-Anglo-Saxon stock.

The resources of Australia and New Zealand are extraordinary. They could feed the rest of the region – particularly if prices were to rise and provide a financial incentive to farmers. Australia supplies Japan with nearly half its coal imports, and nearly 40 per cent of its iron ore. There is the space to provide 'R&R' for the new rich of East Asia, as the string of investments in Australia by Japanese hotel chains shows. Both Australia and New Zealand have been forced to seek new markets in Asia as access to the UK market has gradually been closed. Since the UK market has in any case been growing more slowly than the markets in East Asia, this shift in the direction of Australian and New Zealand exports has been on balance to their benefit.

Australia also brings to East Asia ready access to the ideas, the media, and the cultural vigour of the Anglo-Saxon world, while New Zealand has done some pioneering work on the role of the public sector. Australia's cultural standing within the Anglo-Saxon world grew steadily throughout the 1970s and 1980s, particularly through the press, television and film. This growth seems likely to continue. As for New Zealand, it is redefining the public sector in a way that will probably be imitated through much of the industrial world. It was in the late 1980s the first of the industrial countries to start dismantling the welfare state. By policies such as charging people for visits to the GP, even though the cost could be reclaimed later, New Zealand made ordinary people aware of the real cost of providing these services. The result is that people in New Zealand more than any other country in the world know how much welfare services cost them, and can make realistic decisions as to whether they are prepared to pay taxes to fund them. Just as Sweden, in the 1950s, pioneered the growth of the welfare state, showing the world the extent of the services which might be provided, so New Zealand is pioneering the trimming of universal state provision.

Meanwhile, Australia is acquiring a stock of entrepreneurial skills and vigour from the new immigrants from East Asia, and particularly from Hong Kong, which provided over a quarter of the skilled immigrants into the state of Victoria alone in 1991. In 1947, nearly 73 per cent of new immigrants to Australia were British or Irish, but by 1991–92 three of the five main sources were East Asian countries – the Philippines (5.5 per cent), Vietnam (9 per cent), and Hong Kong (12.3 per cent – up from 5.4 per cent only two years previously). As they establish themselves and prosper, these immigrants also provide a link between Australia and the East Asian countries. If these people are a resource for Australia, they are also a potential resource for the communities they have left.

All human assets are intangible; the benefits they bring are hard to measure. Whatever Asia gains from its relationship with Australia and New Zealand could, in theory at least, equally well be obtained from California, and Japan certainly would consider the west coast of the US as part of its sphere of economic influence. But California has other concerns: it looks south to Mexico, and it would hardly want to become in economic terms a colony of Japan. Nor, naturally, would Australia or New Zealand. They are, however, irrevocably linked by time zones and relative proximity to East Asia – while they will remain politically detached from that region, they are part of its economic future. If the region continues to prosper, it will pull them along with it; if it falters, they will suffer as a result.

Two giants, and other tensions

If one had to single out one feature which will be the most important in East Asia's economic future, it would be the relationship between China and Japan. On paper these two countries might seem natural partners, for each has what the other lacks. China has economic potential, and, with its enormous population and rapid economic growth, is possibly the most attractive market in the world. It lacks manufacturing technology, knowledge of marketing (except through Hong Kong), experience in product development, and investment capital. Japan can supply the best manufacturing technology in the world, brilliant marketing and product development and some 60 per cent of the world's savings. However, it probably faces a period of much slower economic growth. It is also likely to suffer from saturation in many of the main markets for many of its product lines – once an American household has two or three colour TVs, it may not want yet another. In China, ownership of such consumer durables is still very low.

On paper, these two giants ought to be able to lead the entire region into what some expect to be the Pacific century. Yet they are not perfect partners, nor is it easy for them to become so. Quite aside from the historical antagonism between the two countries, each has other preoccupations.

Japan faces the most dramatic demographic transformation of any country in the industrial world, going from being the youngest to the oldest in two generations. It needs to find ways of coping with that. It is committed to its trade relationships with North America and Europe, and must remain so. For most of the 1980s Japan exported more to the US than the whole of South East Asia put together. In 1991, exports from Japan to South East Asia moved ahead of those to the US, but this was largely the result of the build-up of Japanese-owned production facilities in the US itself. Japanese direct investment in the US is substantially larger than its investment in Asia. Japan will become a more important regional economic power, and will inevitably be the main supplier of manufacturing technology to the region. But intra-regional relationships will, for a long time, have to co-exist with relationships with North America and Europe. For the time being, the countries of East Asia need North America and Europe more than they need each other.

As for China, it faces the medium-term task of turning itself from a Communist to a capitalist society. In the short term it has to try to control the new economic zones it has created, which are themselves becoming centres of political power. Japan, of course, cannot help China solve its political problems; nor can it help China with its economic transition. Japan, unlike the US and even Europe, is not a willing buyer of Chinese manufactured products, though it does buy substantial quantities of textiles and some raw materials. The result is a cool relationship. At the moment Japan remains China's main trading partner after Hong Kong, but its need for Japanese technology will tend to diminish as it incorporates Hong Kong and builds closer ties with Taiwan. China has seen Taiwan, Singapore and Hong Kong all develop successful industrial bases without leaning particularly on Japan. It has established its own new economic zones without Japanese technology, learning instead from Hong Kong. On a long view, China and Japan will remain rivals, rather than become partners.

This tension between the two largest economic powers will mean that East Asia is unlikely to develop into a trading bloc as exclusive as either North America or western Europe may become. Attempts to create a trading bloc round the ASEAN countries (Association of South-East Asian Nations)[17] are unlikely to make much progress, particularly since the efforts to corral these countries into a closer relationship have tended to come from the economically smaller and weaker members. Meanwhile other tensions will persist. These include:

- The path to union of the two Koreas (and until that happens, the unpredictability of North Korea)
- Emerging competition from countries at the very start of economic take-off, for example Vietnam
- The internal pressures in Indonesia, in terms of population second only to China in the region, as it develops
- Political uncertainty in Siberian Russia for perhaps a generation

The future of the Koreas issue can be summarized very briefly. Everyone is aware that the two countries will be reunited at some stage, with Germany providing an obvious model, but everyone is fearful about the circumstances under which unification might take place. Until the two countries are joined, there will be, at best, considerable uncertainty, at worst the possibility of military conflict. When they are, there will be a long period of integration, which will be painful in different ways for both sides. Fortunately for South Korea, it has the example of Germany which shows some of the dangers of over-rapid integration.

There is no doubt that the present 'tigers' will be joined by others. Vietnam is the fashionable candidate for take-off during the second half of the 1990s, with French tour groups selling package holidays on the grounds that tourists should see the country before it is ruined by association with the west. But Vietnam faces a long pull from its extreme poverty, and whether the United States is prepared to support it by taking its exports is far from clear. Without the rich market of North America it is hard for any of these countries to achieve rapid economic growth.

From a regional point of view Indonesia is more significant than Vietnam for a number of reasons. These include its size (with 184 million people it is the world's fourth most populous nation) and its great natural resources. Furthermore it has during the 1980s achieved the first stages of economic take-off. In 1967 Indonesia had a GNP per head of $70, half that of India. By 1990 this had risen to $600, the same as Egypt, and the World Bank believes that Indonesia can reach a GNP per head of $1,000 by the end of the century. The country has made enormous progress in reducing adult illiteracy, reducing poverty, and increasing life expectancy. It faces problems of internal religious and regional tensions, corruption, and an ageing leader, but the great leap to developed country status is within its grasp.

As for Siberia, it sits there waiting for more efficient and environmentally-sensitive exploitation than was possible under the economic decision-making of the Soviet Union. This is not yet happening. Eastern Siberia in any case was too far from Moscow to be of much practical economic value to the Russian economy – it naturally looks east and south to countries like Japan. But Asian expertise is not necessarily appropriate for Siberia's needs. The bulk of the world's experience in energy development is in western oil and mining companies, and in particular the Anglo-Saxon ones. Japan cannot solve Siberian Russia's natural resource problems any more than the EU can solve European Russia's industrial ills. The resources are there, but exploitation will be slow, and will involve the whole of the west. These are not resources which will be uniquely available to East Asia.

Three forces will pull against each other in East Asia for the foreseeable future. One will be the desire to get rich, together with the application and drive to succeed in doing so. The second will be the limited economic base on which success has so far been based: exporting a narrow range of industrial goods to the west. The third will be the lack of political cohesion, and the lack of a single focus for leadership. This last has not mattered in economic terms, because the US has been prepared to guarantee the military security of the region, and because the west has not felt threatened by the economic success of countries like Taiwan or Singapore. But it does feel concerned about Japan. The lack of political cohesion in the region could matter much more were the west to take a more robustly competitive approach to East Asia in general.

In the 1990s the sheer momentum behind the East Asian boom should ensure that it continues, in spite of the damage done to Japan by the world recession and the clear evidence of over-heating in China. The region will inevitably look inwards for its growth to a greater extent in the future. As more East Asian countries become rich, the region will become a more important market, in relative terms, for countries like Japan at the top of the scale of economic development. But it is very hard to see it becoming a cohesive political unit, and the fragility of the economic achievement means that there will always be the potential for things to go wrong. The economies of North America and Europe, for all their difficulties, have a depth which East Asia has yet to match.

II

THE FORCES FOR CHANGE

FIVE

DEMOGRAPHY

What we know already

OF ALL THE FORCES that will change the world over the next generation, demography is probably the most important. The numbers of
mouths to feed, the relative sizes of the populations of the industrial
world and the less developed countries, the age distribution of the
west – all these forces will have a profound effect not just on the world
economy, but on societies both rich and poor. The change will be
gradual – the world's population rose by some 93 million in 1992 to
reach 5.5 billion, but in the west we barely noticed the fact that more
than the population of Germany had been added to the human race.
Population shifts have an inexorable effect on the world's living standards, its politics, its environment, and on how people behave towards
each other in societies as diverse as Italy and China.

If, for most people, demography seems abstruse, there is at least no
shortage of information to analyse. There is a wealth of data about
population change – the birth rate, marriage age, number of children,
number of divorces and so on – which for some countries goes back
several centuries. This data sets some curious puzzles: why, for
example, has the birth rate in Catholic Italy fallen to the lowest in
western Europe, while that of Catholic Ireland has remained the highest? And it raises nightmarish questions: can the world feed the 8
billion people the United Nations now estimates will be alive in 2020?

In spite of all the data of demography, it is an area where forecasters
can get things spectacularly wrong. At the beginning of the 1950s,
British demographers predicted that the population of England and
Wales forty years later would be 46.5 million, over 7 per cent less than
the nearly 50 million it turned out to be at the 1991 census. They
did not spot the implications of the post-war 'baby boom' on two
generations, nor indeed the impact of immigration from the former

British colonies.[1] Then at the start of the 1970s, some alarmists thought world population growth would continue exponentially, when in fact the rate of growth had already begun to slow down. Over a shorter timespan, fifteen to twenty years, the errors are likely to be quite small; only estimates for more than one generation ahead are likely to be seriously wrong. We know pretty much how many people there will be in the world in 2010, and can make a decent shot at the number in 2020 or 2025. What is much more hazardous is guessing where and when the world's population growth will level off: the United Nations has estimates of a world population between 7.5 billion and 14.2 billion for the year 2100, but it is perfectly possible that it could be outside even these extreme ranges.

The middle variant of these UN projections, which usually look to the year 2025, are the basis for the discussion in this book.[2] Go back to its 1974 projections for the year 1990, and its estimate for world population has proved remarkably accurate: the forecast was a mere 15 million, or 0.3 per cent, too low – and would in any case have been within the margin of error of the population estimates. True, it overestimated population growth in the developed world and in Latin America, and underestimated population growth in Asia, but not by a margin sufficient to alter the big picture. The projections for 2025 may not be right in detail, but the story they tell will be right in substance.

The story has two parts. The first concerns world population growth, now concentrated almost entirely in the developing world. For several decades, the poorer countries have accounted for a larger and larger share of humankind. The world's population more than doubled between 1950 and 1992, rising from 2.5 billion to 5.5 billion. In 1950 nearly a third of humankind lived in the industrial world; now it is below one quarter. By 2020 it will be less than one fifth. Within the developing world, national populations are growing at very different rates. As countries grow richer, and infant mortality declines, so women have smaller families. In some 'developing' countries – such as South Korea and Taiwan – women typically have families as small as those in industrial countries, two children or fewer. Contrast some African countries where women typically bear seven or eight children.

The future pattern of population growth will depend largely on how powerful a force the apparent link between development and fertility rate[3] turns out to be. In particular, demographers will watch trends in China – up to now, a demographic oddity: a poor country with a low fertility rate. As China grows richer, and political influence on fertility rates declines, will the birth rate rise? Or will a rapid increase in wealth hold it down? As China is home to one-fifth of humanity, a rise in the birth rate would have an immense impact.

Asia by 2020 will probably still have much the same proportion of mankind as in 1990 – some 50 per cent. But the share of Africa will almost certainly have risen: by 2010 it is expected to rise to 15 per cent of world population from today's 12 per cent.[4] Here, the key question will be the effect of AIDS. In some African cities, one in three people are now HIV positive. Such a level of infection, if not curbed, might stabilize population growth or even cause a brief population decline.

What of the other part of the story? In most rich countries, birth rates are now lower than the average of 2.1 children per woman needed for long-term stability. As a result, the population of the developed world will age. The rich countries will be relatively old, the poor relatively young. This change in the age structure of the industrial countries will take place faster in some than in others, but will affect the living standards and lifestyles of people in all of them. The older the population of a country the fewer people there will be of working age to support both the old and the young. Some of the likely changes that will take place are discussed in the next section, but first let's look at some comparative figures for the Group of Seven, the seven largest industrial countries.

These are set out on the graph overleaf.

Two features stand out: the extent to which all mature industrial countries are ageing, and the extent to which some are ageing faster than others.

From a demographic point of view, the two most interesting countries on the graph are Britain and Japan – Britain because it is changing less than any other country, Japan because it is changing more. In 1960 Britain was, with France, the oldest of the industrial nations; in 2020 it will be, with the United States, the youngest. While the long-run trend is for it to age, between 1990 and 2010 it will actually grow younger, in the sense that the proportion of 65-year-olds relative to the whole population will decline a little – though the proportion of very old, the over-85s, will continue to rise. How Britain might benefit from this relative shift will be one of the important features affecting the country's economic performance.

Japan is even more interesting, for it goes from being the youngest of the main industrial nations to being the oldest. No country has had to make such a rapid transformation, at least since the industrial

International comparison of ageing population (percentage of population aged 65 and over)[5]

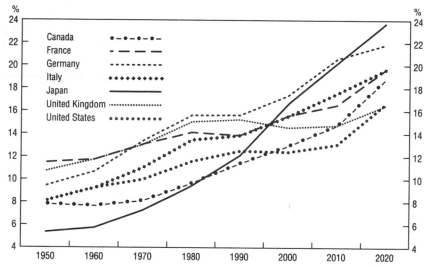

revolution, so the modern world has no practical experience of the full implications of such an adjustment. How Japan copes with this will clearly be crucial to whether its economic progress can continue during the next twenty-five years.

Changes for the other countries are less extreme. The US has been relatively young and will continue to be so; Germany is already quite old and will get even older; France shows a similar pattern to Germany, though in less extreme form; Italy has similarities with Japan, though also in less extreme form; Canada moves from being a society younger than the US to one older.

What might change this picture – or, to put it another way, what level of certainty should be attached to the ageing pattern described in the graphs? In terms of the rising proportion of elderly, the level of certainty is very high indeed, for people will almost certainly tend to live longer. We also know a lot about the number of people who will be of working age. After all, everyone who will be over twenty-five in the year 2020 was already alive when this book was published. Migration may change the balance slightly; and, potentially more important, so may an extension of the length of the typical working life. A change in the birth rate would have its main economic effects only from 2020 onwards, but such a change would have sufficiently important social implications to merit further discussion here.

Again, the easiest way to catch a feel for what has been happening
is to look at a graph.

This shows total fertility rates, the number of children each woman
is expected to have during her lifetime. Replacement rate, the rate at
which a population will ultimately remain stable, is 2.1 children per
woman. All industrial countries experienced some kind of post-war
baby boom, and were still well above replacement rate in the 1960s,
though the rate was falling fast. (In Japan in 1947, immediately after
the Second World War, the total fertility rate was 4.5.) All industrial
countries, with the exception of the US, had moved below replacement
rate by the middle 1970s, with the decline levelling off in most around
1985. Since then fertility rates have stabilized, or started to rise, though
only in one country, Sweden, has the rate reached replacement rate.

This upturn in Sweden, if repeated elsewhere, would have an enormous effect on the older societies of the industrial world. On present
trends, some major countries, in particular Japan and Germany, face
the prospect of a steady decline in their population, starting in the
early years of the next century. We have no experience of the effects
of a slow, steady decline in a complex industrial society. The rapid
falls in population of the past, such as occurred in Ireland after the
1847 famine or in the Americas after the coming of European settlers,
have generally occurred in agrarian societies where, for some reason
or other, there has been an economic or environmental catastrophe.

Comparison of fertility rates[6]

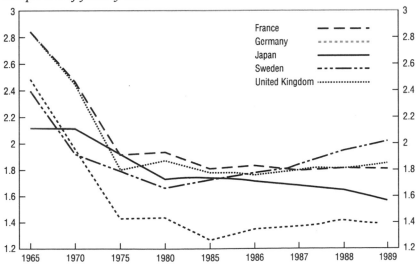

What will happen in countries like Germany and Japan will be quite different: they will not be poor countries facing disaster, but rich countries facing retreat. But what if Sweden is a guide, and the trend changes? Babies may come back into fashion, with families tending to become larger, and with some of the other characteristics of the post-war baby boom being recreated. Some of the implications of that will be discussed later. At this stage it is worth saying that we simply do not yet know whether the rise in Sweden is a one-off, associated with some tax changes which encourage women to have a second baby close to a first, or whether it reflects a significant trend.

What we can be very sure about, though, is that the world's population will continue to grow for another generation and that, proportionate to the total, the population of the present industrial world will shrink. This will have profound effects.

Age and growth

An older industrial world will inevitably be a slower-growing one. There is no doubt that economies with a large proportion of old people, and the prospect of a shrinking population, have a lower capacity for growth (and maybe a lower appetite for it) than 'young' countries. But that does not mean that they will necessarily grow more slowly in terms of income per head. That depends on how they learn to adapt to the difference in balance of their populations.

Population growth, by itself, does not ensure economic progress. All too often it leads to the reverse. One has only to look to Africa to see that a booming population, without economic development, has helped cause impoverishment or even catastrophe. But it can provide a spur. The industrial revolutions of Europe in the nineteenth century, North America in the first seventy-five years of the twentieth, and the growth spurt of Japan since the Second World War have all been associated with rising populations, particularly in the early stages of the process. Population is still rising rapidly in most of the newly industrialized countries in east Asia, but that spur will not exist for the established industrial world for a generation at least, maybe longer.

So the industrial countries will have to learn to adapt. For a start they should recognize that they do not need to grow as rapidly as in the past. A growing population needs more investment in infrastructure and in housing simply to provide adequate shelter. The shanty towns outside the cities of the less developed world show what happens when this investment is inadequate. Countries with a stable population may well choose to upgrade their infrastructure and improve their housing stock, but this costs a fraction of the amount needed to invest in the first place. People in the industrial world, however, will still want to improve their living standards, and if they are to be able to do so, these countries will need to make a number of changes in the way they use the available labour. If the proportion of people of working age is going to be smaller, countries will have to use the available workforce much more carefully than they do at present. This will require large changes in the way the labour market of most industrial societies operates. Some obvious examples of this pattern are:

- Retirement ages have to rise
- Female participation rates in the workforce will climb
- Part-time working (including homeworking) will continue to increase
- University students will be expected to work part-time while studying
- Greater efforts will be made to see the unemployed are in work
- Retraining, maybe several times in a career, will become more normal
- Voluntary labour will be used to a greater extent
- There will be more pressure on children to learn marketable skills

Some of the features noted above are already evident. Every member of the EU is either increasing the retirement age or is considering doing so: by 2020 the normal retirement age may well have risen to 67 or even 70 in most industrial countries. The main motive for this in Europe is cost to the state. Governments feel that if retirement ages are not raised the burden of paying pensions will be so high that working people will not be prepared to pay the tax levels necessary to fund them. But the raising of retirement ages will have important effects on the economies, as well as on public finances. Providing that employers are able to learn new ways of getting the best out of relatively old workers, they will have a ready and flexible supply of labour which they have hitherto neglected.

The proportion of women in the workforce has risen in every OECD country over the last thirty years. Further rises in female participation will, for many countries, be the principal source of new labour. Some of the most interesting thinking on the implications of increased female participation has been taking place in Japan, the country with the most serious potential problem and one which has not made as much use of its skilled women workers as most of its rivals. Here, the aim of the planners is to iron out the dip in female participation while mothers bring up young children. In 1990 some 77 per cent of Japanese women were in the labour force; this fell to 50 per cent at age thirty-two, but then rose again to reach 65–70 per cent between the ages of forty and middle-fifties. The aim of Japanese planners is to keep nearly 60 per cent of the 32-year-olds in the workforce, as well as more than 70 per cent of the forty to 55-year-olds. If more women work, then the labour force in Japan in 2010 could be higher than it was in 1990, even though the total population will be lower, and there will be many more very old.[7] But as with the old, if employers are to make the best use of women workers they will have to rethink the terms on which they employ them.

Both of these groups will frequently want to work part-time, for obvious reasons. The US and UK have perhaps the most experience of using part-time workers, but both countries still categorize workers as full-time or part-time on a fairly rigid basis. This will change as more and more of the workforce seeks to choose its own hours, getting paid for the actual time worked. This could result, indeed should result, in great gains in efficiency, for employers would no longer need to carry a surplus stock of labour – they would merely buy in the hours they needed at any particular time.

University students in the US are already accustomed to providing part-time labour, both in the educational establishments where they are being taught, and in the service industries. Students in general can expect to become a more important part of the labour force. Employers will need higher skill levels, so more people will need to be being trained or educated at any one time, and retraining several times in a career will become normal. But there will be an inevitable squeeze on resources to pay for the education and training – so the students will have to share the costs and the main way in which they will generate the funds to cover these costs will be by part-time work.

If there are fewer people of normal working age, unemployment will seem even more of a waste. Demographic change will tend to reduce the numbers of the unemployed, but it will also change attitudes towards unemployment. From the perspective of Europe in the early

1990s, unemployment appears to be a particularly intractable problem. While the very high levels of unemployment of this period will not decline swiftly, unemployment in the mature industrial world is likely to become a less important issue as the twenty-first century proceeds. Indeed, as discussed in the next section, the whole concept of unemployment is likely to change as the boundaries between a full-time job, a part-time job, self-employment, and living on savings or a pension will become blurred.

The need for retraining will be particularly important if countries are to make the best use of their available workers. A large proportion of the jobs of the late-twentieth century seem to be better performed by young workers. It is regarded as quite normal for companies to refuse even to interview candidates for jobs if they are over forty, while people made redundant in their fifties rarely obtain other full-time jobs.[8] For manual workers it has long been the norm that their earnings peak in their twenties and thirties; recently a similar pattern seems to be developing for many professionals, too.[9] The central way both to boost the earnings of the early-retired, and to boost the supply of labour, is to retrain people who would otherwise live off pensions.

But not all pensioners will need to supplement their income. These people will become enormously useful since many of the new jobs – in particular those involved with caring for other old people – will have to be done by people who are prepared to donate their time. Expansion of the voluntary workforce is an obvious way of using spare time and getting much-needed jobs done. The likely pattern will be a blurring of the distinction between paid and unpaid work: pensioners will work for some payment, maybe in the form of benefits in kind. The growing number of the old will be relatively rich: many will have excellent pensions from funded schemes. They may well not wish to come back into the paid workforce, but will want to contribute to society's welfare. As in late-Victorian England, when there was a substantial number of people with private means, the voluntary sector will absorb their energies.

Finally, if young workers are scarce, there will not only be great demand for them, but also great pressure on them to develop the skills which the marketplace needs. Something of this is evident already in Japan and Singapore (though in both places the culture which encourages children to learn marketable skills predates the present fall in the birth rate). But if, for many types of work, young labour has comparative advantages over older labour, the societies which are going to be economically successful are going to be those which use young labour most efficiently.

Whether they are successful or not in adapting to these changes in the labour market, the structure of the mature industrial economies is bound to alter. For a start, demography is one of several forces pushing countries further away from manufacturing and further towards services. For example, let's look at the two big service industries paid for, to a large extent, through the tax system – health care and education. Most obviously health care is absorbed by the very young and, rather more, by the old, especially in their final year.[10]

Education might seem to be less in demand if there are fewer young, but in practice the reverse is true. The demand for skills continues, even if the number of children declines. The result is that the industry has to change its emphasis from teaching the basics to the young to teaching more specific skills to the not-so-young. It has, so to speak, to move up-market. Instead of mass-producing education for children in schools, it has to become a much more sophisticated producer of education and training for already-educated adults. Growth areas will include higher education, which is still not particularly sensitive to market demand; adult training, a highly-fragmented industry often without proper quality control; and 'leisure learning', teaching skills and knowledge for purely recreational purposes.

To say that might seem commonplace. Everyone, one might say, accepts that these two industries will tend to grow. But the industrial countries have hardly begun to think through the consequences of these changes, still less to grapple with them. For example, it was only in 1993, after the election of President Clinton, that the US started to address the efficiency of its health care system. Universities like Oxford, Cambridge and Harvard still regard it as normal to take undergraduates. Yet they are expensive units for the education of eighteen-year-olds, and might well, in business terms, be wiser to move up-market and specialize entirely in post-graduate work. Interestingly, there is serious discussion in Japan about the possibility of Tokyo University becoming entirely a post-graduate operation. The argument is partly that it is an expensive way of educating undergraduates, but also that the needs of the Japanese economy for post-graduate education will be such that it will not be possible to supply the skills if universities do not specialize at the things at which they are best. The best way, for Japan, of coping with fewer young people is to make sure that those which it does have are educated to the highest possible levels.

These two examples show how the policy-makers in big, established, professionally-run service industries like health and education have not yet fully taken on board the impact of demographic change. The health industry is aware that there will be a need for more nursing homes for the old, and the education industry can see that growth will come in areas which are closely related to commercial needs. But the ideas that an older population will need a health industry with a quite different cost structure, or that education's future lies in a different direction, would seem alien to most professionals in those industries. This is in contrast even to quite ordinary manufacturing industries. The motor manufacturers, for example, are well aware that they have to try to develop different products a generation from now, and they are aware that the structure of the industry may itself change, that the established producers in the mature industrial countries will give ground to new ones in the newly industrialized world. Getting health and education right are two of the greatest challenges for the mature industrial world ... as it matures still further. Private sector operators in both these industries will see opportunities to fill the gaps, as they do already. But the success of the different nations will not be determined by the ability of the private sector to plug the gaps; it will depend on the ability of the public sector to get its pricing and its policies right. The greater the extent to which a country is ageing, the greater the importance of getting health and education right.

Elsewhere in the private sector, other service industries will benefit from the ageing population if they adapt correctly. Retailing will tend to move in the directions already evident: for example, towards mail order (because an older population will tend to want goods delivered). Financial services will grow, developing further the range of added-value advisory services, and using technology to cut the costs of money transfer (older people will need advice on pensions and investments rather than mortgages). Leisure services – restaurants, hotels, tour companies, airlines – will adapt to an older, more cautious customer. Some of these changes are discussed in Chapter 8, but the key point here is that the market will ensure that services do adapt. An older population will have important consequences for the service industries, but since many of these services cannot by their nature be internationally traded, they will not affect the pecking order of nations. Countries which have adapted their service industries well to their older populations may become nicer or at least more convenient places to live, but this will not change their position in the world. Their ability to compete in the production and delivery of internationally traded goods and services, however, will.

Having fewer, and hence more expensive, young people will make many forms of manufacturing more difficult. Even if factories learn to use even fewer people (and as the next chapter points out, they are beginning to reach the practical limits of replacing people with machinery), the other aspects of the manufacturing process like design and marketing will continue to need a lot of labour. The very young, people in their twenties, seem to have a comparative advantage on the factory floor where adaptability counts more; the slightly older, the thirty- and forty-year-olds, seem to have a comparative advantage in other aspects of the manufacturing process like design, marketing and finance, where more experience is needed. So the older a country is, the harder it will be for manufacturers to find internationally competitive staff, particularly on the factory floor. The result will be that actual production will increasingly be carried out offshore, with the goods designed and marketed in the mature industrial world. The motive for moving production offshore has up to now been principally the cheaper labour of the newly industrialized countries; in the future it will be more the differences in the age structure of the two regions.

But this process cannot take place in the internationally traded service sector. Tourism, for example, the largest service industry of all, has an enormous appetite for labour. In 1993, travel and tourism together employed roughly 130 million people, more than any other industry in the world. Demand for tourism will continue to rise, though the things that older and better-educated tourists will seek will be different from services demanded by the young – there will be a boom in all forms of tourism related to culture, history, and education. University towns will be packed with visitors, while the nightclubs of the Mediterranean will be empty. The surge in overseas travel by the Japanese in the second half of the 1980s shows some of the patterns which will develop further: travel to 'safe' destinations, usually in the developed world, generally in organized party tours. All this growth will require yet more labour, often with new skills; the difficulty of supply, when young labour is scarce, will increase. Expect waiters in hotels in London to be foreign students carrying out post-graduate courses at the London School of Economics, while study-tour guests will attend lectures by 'retired' marketing executives from Unilever.

However well the mature industrial world adapts to its new age structure, there will be some loss of dynamism in all younger nations which have achieved industrial take-off. The extent to which this happens depends very much on the quality, attitudes and expectations of the middle-aged and the old in the mature countries. Will the next generation of old people be the same as their parents and grandparents? Or, perhaps because they have been better educated and have better health, will the next generation be (in the purely economic sense, of course) a 'better' generation than those of the past? No-one knows, though in Japan, where the problem is most serious, this argument is often made. The answer will have something to do with education: if people are taught to be flexible in their attitudes (for example by being prepared to retrain several times in a career) they will be more effective producers in their old age. Whether it is possible to teach people to be flexible in their attitudes is another matter. This leads to the question of the social implications of an ageing population.

How old societies will differ from young ones

It is easy to see the characteristics of typical 'young' societies, for there are so many of them in the developing world, but much harder to catch a feel for 'old' ones in the industrial world.

What, rationally, might an old industrial world (which will include Japan and much of North America) feel like? One would expect the values of older people to weigh more heavily in the balance of factors which determine how both economies and societies work. Such a world might include the following characteristics:

- Low inflation (elderly voters will dominate the polls and are likely to be particularly hostile to having their savings whittled away by inflation)
- Low unemployment (because of the fall in the proportion of people of normal working age)
- Low crime (the young commit most offences, while the old probably have lower tolerance of crime)
- Low tolerance (or at least lower tolerance) of disorder, anti-social or even unconventional behaviour, and with this:
- Greater acceptance of authority in controlling such behaviour

This might suggest a return to 'Victorian values', that combination of puritanism, prudery and certainty about what was right and what was wrong which characterized the late-Victorian era in Britain. In terms of the size of income differentials (another characteristic of the Victorian period), most industrial countries have already moved some way in that direction from the egalitarian 1960s. In Britain, pre-tax differentials are wider than they were in Edwardian days: in 1990, the top 10 per cent earned 2.5 times that of the bottom 10 per cent. In 1906 the ratio was 2.4.[11] But while a more middle-aged society is indeed likely to emphasize the values of middle-aged people, their direct influence will probably be quite limited. They will only really have an influence indirectly through the ballot box, by voting in governments which foster the interests and values of the balance of the electorate.

The power of the ballot box is not to be underplayed: after all, one of the most powerful forces helping to cut inflation in the industrial world is the votes of an increasingly old electorate. In an older society it will be very difficult for any democratically-elected government to carry out any cost-cutting exercise, like reducing pensions or cutting funds for health care. But the other ways in which the changing age structure of the population will affect society will be even less direct: the electorate may want lower crime, or a greater degree of public order, but the delivery will be a problem until its attitudes become so widely accepted that its wishes achieve critical mass and start to have a direct effect on people's behaviour. Meanwhile, the indirect effects of demography, particularly through the labour market, will be more important than the wishes of the electorate, expressed through the ballot box.

Changes in the labour market will have an enormous effect on social attitudes, for the whole relationship between employee and employer will become much more defined. It will be a contract to carry out certain functions, and be paid for them. For many so-called employees, maybe a majority of them, it will not be a full-time job as such. If the workforce of most large corporations becomes mainly part-time contract labour, then the idea that the relationship between employer and employee should be anything more than a mercenary one becomes absurd, as does the notion that both sides of the relationship should have some unwritten contractual relationship involving ideas of 'loyalty'. Either side will see itself free to end the contract on the terms specified in the contract itself.

This sort of change in the labour market will put a much greater premium on saving. All employees will have to regard their employment contract as a purely temporary arrangement, and they will probably have to accept that there will be periods of their working life when they are either unemployed or retraining for a quite different occupation. The older a society is, the greater the extent to which its members are likely to depend on income from savings rather than income from work. Increased mobility will further shift the balance in favour of saving, as the more likely people are to have to change jobs, the more they will be inclined to save to help fund the transfer. As savings accumulate and are passed down from one generation to another, a new political constituency will be created, a new *rentier* class.

Here there is a parallel with late-Victorian Britain, when there was a large leisured class which lived off income from investments. This income reached quite a long way down the middle classes, and it became quite normal for people to supplement their income from work with their private means. (This lives on in Britain in 'pupillage', the year of apprenticeship aspirant barristers have to serve completely unpaid, the assumption being that they have the private means to support themselves.) This pattern was not confined to Britain or to the commercial or landed classes. Professional people across Europe were able to provide sufficient private income for their children not to have to think about working. Novelists of the period, such as Thomas Mann, well describe the attitudes of this large leisured class. Indeed private incomes may have stimulated the production of novels: Gustave Flaubert's father, a successful doctor, was able to accumulate enough savings to provide his son with sufficient income to live in comfort virtually all his life.

The larger the group of people who rely, to some extent at least, on income from savings, the greater the political influence of the group. These people can expect to be courted by politicians, who will need to frame policies which will protect savings if they are to be voted back into office. Given the fact that people under eighteen do not vote, it is highly likely that retired people, plus those close to retirement, will become the dominant political force in western democracies: they will be close to having a majority of the votes.

This group of people living on savings will also become significant as an international resource. They, and their money, will be mobile. Already there is a small group of people who choose their domicile for tax reasons. This group will grow, and will be an increasingly valuable human resource for countries to attract. Some of its members may simply want to live off their investments and live in countries which combine an attractive quality of life with an attractive tax regime. Others will have their own businesses and bring jobs as well as capital to the countries to which they move. Governments will increasingly seek to attract both these forms of foreign human capital rather in the way they seek to attract foreign industrial capital at the moment. They will not, for obvious reasons, seek to attract the elderly who do not have private means, and who are likely to absorb large amounts of health care resources.

The ageing of the electorate may well lead to an even larger gap between the expectations electorates have of governments and the governments' ability to meet those expectations. During the early 1990s this is evident in the pressure on public finances in virtually all industrial countries: electorates want governments to spend money on services, but are not prepared to vote the funds to pay for these. Such pressures on public finances will continue. The aspirations of an elderly electorate in 2020 will also be expressed in social ideals, and these may be even more difficult for governments to deliver. The electorate may, for example, put an even higher priority on public safety, and in particular on cutting the incidence of violent crime. While the smaller proportion of young people ought to cut crime – because most offences are committed by young men – crime levels are more likely to be brought down by a change in general social attitudes than by government policies. It is possible for governments to deliver better health care, provided voters are prepared to pay for it; it is much more difficult for a government to deliver lower crime, however much voters want it, and however many new police are hired.

Nevertheless, governments will be forced to use more robustly the variety of powers available to the state to try to meet their electorates' wishes. If older electorates are going to be more concerned about public safety, and have a lower tolerance for disorder than young electorates, then the central issue will be the social price of doing so. Populations are prepared to see a cutback in civil liberties if a majority feel these are being abused – witness the curbing of trade union power in Britain during the 1980s. The key issue for politicians of mature democracies will be to gauge to what extent electors are prepared to give up some of the civil liberties which have been won over the last two or three generations in order to create the more conformist society that the majority will seek.

The rising average age of the population will probably be the most important force determining future trends in social attitudes. There is, however, another shift which at the moment is even more evident: the growth of the proportion of women in the workforce. There is a close relationship between the rise in the proportion of women working outside the home and other social variables, in particular the fall in the birth rate, the rise in divorce rate and the rise in the proportion of children born to single families.[12] The first of these, the fall in the birth rate, has already happened in the industrial world. The big assumption that the UN demographers are making when they predict that, at some time during the second half of the next century, world population growth will level off is that the same process will occur in the developing world as education and job opportunities for women increase.

For the industrial world, though, the great social issue is how long the retreat from the marriage contract – either by divorce, or by not getting married in the first place – will continue. It is very hard to see the rise in women in the workforce not continuing, though at some stage the growth will tail off. But if an even higher proportion of women are to work, will the effect be more families breaking up and more single parents? If so, it is a disturbing prospect for two reasons. The first is simply that people seem to have very little knowledge of the consequences, either for themselves or for their offspring, of rejecting an institution, marriage, which has lasted several thousand years. The second is that, in as far as the effects are known, it seems that children of single parents, and children of divorced couples (including those who remarry), perform worse academically and have greater social problems than those who are brought up in stable, two-parent relationships.[13] Since the people at the bottom of the income scale are most likely to be lone parents, the danger is that a cycle of deprivation is being created, with lone parents passing on poor economic prospects to their children, who in turn become lone parents, and so on.

In some countries, and Britain is a good example, the pace of social change has been quite remarkable. In 1960, 6 per cent of children born in the UK were born to unmarried parents.[14] In 1990 it was 28 per cent – up from 12 per cent a decade earlier – and by 1992 had risen again to 31 per cent. Similar, though in most cases less dramatic, rises occurred in most industrial countries. True, not all children who are born to unmarried parents are born to single parents – roughly three-quarters are born to what are called consensual unions, where both parents live together but have decided not to have a legal union;[15] but while there is an important distinction to be made between the rejection of marriage as a legal institution and family break-up, there is evidence that consensual unions are more likely to break up than people who tie the knot. The trend away from legal marriage may also result in more single families.

Is further weakening of the traditional family inevitable as women form a still more important part of the workforce? If it is, then industrial countries may start to question the social costs of having such a large proportion of women at work. Of course it would be both politically and ethically difficult, to put it mildly, to try to deny women the right to work: quite aside from the fact that they are needed in the workforce, it would be extraordinary were the whole process of female emancipation to be reversed. (Or at least it would be extraordinary in the Christian democracies of the west; such a process is taking place in some Muslim societies.)

But if a further weakening is not to take place, what is the mechanism by which it will be reversed? At some point the frequency of family breakdown will slow, simply because there will always be some people for whom the traditional family works rather well. For it to reverse, there needs to be a redefinition by both sexes of what is expected of a marriage. Historically, social attitudes do move in long swings, and an institution which has worked for as long as marriage has ought to be robust enough to fight back. But, at a guess, the turmoil in family life still has fifteen or twenty years to run before there is a clear reversal, and the proportion of unitary families with husband, wife (but working wife) and children starts to rise again.

None of this should be taken to suggest that there will be a return to the oppressive 'traditional values' typified by the Victorian family in Britain. The economic pressure for women to work will stop that. The real message is more subtle. It is that the countries of the industrial world will be struggling, over the next twenty to thirty years, to find a way of reconciling the trend towards the economic equality of men and women with the social consequences of that trend. Some of those consequences are wholly beneficial: women no longer need to stay with men who beat them up. But some are not: in particular, when families break down children suffer, crime rises, everyone becomes poorer. How countries balance the freedoms that the move towards equality has brought with the costs of those freedoms will help determine whether they are socially – and ultimately economically – successful. A country which has to spend a lot of resources trying to cope with the problems of family breakdown is a country which has fewer resources to devote to other things. In any case, money isn't a perfect solution to social problems: all it does is help with picking up the pieces. Far better not to have the breakdown in the first place.

Age structure is not the only force driving social change. Japan, perhaps the most conformist, though not necessarily the most authoritarian, large industrial country built much of its conformist approach in the 1950s despite its youthful age structure, while the great burst of British exuberance of the 'swinging sixties' took place when it was the oldest industrial country of all. Quite aside from its relatively youthful age structure, the US, with its vast size, its multicultural population and its historical respect for the individual, will remain less conformist than most of its competitors. But in general, as the industrial world becomes older, it will take on more and more the characteristics of the communities we already have where retired people make up a large proportion of the population. More of Britain will become like Bournemouth, more of the US like the more peaceable parts of Florida. In general, the developed world will become calmer and more ordered. By contrast, as the developing world becomes younger, it will become less ordered, and at times more chaotic. This will lead to much greater tensions between the rich and the poor than have been evident for most of the post-colonial period.

The 'haves' and the 'have-nots'

The recipe is dangerous. There will be on the one hand the increasingly old and conformist world of the rich. On the borders of this rich world there will be, on the other hand, a surge in the numbers of young people living in crowded cities who will see daily on their televisions living standards which they can never hope to achieve. True, some parts of this developing world will leap the barrier and become relatively rich themselves, but that may intensify the sense of resentment among those countries and people who fail. Such resentment, in the age of the terrorist and of weapons of mass destruction, is truly alarming. It is overwhelmingly in the interest of both rich and poor parts of the world that the relationship should be managed in such a way as to minimize this danger, but it will not be easy.

The most obvious way in which the imbalance between the two worlds will manifest itself will be in population movements, as in the past – for example from Europe to North and South America through much of the last century and the early years of this. Immigration will be one of the key issues of the first part of the next century, for it is the natural economic response – there will inevitably be great pressure from people on the poor fringes of the rich world to get into it. Already the border between Mexico and the US is in practice almost impossible to police, while Southern Europe finds itself coping with increasing numbers of immigrants from North Africa, and the richer parts of Asia are under pressure from poorer neighbours. On the face of it such population movements might seem to benefit both sides: the rich countries gain useful labour, while emigrants' earnings boost the incomes of their families left behind, but there are two powerful reasons why immigration can do little to ease the pressures of population imbalance: the numbers do not work; and there are strong social reasons restricting it.

The numbers point can be swiftly made. The annual additions to world population are running at between 90 and 100 million a year. Suppose the industrial world were to take even 10 per cent of the increase: over a generation that would amount to more than 200 million people. It is inconceivable that the industrial world could take that number of immigrants; yet to take that number would make only the smallest dent in the population growth that was taking place in the developing world. Immigration into the rich world cannot in any significant way alleviate the pressures of population growth in the poor.

In any case the social arguments against further immigration on any large scale are very strong. Aside from the fact that it would be the people with the best education and highest skills who would be attracted to the industrial world – the very people the developing world most needs to retain – the social pressures that result from the arrival of people with different ethnic and religious backgrounds from the home population are widely recognized.

That said, it is worth noting that different industrial regions will experience different levels of immigration. There are several reasons for suggesting that in the Europe of the first part of the next century immigration will be limited even more severely than it has been in the 1990s. Chief among these is the lack of a tradition of immigration – quite the reverse: it has been the place from which people emigrated to the rest of the world. While some European countries have managed to assimilate immigrants reasonably successfully, Europe as a whole has found it difficult to absorb people of non-European backgrounds. Whatever moral judgement one wishes to make about Europe's difficulties with immigration, the practical point remains that its absorptive capacity is very small. Its population will not, as a result, be significantly altered by immigration during the next twenty-five years. The pressure will exist, but it will in general be resisted.

By contrast, in North America unrest about immigration as such has been virtually unknown – at least since the conquest of the native Americans by successive waves of European immigrants. It can therefore expect both to attract immigrants and to accept them. While this will not have a great impact on the numbers in the countries from which these people come, it will lead to striking changes in the balance of the North American population. The US Commerce Department's Census Bureau has estimated that by 2050 the 'white' population of the US may only just be the majority. The Hispanic population is expected to grow from 9 to 21 per cent between 1992 and 2050, with Asians and Pacific Islanders making up 11 per cent of the population (against 3 per cent in 1992), the black population growing to 16 from 12 per cent, and native Americans rising from 0.8 to 1.2 per cent of the population. On this basis, although the white population will increase in absolute numbers over the period, it will decline from 75 to 53 per cent of the total population.[16] While these trends will only be partially established by 2020, some of the effects of this new immigration should be apparent. By 2020 North America will have already begun to feel more different from Europe in its culture and ideas than it did in, say, the 1980s, simply because a larger proportion of the opinion-formers will have non-European backgrounds. The change in the balance of attitudes caused by new immigrants, particularly those from Asia, will be much more significant than the issue which is currently preoccupying many people in the US: the growth of a large minority speaking Spanish rather than English. The children of the Spanish-speakers will duly come to use English, but the children of the Korean immigrants are likely to keep their Asian cultural attitudes, not least towards families and savings. New languages are more easily acquired than new attitudes.

In Asia, the most useful generalization is that migration within countries will be more significant than migration between them. The most obvious example of this will be a movement within China to what are currently the new economic zones, but which are rapidly developing into semi-autonomous states within a greater China. The new economic zones are already proving a magnet for people close to their borders, just as Hong Kong was, and still is, a magnet to people on its borders. As these regions grow in wealth, they will become an even more potent force for migration, and managing these population flows will be one of the hardest aspects of the transition which China will have to make. The other main patterns of migration within countries will be from North Korea to South Korea as and when the border comes down, and internally within Indonesia.

Japan will to some extent increase its immigrant population, while Japanese business representatives will continue to establish themselves elsewhere in East Asia to manage the plants the country is building there; but it will remain insulated by its strong individual culture. Australia and New Zealand will continue to attract Asian immigrants in sufficient numbers that they start to have a material influence on attitudes in both countries. In Australia in particular, immigrants will help the country pull itself away from its Anglo-Saxon roots.[17]

While cross-border migration will, in some instances at least, have a material impact on countries in the industrial world, it will be too small to have any real impact on the economic conditions in most of the developing world. What can be done to ease the tensions?

The general answer must be for the industrial world to find ways of enabling the developing world to improve its living standards so that its citizens see some progress being made. But how? For most of the post-colonial period the answer to that question has included some combination of trade and aid, with the balance shifting towards trade as the shortcomings of many aid projects have shown themselves. But the opportunities for trade were limited, both by protectionism in the industrial world and by the relatively limited range of goods which many developing countries were able, without technical and marketing help, to supply. By the end of the 1980s, a new element had emerged: the growth of direct investment by the industrial countries in the developing world. The west, instead of importing the people, would export the jobs. This is an extremely promising development, for by making direct investments – building factories, training workers – western enterprises are teaching the industrial world's techniques as well as creating employment and duly benefiting from low labour costs. Given the enormous numbers involved, it would be naive to see such direct investment as in any way 'solving' the problem of the surge in the population in the developing world – and this development, while helping middle-income countries like Mexico or Thailand, does not extend to the very poor, who are unable to supply the quality of labour or the infrastructure to underpin such investment – but it is already one important positive force, and will become an even more important one during the early years of the next century.

There are few other encouraging signs. Some writers see the growth in the world's population as leading to catastrophe: Malthus[18] was right, but a little ahead of his time. Looking one generation ahead, that is surely too alarmist. Whatever happens in the second half of the next century, a global catastrophe purely as a result of population pressure is unlikely by 2020 – on this timescale the economic pressures from population growth should not be unmanageable, just more difficult to manage. If there is to be catastrophe, it will come from something other than demography, though we should be concerned about the interaction between demographic pressure and Muslim fundamentalism. It is likely that there will be an even sharper global divide than is evident in the early 1990s. On the one hand there will be a worried, even frightened, industrial world, which will try to use its technology to preserve its living standards and protect itself from the surge in population elsewhere; on the other hand there will be the burgeoning cities of the developing world, packed with the young and the poor, without the infrastructure which makes the cities of the industrial world effective productive units. In between, there will be the handful of countries, or regions, which will be making the leap from developing to industrial status.

In making this jump, these newly industrialized countries are going to make large calls on the world's natural resources, raising the question about the way in which the environment will be affected by such economic growth.

SIX

RESOURCES AND
THE ENVIRONMENT

Is there a crisis?

SO FAR MALTHUS[1] has been proved wrong. Most parts of the world have not starved. Indeed not only has most of the world's growing population been fed, but a sizeable minority has enjoyed a rising standard of living. Ordinary people in the industrial world have experienced living standards – in terms of housing space, variety of diet, opportunities to travel – which, if available at all, would have been enjoyed by only a handful of the very rich in earlier generations. There is no scarcity of essential supplies. The industrial world is piling up surpluses which it can hardly give away, and pays farmers not to grow more food, there is a such a global surplus of coal that it is hardly worth digging it out of the ground in Britain, while oil is in real terms cheaper than it was in 1960, and there are no evident shortages of minerals. The only important resource which is scarce in many parts of the world is water.

Many people are rightly concerned about the degradation of the environment, of which more later. There are a number of other causes for concern. Some natural resources, such as tropical forests and deep-sea fisheries, are in serious danger of over-exploitation – resources such as these that exist outside the market, that are owned in common, or by the state, or by nobody, tend to be the ones that are vulnerable, while those primary products whose exploitation is privately controlled are not in danger of exhaustion. If they were, their prices would not have tended to fall ever since the 1950s. Indeed, it is the decline in the prices of raw materials which has reduced the economic advantages (and the relative wealth) of the traditionally resource-rich countries like Argentina and Australia over resource-poor nations like Japan and Switzerland.

If there is little evidence of a global resource crisis, there is evidence of regional strains. As the world's population increases, and particularly as living standards in the fast-growing regions like East Asia rise, these strains will become more obvious. The world has some experience of sudden periods of resource-shortage: the Korean War price boom and the two oil shocks are relatively recent examples. This kind of resource shock is likely to become more common, but to remain unpredictable. Within the developed world, countries which are good at providing their citizens with a comfortable lifestyle with the minimum demand for resources will prosper by comparison with those which are wasteful. Quality, not quantity, will come to matter more and more. This will be reflected in consumers' attitudes towards a wide variety of daily needs: food, drink, transport, entertainment. Within the developing world, resource problems will loom even larger in the first quarter of the next century than they have done in the last quarter of this. Coping with these will not be an issue of competitive advantage: the economic and political stability of whole regions will turn on the way in which countries manage their use of natural resources, in particular their production of food and their use of water.

For one more generation at least, then, the world's natural resources will be adequate not just to support its population, but to provide an increasing number of people with modestly comfortable lifestyles. At the same time, there will be periodic disasters. There will also be great scope for political tensions, which may become so serious as to result in conflict. To see where and how these pressure points might arise, one must look at the particular types of resource weakness in three main areas: food, water, and energy. These are not the only concerns – many people would add strategic minerals, and some would add gold. The world's two largest producers of strategic minerals and of gold are South Africa and Russia, both of which face a politically turbulent future. But food, water and energy matter most, for if mishandled they carry the threat of grave environmental degradation, and of mass starvation.

Can the world feed itself?

For the last thirty years or so world food output has grown faster than demand, with the result that the price of staple foods has fallen. The reason is that the 'green revolution' of the 1960s produced high-yielding varieties of rice which enabled the countries of Asia to increase production sharply. Looking ahead, the world will need another revolution of similar scale, but of a rather different nature.

The capacity of the world to produce enough food to feed a much larger population is not really in doubt, provided people are prepared to eat a smaller proportion of meat in their diet. Growing grain or grass and then feeding it to animals is an inefficient use of land, for animals are inefficient at converting plant energy into human food. At present in countries like India, where meat forms a very small proportion of the diet of most people, the total plant energy consumed (actual plant food eaten, plus seed, plus animal feed) is about 3,000 calories a day. By contrast, North Americans, Australians, New Zealanders and the French consume an average of 15,000 calories a day, thanks largely to the amount of meat in their diet. The world's average is some 6,000 calories a day. Some calculations of the world's ability to feed a larger population have been done by the economist Bernard Gilland. He estimates that with some increase in the area of land under crops, and more than a doubling of average yields, the world could feed about 7.5 billion people (the level of population likely to be reached by 2020) with a 'completely satisfactory' diet of 9,000 calories of plant energy a day. Similar changes could support 11.4 billion people on an allowance of 6,000 a day.[2] If these calculations are right, the world could feed double its present population at its present and often unsatisfactory levels of consumption, or provide one and a half times the present population with a decent diet.

There are two difficulties with these calculations. Firstly, whatever happens to total food production, such growth as takes place will not be evenly distributed. Some countries are already facing chronic shortages. These will get worse, for most of them are in Africa, where population growth is fastest. Food production per head in Africa has declined since the 1960s, in contrast to every other region in the world. The little we know about long-term climatic change suggests that sub-Saharan Africa will suffer more from drought in the future than it has over the last two decades. It is much harder to bring new farming methods, or new varieties of crops, even if either were appropriate, to the marginal farmers of Africa than to the larger farm owners of Asia.

Secondly, it is not clear that another green revolution is imminent. Without one, it may not be possible to increase yields by the amounts needed. Some further advances will of course be made, but they will have to be in a different form from those of the past. The success of the green revolution depended on having suitable land, the right climate and enough water. Given these, it proved possible to achieve enormous increases in yields. But these higher yields were often achieved at a cost which is only now becoming evident. These costs include soil erosion, salination and other environmental damage. As a result the sustainability of the advances is now being questioned.[3] Looking ahead, it is quite possible that genetic engineering will bring a green revolution of a different sort. Such engineering could produce more varieties of staple crops which do increase yields. But the environmental consequences of pushing yields yet higher are not yet known, and of course the smaller the rise in yields, the greater the increase that will have to occur in the amount of land taken into cultivation. If farming spreads to land that has up to now been considered unsuitable, this may lead to further environmental damage.

There is an alternative way forward. Instead of the top-down approach which brought the green revolution, where progress originated in laboratories and farmers were told what to do, there could be a bottom-up approach. Here, the aim would be to examine local farming methods, and then try to make marginal improvements to these, so as to improve overall production in a manner which can be sustained in the long run. But such an approach is difficult to organize and put into practice. It can also be desperately slow.

If some parts of the world find it increasingly difficult to grow enough food for a burgeoning population, they will become dependent on imported food, without necessarily having any products they can offer in return. To feed such countries would require an effort that was quite different from the periodic western response to a famine that is brought to the public's notice by television. Keeping the world fed could require a continuing act of international charity, year in, year out. The surplus food producers, in particular North America, would become the lifeline for hundreds of millions of people, mostly in Africa. It is hard, given what is known about population trends in the developing world, not to see the need for some sort of continuing food transfer. The issue is really whether such transfers are manageable, both politically and socially.

Is there enough water?

A shortage of fresh water is probably going to be the most serious resource problem the world will face in 2020. This might seem absurd to most west Europeans, who still think of water as almost free, but increasing numbers of Californians and Australians are already being forced to alter their habits to economize on water.

As with food, the problem is not one of global shortage, but one of uneven distribution. Three-quarters of the fresh water on the planet is held in the polar icecaps and glaciers and so is unavailable for use. Where water is plentiful, people are frequently few, and vice versa. (The most water-rich country in terms of the run-off from rainfall to population is Iceland, with more than 500,000 cubic metres per person per year; the most water-poor is Egypt, with just 0.02 cubic metres.[4]) Even in countries where water is scarce, enormous amounts are frequently used by farmers to irrigate land. Because farmers often pay less for irrigation water than it costs the government to build and maintain irrigation works, they have little incentive to irrigate in the most efficient ways.

There are several reasons to expect water shortages to grow worse:

- Further increases in irrigated land are vital for the world's food production
- The growth in the urban population of the developing world will require a large increase in water supplies
- The normal method of increasing available supplies, building more dams, has grave environmental consequences which are only just coming to be fully appreciated. In any case, most of the world's best dam sites have already been taken
- Where rivers cross national borders, countries may grab what they can at their neighbours' expense

Some 70 per cent of the water people use goes to irrigation. Since 1950 the amount of irrigated land has tripled, and one-third of the world's food is grown on it. Without that increase the world might now be starving. But the price has been environmental damage, which in some areas is now starting to reverse the rise in food production which has taken place. The most serious long-term problem is salination. When irrigation water soaks down into the soil, it absorbs mineral salts from the earth, flushing them to the surface. As the water evaporates, these salts dry out on the fields, gradually destroying their fertility. Some 25 per cent of Pakistan's cultivated land has been damaged in this way. Recovering poisoned fields is vastly expensive.[5] The environmental damage done by ill-managed irrigation schemes is a time bomb which threatens to reverse the progress in food production made by past schemes.

Four countries in particular face serious problems: India and China, which between them account for one-third of the world's irrigated land; Pakistan, 80 per cent of whose fields are irrigated; and Egypt, with a similar percentage of irrigated land, and particular problems from its dependence on one source of water, the Nile. All have suffered to a greater or lesser extent from salination. For them, maintaining their irrigated land will be a constant struggle, for even with regular flushing and the use of salt-resistant varieties of plant, ultimately the salt will win.

Already, several countries are using most of the water available to them. India, for instance, uses 97 per cent of its water for irrigation. The country is currently using half its available run-off, that is the water that falls on a country and is collected in rivers and lakes, and drawing half as much again from underground springs.[6] It has been estimated that by 2025 demand will reach 92 per cent of its entire run-off.[7] Such countries face an awkward choice. Either they must reduce the amount of water used by farmers; or they must make huge investments to develop new supplies. China, also facing severe water shortages, has an enormous project to divert about 5 per cent of the flow of the Yangtze River to the country's semi-arid northern provinces, while further schemes are planned to divert water to the west.

Feeding China will require such gigantic schemes to be successful – or it will require farmers to use water more efficiently. At present only one-third of the water used for irrigation worldwide actually goes into making plants grow – the rest is wasted. Using water more efficiently would bring environmental benefits: overwatering and poor drainage help to make salination worse. The obvious way to coax farmers to irrigate more efficiently would be to make water more expensive. Everywhere from Egypt to California, farmers get their water cheaply while cities are rationed. In the western United States, for instance, farmers in 1992 paid less than 1 cent for a cubic metre of water, while the city of Phoenix paid about 25 cents.[8]

Farmers are a politically powerful lobby, which politicians hesitate to alienate. But cities and their demands will grow. In 1950 there were two urban agglomerations with more than 10 million people: New York/north-east New Jersey, and London. The United Nations estimates that by the year 2000 there will be at least twenty-five cities with populations of more than 11 million, of which only five will be in the industrial world. In practice many of the people in these agglomerations simply will not have access to clean water, just as the inhabitants of London received reliable water supplies only in the middle of the nineteenth century, long after London had more than 1 million inhabitants. Water supplies are essential also for industrial development. Up to now, few cities have found their industrial development circumscribed by water shortages, and that is a considerable achievement. For instance, Sao Paulo, which will by the end of the century have a population of around 26 million, was in 1950 smaller than Manchester or Detroit, yet it has managed to cope with growth sufficiently well to supply most of its population with running water. But Sao Paulo is not in an arid zone. Other cities will have more serious problems. Increasingly, firms in many Third World cities will find that water is cut off or pressure falls during the day.

Providing water for irrigation and for cities will require damming more rivers, flooding more valleys, carrying out more giant water-engineering schemes. Such projects are often hugely expensive, and not only in economic terms. Large dams frequently involve massive changes in the use of land. That means not only the displacement of people from their homes but the loss of farm land, disturbance to water tables, build-up of silt, and other environmental costs. Of course, dams also produce water for irrigation and for hydroelectricity, but serious attempts to measure the benefits from dams suggest that the gains are often smaller than the costs.

The building of giant dams is a post-war phenomenon. More than three-quarters of the hundred very large dams (i.e. over 150 metres high) have been built since 1955, half since 1980. Their capacity is equivalent to 15 per cent of the run-off of the world's rivers.[9] While some are widely recognized as successes, such as the Hoover Dam in the US, others have had disastrous effects, drying out the flood plain below them, and destroying fisheries and crop yields for hundreds of miles downstream. Two extreme cases where attempts to replumb nature have already clearly resulted in environmental catastrophe are the drying up of the Aral Sea and the drying up of the river basin which supplies Lake Chad. Others are, so to speak, in the pipeline.

The damming of great rivers also threatens to become a cause of conflict. Water resources often cross national boundaries, making it very easy for one country to 'steal' the water that should be delivered to another. No-one can predict which of several points of tension will result in armed conflict, but it is easy to list some candidates. They include:

- The diversion of water from the Sea of Galilee into Israel's National Water Carrier
- The Gabcikovo Dam on the Danube in Slovakia
- Threats to dam the upper Blue and White Niles
- The damming of the upper reaches of the Tigris and Euphrates by Turkey, and the Euphrates by Syria

While there is no way of predicting whether these pressure points – or any of the other dozen similar situations around the world – will erupt into war, it is easy to see that control over water will come to be seen as a much more important strategic issue both between countries and within them. Water-rich regions will want to exert their economic power, rather than feel that they are being exploited by water-poor neighbours, even if those neighbours happen to be in the same country, or the same state. Some such tension is already evident, for example in California. It may become much more evident in China, and in Russia, if the proposed large-scale 'replumbing' projects of both those countries are put into practice. Water will become a political issue in much the same way that oil has been for much of the period after the Second World War.

Is there enough energy?

There is no global energy crisis. Set aside, for the moment, concerns about the effect on the climate of the build-up of atmospheric carbon dioxide from burning of fossil fuels; there will be ample energy to support economic growth to beyond the end of the next century. Coal, in particular, and natural gas are in plentiful supply. At present consumption rates there is enough coal to last the world for more than 200 years, and enough natural gas for some 60 years.[10] Oil supplies are tighter, of which more later.

It is fortunate that, oil apart, there is ample coal and gas, for the bulk of the world's energy will come from fossil fuels for another twenty-five years at least, and maybe for a hundred. At the moment they supply between 75 and 80 per cent of the world's total energy needs. It is difficult to see them supplying less than that in a quarter of a century's time, for only in electricity generation are there reasonably competitive substitutes. For all other uses – road, sea and air transport, home heating and cooking and many industrial processes – the world is overwhelmingly dependent on fossil fuels. Even for electricity-generation, where two other sources of commercial energy exist (nuclear and hydropower), fossil fuels dominate, producing more than 60 per cent of the electricity generated in the world. It is hard to see this proportion falling much, if at all, for both nuclear and hydro have serious environmental disadvantages, which will limit their growth.

Nuclear power has been particularly disappointing. In the 1950s it was assumed that it would become so cheap that electricity made from it would not even have to be metered. Nuclear electricity, it was pre-dicted, would simply be supplied to homes for a modest flat fee, as was water. It would be clean, too, in contrast to coal, the main fossil fuel in power station use, and disposal of waste was not perceived as a problem. Those fine hopes have evaporated. The costs of nuclear power have been disappointing, the safety of some nuclear reactors gives rise to concern, and no politically acceptable way has been found to dispose of nuclear waste. While nuclear is a practical method of producing power for advanced industrial countries which are able to manage the technology – it is the main source of electricity generation in France – the experience of Chernobyl shows that if it is not properly managed, it can be disastrous. Humans make mistakes. Even when they do not, things happen, such as natural disasters, which cannot be properly foreseen. It would be astounding if the world did not experi-ence other nuclear accidents on the scale of Chernobyl, either through human error or, perhaps more likely, through some natural disaster such as an earthquake, within the next twenty-five years. These dangers limit the contribution which nuclear power will make to the world's energy balance. The construction of new plants has fallen sharply since its peak in 1980. Thanks to the need to shut down several reactors in the former Soviet Union for safety reasons, and the political difficulties in building new plants in western democracies, nuclear power could well account for a smaller proportion of the world's energy supply in 2000 than it did in 1990. It may well account for still less in 2020.

Rather different environmental concerns limit the potential of the other main non-fossil fuel source of power, hydro. At the moment, hydropower contributes more to the global energy balance than nuclear (6 per cent against 5 per cent) thanks to the giant dam-building spree of the post-war era, but dams have grave costs, as we have seen. The number of good available sites has diminished, each new dam has a cost, in terms of lost land, and that cost will generally be highest when a hydrodam is near the human habitations which need power, since cities also need farm land to feed themselves and building land to expand on.

Hydropower will increase in absolute terms (though not proportionate terms) over the next twenty-five years, and it may well become a useful additional source of energy in some rapidly-growing parts of the world. China currently plans to build a megadam on the Yangtze mainly to prevent downstream floods but partly to provide hydroelectricity. If the Three Gorges dam is built, it will be the biggest dam project ever. But the industrial countries, with a handful of exceptions such as Switzerland, Norway and Canada, simply do not have sufficient hydro-resources to make a real impact on their energy balance. Nor do the newly industrialized countries of South-East Asia, China excepted. The scope for increasing hydropower will always be limited. Even were one to ignore the loss of land, the expense and political disruption of resettling many people, and the environmental costs, hydropower cannot be more than a marginal source of power, helpful in some circumstances and for some countries, but not a solution to a global energy shortage.

No other source of power will do more than take some pressure, at the margin, away from fossil fuels. Of renewable sources of energy, easily the most important is wood, which is the main source of energy for half the world's population. Because most of those who use wood collect it themselves, or buy it from other individuals, it is not included in the general calculations of the world's energy supply. This is a serious omission, for wood provides 15 per cent of the world's energy: more than nuclear and hydro put together. (It supplies 80 per cent of the total energy consumed in sub-Saharan Africa.) But while wood is in theory a renewable resource, in practice its collection is leading to grave environmental degradation in many parts of the world. The acute shortage of firewood in many poor countries will gradually get worse, with the result that many people currently using wood will have to shift to other fuels. How they will be able to afford to buy fuel which previously they gathered for free is an unsolved problem.

Compared with firewood (or indeed nuclear or hydropower), the other sources of renewable energy are tiny. It is perfectly possible to generate power from tidal barrages, from the wind, from solar panels, or from the heat in the earth's crust, but these have, or could have, only local uses. Where it is convenient to have a local independent source of power – for example for running pocket calculators – solar cells will continue to become more widespread. There will be more wind farms, and more tidal barrages. Experiments will continue with wave power. But for at least a generation, until the prices of conventional energy are driven up by approaching shortage, none of these is going to help provide a significant proportion of the world's energy. Nor are they going to provide power for transport, for virtually all of them need to convert the energy through the medium of electricity, and until a much more efficient method of storing electricity than the battery is found, only one form of transport, rail, can be powered by it.

There is no imminent generalized energy shortage. But three particular problems will begin to loom large in the first years of the next century:

– The shortage of oil, the only practical fuel for most forms of
    transport
– Regional energy shortages, made worse by the rising price of
    oil, the most easily transportable fuel
– The effects of using fossil fuels on pollution and climate

Past predictions of the oil market have been spectacularly wrong, but there is little doubt that the oil market will tighten as reserves are used up, and that price will rise as a result. In 1987 proven oil reserves were 32.5 years' consumption. Were there to be no cutbacks in consumption and no new discoveries, there would in theory be no oil left in 2020. That will not happen. Long before that last drop of oil has been pumped from the ground, the price will have risen and either more oil discovered, substitutes developed or conservation programmes put in place. Yet even with improved extraction methods, which enable a larger proportion of a field's reserves to be recovered, even making allowance for some new discoveries, and even assuming continuing conservation efforts, oil supplies will become tight. Just how tight will depend on the development of substitutes. While oil remains in the $20–25 a barrel range it is not worth putting a lot of money into developing substitutes. Were oil $60 or $80 a barrel it would become economic to do so. Plenty of such substitutes exist: the coal gasification programme pioneered by Sasoil in South Africa; the use of alcohol, which is mixed with petrol to power four million of the twelve million cars in Brazil;[11] the experiments in France to convert rapeseed oil into diesel fuel; the use of shale oil and tar sands; the conversion of natural gas to liquid form, and so on. The techniques are there; the problem is simply that the oil they produce at the moment is more expensive than the stuff that flows out of the deserts of the Middle East.

The most sensible expectation is for the price of oil to rise (probably in sudden jumps, if past performance is any guide) until these substitutes come on stream. Oil will therefore tend to become more expensive, both in absolute terms and relative to other fuels, with the result that it will be displaced from uses where there is a ready alternative, such as power generation or home heating. For road and air transport it is hard to see oil being displaced from its prime position within a generation. However, if the real price rises, the effects are likely to be akin to those during the 1970s and early 1980s, when strenuous efforts were made to economize on oil following the two sudden rises in its price.

The oil-producing countries will enjoy some return to the comparative advantage they enjoyed during the second half of the 1970s and first half of the 1980s. The oil-short countries, which include most of western Europe, much of East Asia, and much of the developing world, will be under great pressure to conserve oil. This pressure will be particularly acute when the periodic oil shocks occur, and the world is most unlikely to get through another generation without some repeat of the two oil shocks of the 1970s. The timing of these cannot be predicted, but they are more likely to occur as the underlying supply of oil becomes tighter. So expect an oil shock in 2015, rather than 2000. Regionally, the most vulnerable area will be East Asia, because not only is it short of supplies of crude oil and refining capacity, but it is also growing very fast.

If fossil fuels are to remain the world's main energy source for at least another generation, rising energy use will bring rising environmental worries. Two stand out: local pollution and global warming. These are discussed in the next section, but before turning to them, one further point on energy needs to be made: the case for conservation.

Only conservation is likely to make a material contribution to stretching global supplies of fossil fuel during the next twenty-five years. Until the first oil shock in 1973/4, the normal pattern of energy use for the industrial world was that, for every additional one percentage point of output, energy use rose by half a percentage point. Since then, the industrial countries have learnt to use energy more efficiently. Coupled with the shift to service industries and away from manufacturing, this increased efficiency has enabled most industrial countries to grow without using much more energy. Between 1973 and 1985 the GDP of the OECD countries increased by 32 per cent, but their energy use rose by only 5 per cent. Since then the pace of energy conservation has slowed, but it is perfectly feasible for the industrial world to make further large cuts in its energy use without any great change to the lifestyle of its people. Simply by applying best practice across the industrial countries would cut energy consumption by at least one-third: Japan, with roughly the same GDP per head as the United States, uses only half the amount of energy per person. Allow for climatic differences, Japan's smaller homes and the greater distances of America, and a cut of one-third in the US would still be perfectly feasible. The potential savings in energy use in the former Soviet Union and in eastern Europe are even greater.

But even if the industrial world pares back its energy use slightly over the next twenty-five years, which would mean achieving a better performance than it managed after the spur of the first oil shock, there will be increased demand for energy from the newly industrialized countries and in particular from China. In the developing world the number of vehicles is certain to rise in places like India and Latin America, while air travel seems set to continue growing all round the world. Even with a strong conservation policy in the industrial world it would be astounding if the world in 2020 were using less energy than in the early 1990s. It will be using more, and that additional energy will come in the main from fossil fuels.

Environmental concerns

There are three main concerns. As well as local pollution and the threat of global warming, there is loss of habitat.

Local pollution and loss of habitat are both immediate and inevitable. They result from the pressure from a growing world population on food, energy and water supplies. To house the growing world population means larger cities in the developing countries. To feed these means cultivating more land, frequently irrigated land, which not only puts pressure on water supplies but reduces the habitat for many species, particularly large mammals. Global warming is a more distant and uncertain threat. The combination of loss of forest and increasing use of fossil fuels will certainly lead to a further build-up of carbon dioxide in the earth's atmosphere, but the effect on global climate is less sure.

The problems of environmental degradation will not be equally severe across the world. Much of the developing world will suffer more from pollution, and see habitats disappear. But in many of the recently industrialized countries, the air and rivers are likely to become cleaner and habitats for wild species may even increase. As these countries become richer they will devote more of their wealth to the control of pollution. The technology is available; all that is needed is the money to apply it.

Throughout the industrial world there are 'local' pollution problems, 'local' meaning that the effects of the pollution are felt in the area where the pollution is generated, not that it is unimportant. From the smogs of Los Angeles and Athens to the chemicals in the Rhine or the widespread industrial pollution in eastern Europe and the former Soviet Union, pollution makes life less healthy and less pleasant for people in many parts of the world. With some exceptions, these countries are well aware of the costs of such pollution and have both the technical competence and the funds to handle it. The air of Tokyo is much cleaner than it was in 1960, thanks to vigorous controls on exhaust emissions; the air of London is cleaner than it was in the 1950s before smokeless zones were introduced. The water quality of the rivers and beaches of north-west Europe is steadily improving, thanks to better sewage treatment; coal-burning power stations are being fitted with scrubbers to extract the sulphur; and vast resources are being devoted to cleaning up land polluted by past industries, particularly in the US.

Of course problems remain. The cost of correcting past errors is often either expensive or technically difficult. Eastern Europe, with its appalling heritage of pollution problems, is an example of the first: it *can* be cleaned up, but it will take a generation to bring its filthiest industrial sites up to current western European standards. California is a good example of the second, for the geography and climate of the Los Angeles basin make it a bad place for the polluting automobile. By bringing in tighter emission controls, California has managed to make some improvements to air quality in Los Angeles, but given the rise in population, and hence the number of cars on the road (California has the greatest concentration of motor vehicles in the world), the region has to run hard to stay still – hence its legislation compelling the introduction of a proportion of zero-emission vehicles to be brought in progressively over the next decade.

Even these problems can be solved. Pollution in eastern Europe has already declined dramatically, as loss-making factories have closed; further recovery is simply a question of applying known technology. In Britain much progress would be made if a minority of older vehicles were taken off the roads, for it has been estimated that 50 per cent of the pollution comes from this 10 per cent of the cars.[12] Although it is hardly politically correct to say so, local pollution is no longer a grave problem in the mature industrial countries. Over the next generation these countries will divert a greater proportion of their GDP towards controlling pollution, and as a result people living in these countries will be slightly less rich in terms of their material possessions than they otherwise would have been – but they will live in a cleaner world and doubtless will welcome that.

There is evidence, too, that habitats for wild species will increase in the western industrial countries. Less land will be needed for agriculture, the reverse of the situation in the developing world. Aside from this, people have a passionate desire to protect and preserve wildlife, and feel that the world would be a poorer place if wild birds and animals disappeared. The changing age structure of these countries will further encourage species protection: the young hunt and shoot, the elderly bring out their cameras.

So, in the industrial countries, both the local environment and the bio-diversity will tend either to improve or at least not to deteriorate further over the next twenty-five years. The developing countries face a gloomier prospect. Local pollution is already a grave problem for most of them, particularly those in the early stages of industrialization – according to the World Bank, five of the seven cities with the worst air pollution are in Asia.[13] In the early stages of industrialization, countries are so busy getting richer that they tend to neglect the environmental consequences of their efforts to do so. All the countries which industrialized in the last century – Britain, Germany, France, the US – made a mess of their landscapes as they did so, and Japan did severe damage to its environment in the 1950s, poisoning its seas, its air and some of its citizens. Only in the early 1960s did Japan become rich enough and concerned enough to switch priorities, which it then did with great success. China will be no different, but because it is so large, it has unprecedented capacity to cause environmental damage.

China has a particular problem with energy use. It has enormous coal reserves – around 15 per cent of the world's total – and relies on these for some 75 per cent of its energy needs, but it is relatively short of alternative sources of energy such as oil and natural gas. According to the International Association for Energy Economics, China will become a net oil importer in the middle 1990s.[14] The logical policy would be to burn its coal, and that is what it will do. But coal burnt in homes and factories, or even in power stations without expensive anti-pollution measures, is very dirty. Calculations by the East-West Center in Hawaii suggest that the coal China burns adds more sulphur dioxide and nitrogen oxides to the atmosphere each year than is being cut by the improved environmental controls of the OECD countries.[15] The rest of the world will try to encourage, bully or bribe China to follow environmentally-sound policies as it grows to full industrial status. China's environmental performance will certainly be a factor shaping its trade relations with the United States, for if China's exports can be shown to be manufactured in an environmentally damaging way, the US will have an excuse to impose trade controls on them, but much as China needs access to the US market, trade threats are unlikely to have much influence on environmental behaviour.

The uncomfortable probability is that China will become the world's largest polluter. Indeed, for a while, the faster it grows, the greater the pollution. This will, naturally, affect conditions not only within China itself, but also in neighbours such as Japan, which is already concerned about the atmospheric pollution blowing across the South China Sea. It will also have an influence on the great international issue in environmental economics, global warming.

Before coming to that, there are two other 'local' environmental problems to consider – rubbish and habitat.

The growth of giant cities in the developing countries will mean a growth of local pollution, for cities which are finding it a struggle to supply enough food and clean water to their people are unlikely to be able to afford the adequate disposal of their rubbish. But this is a problem that occurs at a middling level of development; while people remain poor they do not generate much rubbish – instead, they scavenge, combing through whatever is thrown out to see what can be used by someone else. Cairo, which by the turn of the century will have a population of at least 13 million and be the largest city in Africa, copes with its rubbish by elaborately sorting out whatever objects might have some useful value, and recycling them – wages are low enough to make that an economic proposition. In American cities, which are unwilling to allow new landfill sites to be opened to hold their rubbish, the only alternative will be to create less rubbish in the first place, for example by following the German-style path towards simpler packaging.

It is possible to be quite hopeful about the world's ability to feed itself, to supply clean water to its people, even eventually to cope with the many problems of its new giant cities. But it is hard to be hopeful about the preservation of habitat for wildlife in many parts of the world. The population pressure is too great. The large mammals at the top of the food chain, the rhinos, elephants, and tigers, are most vulnerable. If these large species disappear, then the countries in which they live will merely have followed the path first trodden by the industrial world – Britain hunted its wolves to extinction, the US nearly lost its bison. What is different is that the rich world now perceives that it has an interest in trying to preserve these species. People in developed countries would feel the world had become a poorer place if there were no pandas or black rhinos; a century or more ago, there was no such pressure to preserve the wolf or the bison. The rich countries will hope to find ways of encouraging developing countries to protect their wildlife, and many individual projects may be successful, but several species of large mammals may well have vanished from the wild by 2020.

The most contentious environmental issue of our times is climatic change, and in particular global warming. There is no doubt that the accumulation of carbon dioxide and other 'greenhouse gases' in the earth's atmosphere will, in principle, cause the climate to grow warmer, but this 'greenhouse effect' (so called because of the way the gases trap the heat in the earth's atmosphere) will be offset in several ways. For example, the extra warmth will cause more water to evaporate, and create clouds which will help to cool the earth. Nobody can predict how fast the earth's temperature will rise, how far, or where the main changes in climate will take place. Some parts of the world may gain if the climate becomes warmer and wetter, because they will be able to grow more food. Other parts of the world will lose, for climate change may speed up the advance of the deserts. But the effects of global warming will be quite limited for a generation at least.

Even if the earth's temperature warms by enough to start melting the polar icecaps, leading to a rise in the sea level (and scientists seem less sure than they once were that such a rise is probable), it would be a couple of generations before the rise became evident. There are good reasons for seeking to cut the amount of fossil fuels being used, the best being that it is unwise to conduct a giant experiment with the earth's weather, when we know so little about the long-term consequences of what we are doing, but the costs of stopping the build-up of carbon dioxide or other gases would be large, while global warming will not be a significant factor in the world economy in the year 2020. A more immediate problem may be the consequences of the thinning of the stratospheric ozone layer, worries about which led to one of the swiftest ever international responses to an environmental threat, the Montreal Protocol in 1987. The industrial countries now plan to stop production of CFCs, the chemicals which seem to have caused the depletion, by 1997. A more immediate threat to the economies of many of the world's poorest countries than global warming is a deterioration of local weather conditions, brought about largely by deforestation.

The degradation of the environment will be a greater preoccupation in the year 2020 than it is in the early 1990s. The industrial countries, and increasingly the middle-income countries, will be spending a greater proportion of their resources to try to correct the damage, and as a result will be cleaner and in many ways nicer places to live. The present generation of newly industrialized countries will be working hard to improve the quality of their environment, and will be achieving much higher standards of air and water quality and solid waste disposal in their cities. They will have the advantage of technologies developed in the rich countries under the influence of their tough environmental controls. But other countries (or regions) at the earliest stages of industrialization will be struggling with even more serious problems than they do at present.

So when people in western democracies look out of their windows they will see cleaner air; when they swim on their beaches they will enjoy cleaner water; when they walk in the country there will be a greater variety of crops and wildlife. But when they turn on their televisions they will see even greater hardship than they do today. And if they travel to the new giant cities of the developing world they will feel as visitors to London felt in 1850, or visitors to New York in 1920 – a mixture of wonder and horror – except that London and New York were better able to cope with their problems then than Lagos or Manila will be in 2020. The world will be managing, just, to cope with its larger population, but the signs of strain will be evident. The effects of the environmental deterioration which will have taken place will not yet be so evident as to make the world feel very different from the way it feels today, but people in the industrial world will be sufficiently worried about the next generation – the years to 2050 – that they will put great pressure on governments to intervene, to take charge. Resources and the environment will become hot international political issues.

The politics of natural resources

Until the Second World War the main aim of the industrial world in its relations with the developing countries was to exploit their natural resources. During the post-colonial era the aims have been more mixed, with the west competing for influence against the then Communist world by offering various forms of assistance under the general guise of 'aid'. The end of the Cold War has provided an opportunity and a need for a new look at the relationship, for except in very unusual circumstances (such as Kuwait) the west no longer needs to guarantee a state's external security. The industrial world will come to rethink what it wants both of the resource-rich countries and of the developing world.

Some familiar themes will continue, for the industrial countries (including the NICs) will continue to have an interest in protecting the security of supply of Middle-East oil, and the strategic minerals of southern Africa. Other new relationships, or the resumption of old ones, will develop. Western Europe will want to maintain, and if possible increase, its access to resources in Russia and the other countries of the former Soviet Union, and in particular its access to natural gas. As a result, Russia will move back to the position it held before the First World War as the main supplier of many raw materials to the more sophisticated countries to the west. Japan will seek access to Siberian raw materials, and will trade technology and money for security of supply.

Other, less obvious, aims will also grow in importance. The industrial world periodically has to supply emergency food aid to the developing world. As the frequency of such intervention increases, it will want to influence the social, political and environmental conditions which created the food shortages in the first place. It will become more interested in the environmental problems that the world's quest for water will create. It will become more concerned about cross-border pollution, and about carbon-dioxide emissions. Environmental issues will loom larger in trade policy, and not just because they provide a politically correct excuse for protectionism – as the cost of producing goods in the west is increased by environmental levies, western companies will be loath to allow imports from countries which have lower environmental standards, and hence costs. In addition, individuals in the west will want to use whatever influence they have to protect habitat for the wild creatures of their children's storybooks.

The objective of colonialism, where the west exploited the natural resources of the developing world, will thus be turned on its head. Under the new relationship the west will bully and bribe the developing countries not to exploit their resources, or at least to exploit them only in the most environmentally-friendly way possible. Whether the west will be effective in achieving its aims will be quite another matter, but expect it to try. Thus Japan will seek to persuade China to burn less coal, and will probably find itself paying for scrubbers on Chinese power stations. The United States will demand higher environmental standards from the countries of South America in exchange for access to its market, as it is already doing with Mexico in the negotiation of the North American Free Trade Agreement. The EU will find environmental degradation a good excuse to keep out agricultural products from countries like the Ukraine. The whole industrial world will find itself under pressure to intervene in Africa, as the rising number of people puts more and more pressure on the food supply. And since, by 2020, much more will be known about the scale and effects of global warming, countries will have to decide whether to restrain the use of fossil fuels for the benefit of future generations. The more frightened the industrial countries become about pressure on world resources, the more aggressive they will be in asserting their aims and values. The environment is unlikely to become a source of armed conflict between the 'haves' and the 'have-nots' – it would be disastrous were that to happen – but it will be a continuing source of tension and concern.

SEVEN

TRADE AND FINANCE

The opportunities that markets create

THE SINGLE GREATEST change in the world economy since the Second World War has been the extent to which it has gone international: money has become international; physical trade has become international; service trade is increasingly becoming international.

Whereas a generation ago the various national financial systems were insulated from each other, they are now all driven by the same force: the power of the international markets. One by one the barriers which stopped the markets exerting their power have broken down. Exchange controls have either been abandoned or become ineffective; exchange rates have come to be determined principally by market forces; long-term interest rates are set entirely by supply and demand for funds, rather than government decisions; even short-term interest rates are heavily influenced by the view of the markets. As a result of these freedoms, the financial services industry has been able to create a vast array of products which enable both borrowers and savers to take advantage of financial conditions around the world. A company in North America, Europe or Japan seeking to raise capital can do so in any of a dozen or more currencies, in as many countries, and on an array of different terms. A private individual in Britain wanting to take advantage of the faster economic growth of the newly industrialized countries has a hundred or more different funds specializing in investment in these areas into which to place his or her savings.

Inevitably the freedom to move money around the world is not absolute. There are two main sorts of restrictions: those imposed by national governments, and those which the markets themselves put in place for commercial reasons. The first kind ranges from the system of central bank loans and foreign exchange intervention which held together the EU's Exchange Rate Mechanism (ERM), to the exchange controls still imposed by some countries in an effort to make their citizens keep their money at home. The second sort includes limits on the willingness of British banks to lend money to certain types of small business which have in the past run up many bad debts, or the fact that small savers receive lower returns for their cash than large ones. But within these limits there is enormous freedom for money to flow around the world; more freedom, in fact, than at any stage since the beginning of the First World War, when in any case the flows were much smaller.

The rise of the power of the financial markets, together with their increasingly international nature, has inevitably reduced the power of individual national governments. They have to frame their economic policies with an eye to the way these will be received by the world's financial community. If they fail to do so, they will be punished by either a run on the currency or higher interest rates, or both. (This reduction in power will be further explored in Chapter 9, which looks at the way in which governments' role is changing.) This internationalization of financial markets has an equally important impact on the way companies behave and on the economic relationships of different countries with each other. In effect, it gives all large companies equal access to funds, and means that any large company will increasingly be owned by investors scattered around the world, rather than confined to the country of its corporate headquarters. Large companies are gaining the freedom to base themselves wherever they want. Finally, the growing freedom of financial markets limits the ability of governments to set trade controls that work, or, more dangerous than trade controls, controls on capital movements, or on the assets that companies will increasingly hold in many different countries.

The effect on national economies of internationalization is particularly important, for the fact that enormous amounts of money are freely available for projects which are deemed by the markets to be commercially attractive gives developing countries the opportunity to grow much more rapidly than they otherwise could. They can bring in foreign commercial funds to finance economic development, rather than wait for a foreign government to approve some small aid package, or for domestic savings to build up enough to provide the finance. Providing there is confidence both in the investment project and in the stability of the country itself, virtually unlimited amounts of money are available. But there is a price to be paid by the debtors, and not just in servicing the debts – the countries with a strong flow of savings which are not currently needed at home can use these savings to buy the companies, resources and even the skills of other nations, and financial power buys economic influence.

These international flows of funds can have a number of different results, some favourable, some not. One favourable outcome can be that economic take-off is achieved much more rapidly than in the past. This happened in the 1970s in South Korea, which used foreign bank loans to finance its economic development. But South Korea invested wisely. Many Latin American countries also borrowed heavily but squandered the money, using it to support higher consumption rather than productive investment. Eventually these countries were forced to reverse their policies, though not before western banks had lost a great deal of money from dud loans.

Both these examples of cross-border investment involved money channelled through the banks. The middle 1980s saw one of those big shifts which take place periodically in the financial services industry – the securities markets were replacing banks as the main intermediaries between savers and borrowers. This change had two main causes:

– The debt crisis of the 1980s, initiated by the Latin American defaults and aggravated by other bad loans, particularly to property companies, left the banks greatly weakened
– The growth of savings institutions, in particular insurance companies and pension funds

The debt crisis forced the banks to adopt much more cautious lending policies, and convinced many borrowers that it was unwise to rely so much on bank funds. But even without the banking crisis, the longer-term rise in the importance of the savings institutions would have diminished the relative role of the banks. Pension funds and insurance companies owe their growth largely to the ageing of the population of the industrial countries, for as people get older they need to save for their retirement, and most countries offer tax breaks to encourage them to do so. The Anglo-Saxon countries, the Netherlands and increasingly Japan all have substantial private-sector pension funds, and other European countries are rapidly building these up. Eventually, as the pensioners start to draw down their pensions, these funds will cease to grow, but by the time that happens, new pension funds in the newly industrialized countries will have grown up too.

Pension-fund managers have to think a long way ahead, for they are investing for people who may not want to draw down their savings for up to forty years. So they need investments which either are likely to do well over this very long period, or mature in twenty or thirty years' time when the pensioners need the money. This leads pension funds to seek two sorts of asset: those which are likely to grow in capital value over a long period; and those which mature at specific dates in the future. The first need leads to investment in equities, for historically these have produced a better long-term return than any other form of investment; the second need leads to investment in bonds, which have the advantage of specific maturity dates. Equities and bonds are, of course, instruments of the securities market. One key practical difference between a bank loan and an equity investment is that in the case of equity there is a shift of ownership; buyers of shares technically own part of the company that issued them. This has important implications for the relations between countries, and for companies around the world. Countries will have to come to terms with large proportions of their assets being owned overseas; and companies will have to accept that they are at least partly owned by 'foreigners', people who are not residents of the country where they are headquartered.

Both these features are already evident to a limited degree. There are many examples of the first, though up to now companies deemed essential to national interest have been protected. The best example of the second has been the move of the United States from creditor to debtor status. The movement of money across borders during the 1980s allowed the US to run a large current-account deficit – it was consuming much more than it was producing, and as a result was passing the ownership of many of its assets to the countries which were financing it, of which the most obvious was Japan.

The consequences of both these shifts are discussed in the next two sections. Meanwhile, note that investors moving money across national boundaries will increasingly want to control how that money is deployed. They will not make the mistake of the banks in the 1970s and early 1980s, lending vast amounts of money to countries about which they know little, on terms that do not adequately compensate for the risk. Instead a country accepting an inflow of funds will have to offer in return either a change of ownership, or at least some loss of national control. The change of ownership happens most obviously with Japanese purchases of office blocks in the US or Europe. The loss of national control obviously happens when, for example, a Japanese car firm builds a plant abroad, but it even happens to some extent when foreigners buy the bonds of another country – the US relied heavily on inflows of foreign capital to finance its budget deficit in the 1980s, and the interest rate on such debt was largely determined by the rates which Japanese investors were willing to invest.

Much the same considerations apply to developing countries. Risk money is available either in the form of direct investment by companies, or through portfolio investment in the shares of companies (or funds which invest in those shares) in the developing world. But this money will continue to come forward only if the returns are above average, to compensate for the above-average risk. Governments in the developing world have come to realize that if they wish to gain access to foreign capital, they need both to create a climate of political stability, and to acknowledge that investment funds will come only if they are likely to make good profits for the investors. This is a sharp contrast to the attitude of many such countries in the 1960s and 1970s, when they followed policies, such as nationalization, designed to frighten foreign commercial money away, competing, instead, for the aid budgets of the Soviet and western blocs. Then the price extracted by the donors of aid was political influence; now it is commercial influence. Countries still want to retain as much control over their national assets as possible. Managing this balancing act will be one of the main aims of policy in the developing world.

The key to political influence will always be national wealth. In the days of the Cold War, that wealth was used to build up armed forces, and to support friendly regimes. In the post-Cold War world, countries wishing to have influence are more likely instead to build up overseas assets. To do so requires accumulating savings and deploying part of those savings overseas. Japan provides the most dramatic example of such a policy, but it seems likely that other East Asian nations will follow suit. Look, for example, at Taiwan. Its income per head is still somewhat lower than that of the fully-fledged members of the industrial world, but it has built up the world's second largest stock of foreign exchange reserves. The savings ratios of the tigers of East Asia are double that of the established industrial countries. At this stage of their economic development they need these savings ratios to support their rapid economic growth; some shading-down of the savings rate is likely later on. But if they continue to save at higher rates than Europe or North America as their economies mature, they could find themselves building up balance-of-payments surpluses as large as that of present-day Japan. If East Asia supplies the bulk of the world's savings, it will build up foreign assets which will give the region a powerful degree of influence over world economic relations.

The countries that save

All countries save, but some save more than others. The most ferocious savers in the world are the Japanese. Until the 1980s these savings were used largely within Japan itself, but from about 1980 onwards they flooded abroad. Japan's current account, negative in 1980, went into a surplus which increased steadily through the decade, reaching a peak of $87 billion in 1987. After falling back to $36 billion in 1990 the surplus again surged forward to $118 billion in 1992. The result was that Japan's net external assets, negative in 1980, were in surplus to the tune of $514 billion by 1992.[1] The surplus was used in a number of ways. Part of it was transferred abroad to invest in local plants, part went to buy property in the US and Europe, and part went simply to buy US Treasury securities, thus helping to finance the US government's annual budget deficit. American people consumed (and in 1993 are still consuming) the savings of the Japanese.

As Japan acquired overseas assets, the United States relinquished them. In 1981 the US was the world's largest creditor, with net external assets of $374 billion. America slipped into debt in the first half of 1986 and by 1992 this debt had reached $521 billion.[2] The indebtedness of the United States continues to rise. This extraordinary switch is shown in the graph opposite.

The transposition of the net-asset positions of the United States and Japan is a dramatic change. It is dramatic not only because of its scale, but because of what it reveals about the changing nature of international capital flows. Huge sums of money have moved across borders in the past – after the Second World War European reconstruction was financed by flows from the US under Marshall Aid, and for much of the subsequent post-war period there were large capital flows to developing countries through the World Bank and other development institutions, and directly from governments. The ways in which the flow between Japan and the United States differs are that the flows have become much larger and the control over them has shifted from governments to markets.

International comparisons of external net asset positions[3]

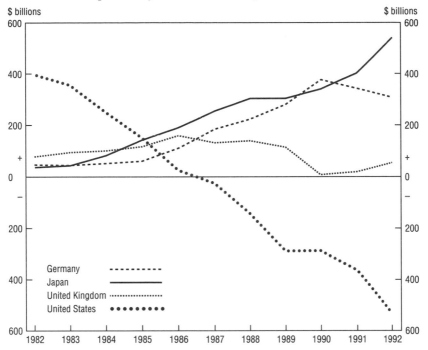

The only comparable market-driven international investment boom was between about 1870 and 1914. Then, the world did not, however, have to face the consequences of these flows for long: most of the overseas assets built up by countries like Britain, France and Germany were run down to help pay for the war, or became worthless, like their holdings of Tsarist bonds. After that, for two generations, cross-border investment languished because not only did investors feel insecure about sending their savings overseas, but capital controls made foreign investment difficult, sometimes impossible.

The world has now moved some way back towards the situation at the end of the last century, except that in the place of the half-dozen European countries which supplied the bulk of the world's international investment funds, there is now one Far Eastern one: Japan. Japan is not the only creditor nation, but it is by far the largest. Neither of the countries in second and third position, Germany and Britain, is likely to build up external assets on such a massive and potentially destabilizing scale. If it weren't for unification, Germany might have joined Japan as a chronic surplus nation, but the costs of absorbing

East Germany pushed the current account into deficit. Britain, whose oil exports created a current account surplus in the early 1980s, enjoyed a brief moment of glory in 1985/6 as almost the largest creditor nation, but the import boom of the late 1980s meant that Britain's net assets were run down even faster than they had been built up. Indeed Britain was saved from becoming a net debtor only by the fact that the country's overseas investments, to a large extent in foreign shares, had performed well and showed large capital gains.

So, for the moment at least, Japan's surplus dwarfs all others. Japan's net assets will continue to get larger, for it is hard to see how the current account deficit will be cut for at least a decade. Assets will build up partly because they will earn interest which can then be reinvested, and partly because they will be swollen each year by each year's current-account surplus. It is perfectly plausible that Japanese external assets will reach $2,000 billion by the year 2000, maybe much more. Indeed it becomes harder and harder to see quite how the surplus will stop growing – or, from the debtors' perspective, how these debts will be cleared. So it would seem that the Japanese surplus will continue to grow and Japan will as a result own an ever larger proportion of the world's property and financial assets.

Yet common sense says that no trend can continue for ever. If this one did, Japan would eventually own every company, every factory, every farm, even every home in the US. That will not happen. So the fascinating question is what might change this position. There are a number of possibilities, of which only one is at all attractive.

First, of course, the assets could be stolen: the debts repudiated, as took place in Bolshevik Russia, the assets nationalized at knock-down prices, as took place in many developing countries during the 1950s and 1960s, or the real value of the debt wiped out by inflation, the method used by many industrial countries to cut the burden of their national debt during the 1960s and 1970s. But either of these 'solutions' to the problem of international indebtedness would carry enormous costs. It is almost unthinkable that the US would nationalize Japanese assets for to do so would break up the whole liberal trading environment of the post-war era. Nor is inflation a credible option – inflation fast enough to reduce the real value of Japan's US assets would cause enormous damage to the US economy itself. In any case, any rise in inflation would be met by a rise in interest rates, for markets are wise to inflation in a way that they were not in the 1950s and 1960s.

Second, there could be another global catastrophe like the First

World War. That would certainly clear the debts quickly, but of course the costs to the entire world would be even more devastating than rapid inflation. Military catastrophes, albeit fortunately on a rather smaller scale, do occur. Kuwait looked as though it would accumulate enough money to be able to buy dominant stakes in much of Europe's industry: it had taken key interests in such western giant companies as British Petroleum and Daimler-Benz, and its apparently predatory approach to its investments was starting to arouse serious concern; but after the Gulf war, more than half of Kuwait's assets were required to help pay for reconstruction, and the country ceased to be seen as a potential threat. However, it is hard to envisage the circumstances under which Japan would need to repatriate funds to pay for some military disaster.

The third is a possibility which is much debated in Japan itself. At some stage before the end of the century the next large earthquake is likely to strike the Tokyo region. While the Japanese authorities are well prepared for such an eventuality, and all modern buildings are constructed to withstand earthquakes, there will be serious damage. This is likely to lead to some repatriation of capital. Were the earthquake on the scale of the great Kanto earthquake of 1923, the estimated costs of rebuilding would be about $1,000 billion.[4] It is also likely to damage the country's industrial capacity, given that so much of its GDP is generated in the Tokyo region, so exports would be likely to suffer too, maybe eliminating at least for a while the surplus which led to the accumulation of overseas assets.

The fourth, more benign, possibility is that, as Japan ages, its people will seek to enjoy the fruits of their hard work. Japan, as Chapter 5 showed, is going through a once-and-for-all shift in the age-structure of its population, moving from being a very young country to becoming a very old one. As it becomes older it will not only no longer need to save, so to speak, for its old age, but it will positively need to spend the accumulated savings. It will, under this argument, be running down foreign assets by 2020, and using the funds to help pay the pensions of the large numbers of elderly people. The building-up of foreign assets will have been a temporary situation brought about by Japan's unusual demography.

Maybe the adjustment will be brought about by some combination of the last two possibilities. Meanwhile, the fact remains that in a world of free capital movements, countries which save, like Japan, will end up owning large swathes of the rest of the world. How this might affect companies is examined next.

The impact on companies

The internationalization of financial markets is one of the forces that will make it increasingly difficult for one large company to acquire a competitive advantage over its rivals. There are two processes at work. On the one hand companies are the main vehicle for international investment, either by building plants overseas, or by buying local companies. On the other, they frequently find themselves bought by foreign interests, or at least they do in the Anglo-Saxon countries.

Overseas investment by companies has been one of the great forces internationalizing the world economy during the 1980s. It brings enormous benefits, for as companies invest abroad they transfer skills and technical knowledge as well as money. During the second half of the 1980s the amount of corporate foreign investment soared, rising in value from around $50 billion a year in 1980 to 1985, to nearly $200 billion in 1989. One projection reckons that this might grow to $800 billion a year by 2020.[5] It may well be more. Indeed international production is replacing international trade as a way of getting products to foreign markets. In 1990 world trade totalled $3,800 billion, but the production of companies in countries other than their home base was $4,400 billion. US-owned companies outside the US sold twice as much as the US exported.

Does it matter whether companies set up new plants abroad, or buy into existing companies? Probably not. On the face of it, it might seem that spending money to build a new plant increases a country's industrial capacity in a way that buying an existing firm does not. Japan's overseas investment tends to follow the former course (though not always: witness its purchases of Hollywood studios), whereas Britain's investments frequently take the form of foreign takeovers. But in each case the investment makes sense only if the new owner is able to improve the company's performance as a result. Buying a foreign firm frequently needs to be followed by new investment. Even if it does not, the new buyer has to manage it better than the previous owners for the purchase to be successful. Transferring management skills is just as important an aspect of international investment as building foreign factories.

This process of replacing exports with local production is absolutely crucial, for it means that goods will either be made close to their markets, or where costs are lowest. They will not necessarily be made where the company happens to have its headquarters, or its origins. The choice of where to produce will depend on a number of things. Where there is fear of protectionism, as with cars, there will be a tendency to produce locally as a way of fending off such pressures. Where labour costs make up a large proportion of the total costs, there will be a tendency to shift production to countries where wages are low. Anyone looking around the world can see this process taking place. What is not so obvious is the fact that the profit is less and less in manufacturing, and more and more in design, branding and marketing. The manufacturing cost of a product like a CD is less than one-twentieth of the retail selling price. Even in a complex product like a car, it is only around 60 per cent, and falling. Location of the manufacturing facility is therefore diminishingly important, while ownership of the design, marketing and distribution matters vastly more. This shift – already evident in luxury branded products – will continue. No-one cares terribly where Chanel or Dunhill make their products: the value is in the brand.

While company activities have become much more international, so has their ownership. Most companies at present think of themselves as national entities. They may call themselves multinationals, have offices, plants and subsidiaries all around the world, and have many foreign shareholders, but executive control still rests in the country where the original national business grew up. Thus IBM or Exxon remain essentially US companies, run by Americans; Toyota is certainly Japanese; British Petroleum is largely British. There is only a tiny handful of true multinationals, of which Shell and Unilever are the best examples: both are the result of Anglo-Dutch mergers, but are heavily influenced by their US arms.

While companies remain principally owned by nationals of the country where they are registered – as in the case of IBM or Exxon, say, where US shareholders own a majority of the shares – then there is no problem of national identity. Toyota's plants in the US or in Britain are clearly responsible to the head office in Japan, where all the important decisions are made. Any well-run company will seek to take into account local customs and preferences: good local employees will proceed up the corporate ladder and the company will fund local art exhibitions, sports centres or other good causes and generally try to act as a good citizen, because it is in its commercial interest to do so. But the decision as to whether IBM should open or shut a plant in the UK is not made in Britain, any more than the decision whether

Toyota should open or shut a plant in the US is made there. There are inevitable and quite proper limits to local democracy in large corporations.

However, as the ownership of a company becomes nationally more diverse, the idea that the company is American, British, French or Japanese becomes less relevant. Sometimes a company changes nationality because it is bought by a foreign entity – one might imagine that the change of nationality is then explicit, but even that is not clear-cut. Consider the case of Rowntree Mackintosh, the British sweet manufacturer which was taken over by Nestlé. That might seem a clear transfer of control to Switzerland, and in management terms it was; but in terms of ownership of the global confectionery industry, if the owners of the shares in Rowntree kept their money in Nestlé shares, then nothing changed: instead of owning 100 per cent of Rowntree, the British shareholders would own, say, 10 per cent of the very much larger Nestlé. All large companies take the views of their big shareholders seriously, briefing them at regular intervals, and in general terms seeking their judgements on corporate strategy. If a majority (or even a large minority) of those shareholders happen to be in one country, the management has to pay attention to them even if the headquarters of the firm is located somewhere else.

This happened in the case of Reuters, the UK-based information group. Before the 1980s it was entirely owned by British newspapers, but when it was floated on the stock market and the newspapers sold their shares, many of them were bought by US interests. By the late 1980s some 30 per cent of its shares were owned by foreign interests, mostly in the United States. It was not yet an American company, but it was moving that way. It so happens that the financial institutions which control Reuters' stock are also among its main customers, so inevitably they pay close attention to it as a business; but it would be inconceivable for Reuters to follow business practices to which its large US shareholders objected.

To take yet another example, Glaxo, ranked by market capitalization, was in 1993 the largest British pharmaceutical company. But how British is it? Its chairman and chief executive were both UK nationals, as were nine of its board of directors but seven other members of its board were non-British; 33,000 of its 45,000 employees were located outside the UK; and only 11 per cent of its sales were in Britain.

Large 'British' companies like these are unusual in having such a high proportion of their shares held overseas, but they are far from unique. In the Netherlands, even as early as 1985, NV Philips had an estimated 60 per cent of its shares owned abroad. The comparable figure for Olivetti, the Italian electronics group, was 48 per cent; for Matsushita, the Japanese electronics group, 21 per cent; and Credit Suisse, the Swiss bank, 25 per cent. Even Coca-Cola, that symbol of US cultural imperialism, was just a little bit non-American – 5 per cent of its shares were owned abroad. With the boom in foreign ownership the percentages will have grown since then.[6]

This internationalization of corporate ownership has many advantages. From a company's point of view an international spread of shareholders provides a defence against protectionism: it has a local lobby of share owners whose interests would be damaged by trade barriers. It also has a wider range of sources of new external capital, for if its home capital market is heading downwards, there is always a chance that some foreign market is going in the opposite direction. However, voters tend to become unhappy if too many of their country's most successful companies are owned by foreigners, and not just in sensitive areas like defence equipment.

For the moment, most countries still feel that they have retained enough control over their large companies. Foreign ownership has bred occasional rows, as when Kuwait bought 21.7 per cent of BP against the UK government's wishes, but these are rare. However, they may become more frequent if cross-border capital flows continue to increase. It is quite possible that international portfolio investment will become a contentious issue rather like international trade: most people accept that it makes an important contribution to international prosperity, but it also breeds tension.

What might seem a threat to a country could be a liberation for a company: a multinational company will be bound less and less by the conditions of the 'home' country. If a company can, so long as it is above a certain minimum size, attract capital from investors anywhere in the world, then it is not bound by the conditions of a local capital market. If it can locate plants anywhere, it is not bound by the competitive advantage (or disadvantage) of having its main production base in any one country.

This freedom will extend to people, for companies can buy top talent from anywhere. Many senior executives already see Europe and North America as a single market. Expect Japan to be drawn into this international market for skills, as its production experts are poached by other countries seeking their technical and human-management skills.

(In soccer there is already a completely international market for both top players and managers.)

The current fashionable thesis is that the main asset of a large company is its human skills: the collection of individuals who work in it. It follows that the companies likely to be most successful will be those which train their people best and which nurture those skills. But these human skills can increasingly be bought on the marketplace, just like any other resource: top managers are becoming an international commodity; research facilities can be located near to the best universities; production is anywhere. It is easy to see how countries can develop their comparative advantages by educating their people to build skills that other countries will find hard to match; but what constitutes comparative advantage for a company in a world where everything, including talent, is for sale?

Encouraging entrepreneurs . . . and intrapreneurs

Some benefits will continue to accrue to companies from their culture. Companies that operate in a climate of intense product innovation, as in Japan, will find it easier to develop new products. If a country has a large pool of skilled engineers, as does Germany, it will be easier for companies based there to produce high quality manufactured goods. So some barriers to internationalization will remain. Culture will keep countries apart. Cultural taboos will ensure that hostile takeovers will remain virtually impossible in Japan and much of South-East Asia, while friendly ones will continue to be difficult. A US software firm seeking to buy a Japanese computer manufacturer will continue to find it much harder to do so than a Japanese electronics firm trying to buy a Hollywood film-maker. However international the capital markets become, costs of funds will vary a bit from region to region, partly because the markets for small savings are still segregated and national, and partly by differences in the willingness of people in the different regions to save. As a result, companies in some countries will always find it cheaper to borrow than others. And of course companies will need to stick to things that they know about – the corporate history books are full of disasters involving firms that have strayed into areas where they have no experience.

But when all this is said, the fact remains that big companies the world over are becoming more and more alike, so how might a country encourage its companies to gain an edge? The answer is entrepreneurship:

- Countries can encourage large companies to become more entrepreneurial
- They can encourage the growth of new companies, for comparative advantage between countries will depend on the speed at which it can build new enterprises

The first approach is easy to explain. If all large companies start with more or less equal advantages, the ones that do best will be those that are best at assessing comparative advantage around the world and then finding a way to exploit it. A lot of the skill, certainly for companies selling goods or services directly to the consumer, will come in spotting gaps in markets or identifying social trends.

A good example of this is Virgin Atlantic, a British airline. The success of Virgin breaks all the standard business-school rules – the founder, Richard Branson, had no experience of the industry (his background was in the music business), the industry was overcrowded, the costs of entry appeared to be high – many competitors were subsidized by their national governments, the business was highly cyclical, and it was virtually impossible to differentiate a product, for all airlines flew the same aircraft to the same places. But Virgin spotted a gap in the market among business people who wanted first class space, but did not want the level of 'service' that went with it. Virgin's solution, 'Upper Class', gave them the space for business-class prices, and gave Virgin a yield well above that of competing airlines. This, coupled with the founder's talent for publicity, enabled the airline to succeed, when rationally it should not have done so.

Virgin Atlantic is relatively small, and is therefore also a good example of the second line of approach. It is tougher for the giants to be entrepreneurial for it is the one business skill which is both impossible to teach and hard to develop within a large and inevitably bureaucratic company. Because it is so hard to develop, there is an enormous reward for companies which can find ways of cultivating it. Indeed one of the great challenges for the giant corporations of the next twenty-five years is how to behave like smaller, more nimble creatures. This has been widely recognized in the management literature, and the dreadful word 'intrapreneurship' has been coined to describe the process where large companies seek to develop entrepreneurial characteristics within their organizations.

The great test-case of the ability of large companies to behave like small ones will come with the reforms IBM is trying to bring in to compete with the burst of entrepreneurial companies in the PC business. The most successful US companies of the 1980s and early 1990s – Apple, Microsoft and Intel – were all essentially the creation of a single individual: Steve Jobs at Apple, Bill Gates at Microsoft and Andy Grove at Intel. If IBM manages to recast itself then it will become the standard-bearer for all corporate giants throughout the world. If it fails, then it will illustrate graphically that a country's fortunes will be determined less by the performance of its big firms, and more by the success with which it fosters new ones: the number that are created, the speed at which they become successful, and the quality of the goods and services they produce.

There are limits to the extent to which governments can actively encourage the creation of new businesses, but they can remove blockages. Setting a generally pro-business climate helps. The US has an excellent record of creating new businesses, and during the late 1980s Britain, by then several years into the Thatcher experiment, was creating more small businesses than the rest of the EC put together. It is perfectly plausible that by the early 1990s China was creating as many new businesses as the rest of the world put together. In Russia, by contrast, the climate for creating businesses has remained hostile, while one of the EU's most serious long-term economic problems is that it too is bad at generating new businesses.

The disadvantage for small firms is that they will find it much harder to escape from their national confines than large ones. They will not have the easy access to international capital markets. They will not be able to attract international management talent. They will not find it easy to shift production abroad. Yet since a large proportion of the manufacturing production of a typical industrial country comes from small, often family-owned firms with less than 200 employees they are obviously enormously important to the economy. In Britain, 41 per cent of manufacturing production comes from companies with less than £100,000 a year turnover.[7]

While it is easy to agree that such enterprises are obviously important, both for economic growth and for employment, it is much harder to pick out common themes and develop common policies to encourage them. We know quite a lot about company creation and quite a

lot about self-employment, two measures of the adaptability of economies to changing competitive conditions. Some countries clearly are
better at creating companies than others. Yet self-employment is not
always a good measure of an entrepreneurial climate; it may reflect
the structure of the economy rather than a desire to start businesses.
For instance, most small farmers are self-employed, while few people
in manufacturing industry are. It is worth encouraging business start-
ups. The vast majority of new businesses fail, but the more that are
created the more efficient the service sector in general. It is quite
impossible to predict which new businesses are likely to succeed, or
even to predict the sectors which are likely to be winners. There are
no rules for success in entrepreneurship. So the best policy is to encourage as many new ventures as possible. Maybe, too, there is a case
for encouraging immigration of entrepreneurs. Some of the most
successful business people around the world have been immigrants –
including Intel's Andy Grove – while Australia's top 200 richest citizens
include thirty-five who came originally from eastern Europe.[8] As the
proportion of relatively rich private individuals in the developing
countries increases, these too ought to become attractive 'catches' for
countries.

Still, before leaving this subject it is worth recording that large
companies will take a long time a-dying. It could be argued that the
decline of the corporate giants is inevitable,[9] but while there will
be substantial changes in the pecking order of different companies and
different industries, there is no doubt that some very large companies
will exist, and some will prosper.

There are at least three reasons to be confident about this. The first
is that there will always be opportunities for entrepreneurial companies
to extract profit from shrinking industries. Some have made a business
out of this: the Anglo-American conglomerate, Hanson plc, has spotted
that it is easier to make money out of low-technology declining industries, like tobacco, than high-tech expanding ones, because there is
less competition.

The next is that many large firms own a body of proprietary knowledge and expertise which would be difficult to replicate even were
their key employees to be tempted away, in particular technical standards and expertise. There is nothing to stop a competitor from introducing a new form of, say, video cassette recorder, but the fact that
millions of people around the world have already bought VCRs and
are loath to switch technologies means that the competitor has to be

able to offer a substantially better product. The oil companies and the drug companies, for instance, possess a body of knowledge among their employees which would be very hard to replicate simply by hiring away a few people. A generation from now the big oil companies and the big drug firms will be pretty much the same as they are at present: entry into these businesses is vastly harder than entry into, say, computer software.

Finally there is the durability of brands. Brands are protected in a slightly different way, but have proved to be profoundly durable. Johnny Walker's Red Label has been the best-selling Scotch since at least the mid-1960s, and in fact received its Royal Warrant from George V in 1933.[10] New perfumes are launched every week, often with celebrity names attached, but Chanel No. 5, a perfume launched in 1921, continues to be one of the world's largest sellers. British chocolate brands are another case – the bestselling Kit-Kat and Mars Bars are over sixty years old and Cadbury's Dairy Milk nearer a hundred.

A look forward

Since 1945 markets have gradually re-emerged as the main place where financial decisions are taken. Their reinstatement has been gradual: there have been small steps, such as the lifting of exchange controls by the European countries, a process which has taken more than forty years and is still not entirely complete; and giant steps such as the collapse of state control in eastern Europe and the former Soviet Union. The central question is whether this process of liberalization will come to an end and give way to a gradual rebuilding of administrative controls.

Some day the pendulum will undoubtedly swing back, but that time may be far off. There are two good reasons to believe that the advance of the markets is set fair for at least another generation:

– The economic defeat of Communism has made it self-evident that market economies work better than centrally-planned ones
– China, probably Russia, and possibly India are all committed to market reforms, which will shift the global balance in that direction

The success of West Germany compared with East Germany, where the same people prospered under one system but failed to do so under the other, was the nearest thing to a controlled experiment that economic life ever sees. Similarly, the success of the expatriate Chinese communities compared with the economic stagnation of mainland China really leaves no doubt as to which system better meets the needs of ordinary people. In the 1990s, this argument can be made with greater confidence than would have been possible even in the early 1980s. To choose a centrally-planned system over a market one now would simply look perverse.

In addition, the very fact that so much of the world is adopting the market system itself makes the shift more durable. It is not just China and Russia which have made what is probably an irreversible shift away from centrally planned economies; India is also trying to abolish some of the controls which have hampered its economic development. If these three giant economies are set on change, the change is in practice universal because, on a global scale, small countries like Cuba and North Korea, which remain centrally-planned, are not relevant to the world economy. Even they will eventually change, if Vietnam is any guide. It is surely astounding that Vietnam, less than twenty years after a bloody civil war which ousted the market economy of the south and imposed the planned one of the north, should be turning policy through 180 degrees and adopting the system it had fought so hard to destroy.

So the whole world will play by the same economic rules. The rewards will go to those who best understand those rules, who understand that saving is the key to success in the market system, and who learn how to deploy those savings both at home and abroad. If Europe and North America continue to save a smaller proportion of their income than East Asia, then the 'new' industrial countries of Asia will be able to use the capitalist system to secure a real influence over the companies and maybe even the governments of the 'old' industrial world. To some extent, savings ratios in East Asia ought to fall as their population ages – a high level of saving is associated with a young population putting money aside for its retirement – but if, nevertheless, Asia becomes the main capital exporter to the world, it will gain enormous power.

The most serious threat to the further advance of the market system would be the re-emergence of high inflation. It is not just that markets cannot take correct decisions if their yardstick, money, is distorted by inflation; it is also that the social costs of inflation are high, for the losers are usually the poor and the old, while the gainers are the young and the financially sophisticated. The combination of inefficiency and social injustice is deeply destructive.

Is the long-term downward trend of world inflation secure? The first half of the post-war period was characterized by rising inflation, the second by falling inflation. From the perspective of the early 1990s inflation seems set to continue on its downward path, but since the trend is little more than ten years old – the peak in most countries was only in the early 1980s – it is too soon to be sure. As noted earlier, some governments will see inflation as a tempting way to whittle down the large budget deficits that most industrial countries have accumulated and find hard to service from taxes.

There are two more reasons to expect inflation to continue to wane. The first is demography. The rising proportion of older people in the industrial world is likely to want to vote for low inflation, not just out of natural conservatism, but because their real incomes are more likely to be protected in a period of stable prices. The second is that the financial markets are well aware of the dangers of inflation and generally punish governments which devalue their currencies by pushing up long-term interest rates. So the rise of market power is a force for keeping inflation down: governments in Europe and Japan are being forced to give a greater degree of independence to their central banks in an effort to convince the markets that they are committed to price stability.

How fast towards 'managed trade'?

A final note of caution. If the new industrial world of Asia seems to be benefiting from the market system more than the old industrial world of North America and Europe, then the liberal market economy will come under strain. The main financial mechanisms of the market system – the foreign exchanges and the securities markets – will not be threatened, and there will be no return to nationalization, for that is a form of corporate organization which has clearly failed. The strain will show in attacks on free trade.

The multilateral free-trade principles, established after the Second World War in the General Agreement on Tariffs and Trade (GATT), are already under pressure. An increasingly large proportion of trade in goods is subject to specific market-sharing agreements, while free trade has never been extended to agricultural products, nor to many services. It may simply be that the whole process of trade liberalization has come to a halt: we may have reached a plateau from which further advance is politically impossible. If that were to have happened it would be very sad, but it is unrealistic not to accept the possibility. The first forty years after the Second World War were devoted to freeing international trade; the next forty may have to be devoted to preserving as much of that progress as possible, while seeking to make a second-best solution, managed trade, as workable as possible.

Some of the tension will be between the established blocs, but it is so overwhelmingly in the self-interest of the existing industrial world not to permit a trade war to develop that these tensions should be manageable. The more likely areas where trade barriers might be really damaging would be between the mature industrial areas and the newer, low-wage economies seeking to export to them. Western Europe needs to manage its relationship with the members of the former Soviet Union so as to give them some hope of greater access to the rich west, and North America needs to open as far as practicable its markets to the producers of Latin America – and not just Mexico.

North America will be particularly loath to extend to China the access to its markets which it gave to countries like Japan and Taiwan. Japan, Taiwan and the other newly industrialized countries of East Asia either have been staunch political allies of the US for the entire post-war period (for example, Japan and South Korea) or they are too small to present an economic threat (Singapore or Hong Kong). As the US begins to feel threatened by, most obviously, Japan's export success, it starts to haul up trade barriers; it is, however, inhibited because Japan remains a political friend. China, the only potential rival for world leadership in the next century, enjoys no such relationship. Nor can it unless and until it establishes something more akin to a western market economy and shows greater respect for human rights. There need be no particular economic antagonism between the two giant nations, but America owes China no debts.

The US trade relationship with the EU, and the EU's with Japan, are both tense, too. They will continue to be tense through the 1990s, particularly if the period of relatively slow growth persists, or if the winners seem to be following 'unfair' practices. What is deemed unfair is likely to be redefined. It may simply be that running a large current

account surplus is deemed unfair, whether or not the country concerned has a genuine comparative advantage. It is certainly very
unlikely that any country will be allowed to follow the predatory export
practice of the Japanese in the 1970s and early 1980s, selecting a
particular product-line – for example motorcycles – and seeking to
drive out domestic producers in that market.

The present tensions will certainly last into the first part of the next
century. Some retreat towards managed trade between the three main
blocs seems likely, but this need not be a grave threat to the world
economy – it would merely mean that some of the benefits of specialization would not be obtained. But if one looks beyond, perhaps, 2010,
it is quite possible that managed trade will be so established, and local
production so commonplace, that tensions will start to shift from trade
in goods to trade in services and, more important, to financial practices
in general.

The world has learned to live with barriers in trade in services: as
a result some countries which have a relatively underdeveloped service
sector have not been able to benefit from the advances made elsewhere
in the world and are consequently poorer. Japan, much of continental
Europe, most of the newly industrialized countries and almost the
entire developing world come into this category, while other countries
which have efficient service industries, particularly the US but also the
UK, have been unable to export their skills as successfully as they
might. But while the failure to liberalize further the world trade in
services would be a loss, it would not be a catastrophe. The pressures
for increasing service trade are strong. It is already growing at twice
the rate of international trade in goods. Some continued growth is
inevitable and welcome.

Tensions in financial practices in general are far more dangerous.
Suppose that a populist government in the US objected to Japan owning large parts of California and decided to confiscate these assets.
Unthinkable? Perhaps. Suppose East Asian savers owned half the
national debt of the US, on which US taxpayers were having to pay
very high real interest rates. Might there not be some debt reconstruction plan to cut the interest rates and in practice halve the value of
that debt? Suppose a Middle East country found itself controlling a
large European technology company, having bought the shares perfectly legally, but giving rise to worries about a European asset passing
into foreign hands. Might the EU not bring in legislation which
deprived the foreign holders of voting rights on the shares?

The whole post-war economy has been built on the sanctity of ownership of financial assets. Nations which broke the rules, for example developing countries which nationalized foreign assets, or Latin American ones which failed to service debts, found that they were punished by the closure of the world's financial markets until they reached an accord. But in the past only poor countries broke the rules. In the future, there will be a great temptation for rich countries, beset by rising public debts, to find some way of cutting the burden on their taxpayers. It is much easier to claim that this is morally justified if the losers are foreigners who have built up the debt by predatory trade practices.

This is not to say that a great international default, akin to the defaults which accompanied the First World War, will inevitably take place. It is to say that very large international transfers of funds, where people in one country end up owning enormous assets in another, is not a stable situation, and will be a source of continuing tension which will need to be handled with great care on every side.

If there were to be a default, there would have to be a trigger. The gravest threat would come if some financial or economic catastrophe took place, akin to the great depression of the 1930s. Of itself it might be manageable, but mishandled it could reverse the trend towards liberal market decision-making and make it much harder for the world economy to recover. The lessons of the 1930s will linger in people's minds for a while. But they will grow dimmer over the years, and, as time passes, the dangers will increase.

EIGHT

TECHNOLOGY

Incremental advance or radical change?

TECHNOLOGY SEEMS TO BE moving so rapidly that there is a great temptation to assume that life in the future, at least in the developed world, will be transformed by wondrous advances of which we at present know nothing. The reality is quite different. There will be important changes which will indeed alter the lives, and certainly the jobs, of many people a generation from now, but the technologies involved will be ones that in some form already exist. The issue is which of the existing technologies will have practical commercial applications in the future and which will not.

To catch a feeling for the possible advances, or lack of them, think back to the 1960s. In some areas there has been no advance at all since then. Houses might be better insulated and more thoroughly equipped, but the basic home has hardly changed, in fact, for two hundred years. Few modern US homes could be more practical or comfortable than Thomas Jefferson's Monticello, built at the end of the eighteenth century; the most prized homes in London are Georgian; the most expensive apartments in Paris are in the early nineteenth-century blocks in the 16th arrondissement. Homes won't be much different a generation from now, for at least 60 per cent of the industrial world's homes of 2020 are already built. Housing stock turns over only slowly.

In other areas there will be an incremental advance, essentially making available to ordinary people what has been the privilege of the rich. It was possible to fly across the Atlantic on a Boeing 707 at the beginning of the 1960s in the same time as it now takes in a 747, but the real cost has more than halved. The real cost of the motor car has fallen by less than this, but incremental advance means that the comfort and performance of the ordinary car of 1990 (although not the charm of design) is similar to that of the luxury car of 1960. The consumer durables that already existed in a wealthy US home of 1960 now exist in a middle-income European home of the 1990s.

There are some areas where radical advances have made possible a dramatic reduction in the cost of a familiar service, or brought into ordinary homes technology that was previously available only in the laboratory. An example of the first is the fall in the cost of international phone calls. A three-minute transatlantic call in 1960 cost £3, equivalent to £30 in 1990 money; in 1990 the price had fallen to £2.33. (Incidentally, it cost £15 in 1930, equivalent to £470 in 1990 money.)[1] The service is identical; the actual telephones on which the call is made might even be the same instruments; but the reduction in the cost has led to radical changes in the way the telephone is used. The obvious examples of the second would be the personal computer and the home fax. Computers with the power of a PC existed in the early 1960s, as did facsimile machines, but both were so expensive and bulky that they were available only to large companies or defence establishments. The integrated circuit, the key advance that brought both into the home, was invented as early as 1958.

Anyone writing in the early 1960s might have forecast that both these devices would come down so much in cost that they would move into the home. Some people did. But people also assumed, wrongly, that other advances would be made. For example, it was widely predicted that electric cars would take over from petrol and diesel ones, but the failure to develop a practical, cheap way of storing electric power has foiled that. It was expected that vertical take-off planes would provide city-centre to city-centre air services, but technology has failed to solve the noise and cost problems. Few people managed to predict the new products and services, driven by social change, that have been made possible by improved technology.

A good example of an unexpected advance is food retailing. All retailing has been revolutionized by the combination of bar-coding and electronic tills, which can tell the retailer precisely what is being sold and at which outlet the instant the sale is made. In many parts of the retail sector this simply allows greater efficiency: the right goods get into the right shops at the right time. In Japan, where point of sale technology was first developed, it has enabled very rapid shelf turnover in the array of neighbourhood convenience stores. For example, 7-Eleven, part of the Ito-Yokado group, manages to turn over its shelf space three times a day, by transmitting sales data directly to its warehouses. As a result, a chain of very small stores (space is very expensive in Japan) is both efficient and highly responsive to customer demand.

In combination with developments in food manufacturing technology, the system has also made it practicable to supply supermarkets with freshly prepared foods on a daily or even hourly basis. This has enabled high-quality chilled food, from sandwiches to complete prepared meals, to displace lower-quality frozen food, just as frozen food displaced tinned food. Ready-made meals became available during a period where female labour was displacing male labour, leaving wives and mothers without the time to cook elaborate family meals. In Britain, a world-leader in food technology, people bought their dishes ready prepared by Marks & Spencer instead, and Britons eat more sophisticated food as a result. Without the technology Marks & Spencer would have found it much harder to promote its quiet revolution in British eating habits, for it would not have been able to match supply and demand without wastage. (A further technical advance encouraging the use of prepared meals, both frozen and chilled, has been the microwave cooker.)

Another example of technological advance is the fast-food outlet referred to in Chapter 2. US chains – of which McDonald's is the prime example – have developed a way of turning what has been a craft-based service industry into a mass-manufacturing one. Instead of food being cooked by individuals of varying talent, McDonald's developed a means of getting consistent quality into a multiplicity of outlets, using low-skill and hence low-wage labour. (The low wages in the US make it almost as cheap to eat out as to eat at home.) The technology itself was not particularly innovative, but its use was.

So the advance of technology is not just a scientific process where boffins in white coats invent something which, after a while, ends up in the home or the office. The process is an immensely complex interaction between the direction in which research is pushed, the price of a particular technology, and how that technology fits in with society's changing wants and needs. To guess correctly the direction of technological advance thus involves guessing both the future of technology itself, and the changing patterns of people's lives.

The next sections of this chapter attempt to set out some broad guidelines. One is that, as far as mechanical change goes, the laws of physics suggest that advance will only be incremental. In electronics, advance will continue to be extremely rapid, and will have an enormous impact on life and work patterns. A further proposition is that inventing new technologies will be less important over the next generation then finding ways of applying existing ones – this approach will be developed by governments to run countries more efficiently, rather than for consumers who want new toys.

Developing technology so that it performs quite different functions from the one for which it was originally intended is the standard path of technological advance. The steam engine, developed for pumping water out of mines, revolutionized land and sea transport. The steam turbine, developed for ship engines, has been largely displaced in that role, but has become the principal method of generating electricity in the world. The internal combustion engine, developed and still used for land transport, made possible powered flight. The personal computer was developed for home use, but its main economic impact has been in the office, where, except in a few specialist functions, it has ousted the mainframe. The video camera was developed for use by the television industry, but has become an important tool for security and most recently has become a consumer durable. New technologies will doubtless become available by the year 2020, but it will be yet another generation before these have a material impact on the way ordinary people, even in advanced countries, live their daily lives. Meanwhile, changes in the cost of existing technology, coupled with changes in society, will make the world in 2020 feel quite different, often in surprising ways.

The following sections do *not* look at which countries are likely to develop new technologies, or what technology policy governments should adopt (these are hotly contested issues in the business and academic literature) for one simple reason: what matters most is not where technology is developed, but how effectively it is applied. All industrial countries have access to the same technology, be it in manufacturing, services, medicine or even military equipment. The countries which develop the technology will benefit in royalty payments, but they will be unable to gain a comparative advantage for long. The speed of application will depend on a wide variety of factors including the inquisitiveness of consumers and, perhaps most interesting, the willingness of societies to use technology to shape behaviour.

Electro-mechanical technology – what progress?

Advances in electro-mechanical technology – the technology which gives us things like cars, washing machines, or aircraft – will not be sufficiently radical to make any great change to people in the industrial world within twenty-five years. Electronics, as we shall see, is different, and electronics will increasingly be coupled with mechanical products to improve their performance. But while there are a few promising new technologies, such as superconductivity and ceramics, which may prove practical propositions by the middle of the next century, there is nothing obvious which is close enough to mass use to change people's lives in the next twenty-five years. The vast array of non-electronic consumer goods to be found in a home of the second half of the twentieth century will continue to be found in the home of the first quarter of the twenty-first. There will continue to be progress, but it will be much more akin to the progress between 1965 and 1990 than between, for example, 1900 and 1925. There will be no completely new product, like the car or the aeroplane, which will go from prototype to mass market. Instead the existing range of products will be rather cheaper in real terms, and rather better.

This progress will not always be evident. Just as Londoners in the 1990s often find themselves in underground trains and buses that were built in the 1950s and 1960s, so travellers in 2020 will still be using trains, buses and aeroplanes built in the 1990s. Even when the technology is newer, it will in substance be similar to that of the present, although designs will be refined and modified. Thus it would be reasonable to expect the next generation of civil aircraft to have a seat-per-mile cost of two-thirds of the current new fleet, and it would be reasonable to expect a similar improvement in the efficiency, safety and reliability of motor transport, but the basic technology of aircraft and the internal combustion engine will be unchanged. Concern about air pollution may mean that some motor vehicles in the industrial world will have hybrid diesel/electric engines. But the internal combustion engine will still dominate transport in the cities of the developing world. It seems unlikely that battery technology will have advanced sufficiently for purely electric vehicles to have moved beyond specialist city/delivery use.

Other areas of steady advance in energy efficiency will include power generation and home insulation. The thermal efficiency of large power stations will continue to rise, while small flexible generating stations, based on aircraft-engine technology, will have replaced many of the less efficient thermal generating stations of the present. As a result, by 2020 power stations will be thermally so efficient that yet further gains will be hard to achieve. This rise in thermal efficiency is important because electricity will account for a significantly larger proportion of energy use. There will be a correspondingly large rise in the thermal efficiency of homes: legislation in all the industrial countries designed to cut carbon-dioxide emissions will have improved insulation standards to such an extent that heating (and even air-conditioning) costs will become a much smaller part of the household budget, and this despite some rise in the real cost of energy.

Fabrication costs of most consumer durables will continue to fall, partly through improved production methods, partly because any product with a high labour content will be made in low-wage countries. The result will be that the real cost of a washing-machine, cooker or fridge will be somewhat lower than it is now. Where electronic technology is involved along with mechanical, the fall in costs will be greater: expect a video cassette recorder to be one-fifth of the 1990 real price in 2020.

Parallel to this trend of incremental improvement will be a change brought about not so much by advances in technology but by changed social conditions. For two reasons, there will be a modest return towards making goods which can be repaired, rather than replaced. First, environmental considerations will put pressure on manufacturers to take back products at the end of their life. It is – and will continue to be – expensive to take a car, or a washing-machine, to bits, and there will therefore be a market for products which have a long service life. Second, a combination of a relatively affluent population and concern about waste will create a market for products which are durable. This trend will be reinforced by the combination of low inflation and low interest rates, for that will remove the need to get the most rapid payback possible. Not only will there be a greater demand for quality, rather than quantity, but it will be economic to meet that demand – rather in the way that the best-built homes in Europe were built at the end of the nineteenth century, after a long period of stable prices. Builders of late-Victorian houses in Britain, or grand blocks of flats on the Continent, built houses with larger rooms and more overall living space than the buildings of fifty years earlier or later because the secure middle class had either accumulated enough wealth, or were prepared to borrow at the prevailing low interest rates, to pay for this luxury.

While the goods of the early part of the next century will continue to look very much like those of today, the way they are made will continue to alter. The most striking change in electro-mechanical technology may be the inexorable retreat from very large factories. This will have important social consequences. The factories themselves will not disappear entirely, but fewer and fewer people will work in them, and their unit size will continue to decline, so that new plant will be much smaller than old. The whole trend towards very large plants originally took place because it seemed to be the only way to get economies of scale. Now it is apparent that the savings which can be made from such economies of scale are frequently more than offset by the cost and time involved in building very large plants, and the difficulties of running them once they are built. The combination of a series of small, incremental changes in plant construction and design, and a handful of specific technical advances (from mini-mills in steel-making to instant print shops in printing) has made small and medium-sized plants competitive with the giants.

The advantages of small plants are partly managerial. Since people seem to prefer to work in small units, it is easier to motivate them – to generate the team spirit which generally results in improved productivity. If labour relations are better, strikes are naturally less frequent, and the amount of central management time needed to be spent on worker relations is correspondingly smaller. Small plants tend to manage themselves, learning as they do so.

Moreover, in mature industrial economies, where demand grows relatively slowly, large units involve a bigger exposure to risk than smaller ones. The smaller the individual unit, the greater the flexibility of production. Companies can switch production between countries; they can make batches of new products to test market acceptability without disrupting their main product lines; they can build a new plant without having to commit vast sums of money; and they can get new plants up and running far faster.

In Japan such changes are now being seen as the end of the era of mass-production. The factories of the future, it is argued, will produce batches of individual products, crafted to meet the needs of particular markets, instead of long lines of identical items. Computer technology will be used to match demand to supply. To some extent this has already happened – during the early 1990s there was an enormous proliferation of products developed by Japanese producers. But customers may not actually want a vast variety of products. Certainly, Japanese manufacturers were accused of what came to be called 'product churning' – introducing large numbers of variations, often with only cosmetic differences, which cost more and confused the customer. A consumer revolt in the early 1990s recession forced Japanese manufacturers to return to basics. Perhaps the closest historic parallel was the planned obsolescence of the US motor manufacturers in the 1950s and 1960s, when models were needlessly changed each year to try to persuade customers to buy.

It is impossible to predict how customer taste will move in the long term. What is certain is uncertainty, and the greater the degree of uncertainty, the greater the case for spreading investment risk as widely as possible. Small plants may not spring up in every town to replace the conventional factory system, but plant size is likely to continue to fall.

Enthusiasts for technological advance argue that a number of new technologies should be practical possibilities by 2020. That may be so, but they will not be very important ones. If this seems unduly dismissive, consider the implications of the usual top of the list candidate, superconductivity. This is an essential part of the technology for high-speed or 'mag-lev' trains, which are located on (or rather just above) the track by magnets, which also power the train. The technical attraction of this technology is that it would remove the need for wheels and engines, which, though the essential moving parts of present generation trains, limit their speed. Few people doubt that such technology can be made to work – prototypes with an average speed of 350 m.p.h. are running in Japan – but even on favourable assumptions, such trains are unlikely to be in commercial use until the second or third decades of the next century. Interesting, yes, but unlikely to make a significant change to lifestyle.

Another important candidate is carbon fibre technology. This is already used in much sports equipment – skis, tennis racquets – and in aircraft. If it continues to advance in performance and the price comes down, it might start to be used more significantly in cars. The reduction in weight would enable a sharp jump in efficiency, which in turn would make the electric car a more practical proposition. If this were combined with advances in fuel cells (another candidate) it is possible that by 2020 the steel car driven by an internal combustion engine would be nearing the end of its reign, but that looks too early for the mass market; it is more likely to be 2040 than 2020.

The technical changes that will really affect people's lives in 2020 are much more mundane: things like the change in factory size, quieter and less polluting vehicles, safer road surfaces, better insulated homes. Technological development will be used mainly to hold down costs, particularly of large infrastructural projects: to find cheaper ways to replace worn sewers and rebuild the transport systems of the big cities of the west; and cheaper ways to build such infrastructure in the new cities of the less developed countries.

There have been periods in the past when mechanical technology has suddenly advanced, as in the wake of the invention of the steam-train, the internal combustion engine, or the gas turbine. This is not such a period.

Electronics: the race continues

By contrast, the electronics revolution has hardly begun. The easiest way to put into perspective the state of electronics technology is to think of it as being in the position of the aircraft industry in 1950. By then it was possible to see that aircraft would take over from ships as the main means of long-haul passenger traffic. It was possible to fly to Australia in three days, and across the Atlantic in less than twenty-four hours; the first commercial turboprop airliner, the Vickers Viscount, was carrying out its test flights, and research into its even more efficient successor, the jet airliner, was under way. But while it was easy to imagine that air travel would become the norm for the relatively rich, it was harder to envisage the social consequences of it becoming extremely cheap. The cheapest London to New York return airfare in 1960 was £154.35, equivalent to £1,543.50 in 1990 money. By 1990 the price had fallen to £323.[2] Cheap air travel has not just created the package holiday to the south of Spain or to Florida; it has had a host of other consequences, ranging from inter-continental migration and drug smuggling to making strawberries from Kenya available on the Christmas supermarket shelves of Europe. And so it is with electronics. It is not too difficult to see how the technology will develop, but it is much harder to think through its possible social consequences.

The starting point is that computer power, and with it communications, will become so cheap that for anyone in the developed world it will seem virtually free. The leaps in the power of PCs that occurred during the 1980s have at least another decade to run before the miniaturization of chips will start to reach practical limits; the next leap beyond that will be the use of optical, rather than electronic, signals in computers, which theoretically will lead to another step-change in computer power. In practical terms the power of the next-generation-but-one computers will be enough to do more or less anything that most businesses will want of them. The hardware has already become so good that the usefulness of computers is determined by the software: the virtue of more power is to enable more user-friendly software to be put in place. At some point in the next twenty-five years a stage will be reached where it is no longer worth putting effort into making more powerful computers, just as there is no point in making more powerful cars. We are by no means at that point, but it is not difficult to envisage the consequences – that any home or any small business will be able to afford enough computing power to be able to compete against a multinational corporation. There will be no comparative advantage in size in the collecting, storing and processing of information. The mainframe will have gone the way of the battleship.

Communications will have experienced a similar revolution. It is easy to see that the mobile personal telephone will have replaced the fixed-station telephone. If almost everyone carries a personal telephone as a matter of course, there will be no need to know where someone is when talking to them. Home and office phones will doubtless be retained, but may well be used more for data transmission and video links than for ordinary chats. A new etiquette will have to be developed – when people take calls and when they do not – so that individuals answer calls on their personal phones only when they choose, and otherwise have them diverted to a recorder.

It is still hard to be sure what technology will connect homes and offices. The telecommunications industry predicts that optical fibres will replace both the thin wires of the telephone, and the coaxial cables of the cable TV networks – for large-scale business use, this is starting to happen. If homes and offices are cabled by optical fibres, the potential volume of data which could be transmitted into and out of them would multiply many thousandfold. A package of A4 documents could be faxed across the world in a fraction of a second, rather than taking minutes, and the result would be much higher quality. More important for computer-to-computer communication, signals would no longer need to be converted into analogue form to suit the world's phone systems, but could be sent digitally. In fact, it is perfectly possible that data compression will reach such a stage of development that the regular phone wire – 100-year-old technology – will be adequate for most household use for another twenty-five years. One technology racing forward, data compression, may make less necessary another technology also racing forward, fibre optics.

The expansion of TV channels will continue, so that the structure of the broadcast media becomes much more akin to the structure of the print media: a few national and international products, but a multiplicity of special interest channels, the equivalent to specialist magazines. Meanwhile compression of data is at last making the video phone a practical proposition on existing phone lines. (The video phone is a good example of a technology that has failed to live up to early expectations, taking a full generation between being first demonstrated and reaching the shops.)

Television will eventually make the leap to high-definition standards – the timing is determined simply by the speed at which costs can be reduced – but in social terms TV in general seems certain to face a retreat, with more and more channels being introduced, but being watched for fewer and fewer hours. There seems to be a practical limit to the amount of time people are able or prepared to spend in front of a screen. The longer they spend on the computer, the word-processor, the trading screen, the less time they have to watch conventional television. The higher the educational level, the fewer hours of TV watched, with the result that it is virtually impossible for advertisers to target high net-wealth individuals through television. The video phone will be a serious blow to conventional television – though maybe teenagers will develop ways of watching TV and watching their friends on a video phone at the same time!

It is the social consequences of the electronic revolution that are the most interesting. Consider the implications of virtually free communications for three areas: the workplace, which for many will cease to be a central location; the home, which for some will not need to be even in the same country as the place where the employer is located; and the external environment: the country, the town, or the street.

There are four main changes which the electronic revolution has brought to the workplace. First, it has made information almost infinitely available, but at the cost of creating an overload of poor quality information. It has therefore made understanding and manipulating that information a more complex, specialist craft. Second, it has cut the entry costs into many businesses, sometimes dramatically. Third, it has helped to change the nature of the employment contract, encouraging a return to piecework where pay is related to the performance of certain specific tasks, as against salaried employment. Last, it has for some service industries made the office redundant, for much of the work can be done from home. A good example is the directory enquiry service of BT.[3]

Much has been made of the idea that we are entering some kind of 'information society', where knowledge is king. The reality is more mundane. Information is of two main kinds: that which is available to all, and that which is particular to an individual business. An example of the first is the information on the various electronic data bases, which give access in theory at least to most of the material published in the industrial world; an example of the second is the sales figures which a retailing group has from its point-of-sale tills.

The data bases are available to anyone at a cost which any small business seeking information on a particular topic would find perfectly acceptable. In practice the vast bulk of this 'information' is rubbish, the intellectual equivalent of junk mail. The volume is such that nobody could hope to keep up to date with it, even in a quite narrow field; but that is not necessary. Instead, people need filters to separate the quality information from the junk, and to apply judgement to what remains. The filter could be the forecasting department of a multinational; it could be a specialist consultancy; it could be a university; often it is simply a talented individual.

This process is already unfolding. Many large multinationals have a research division: Shell is a good example.[4] Others have set up special quasi-academic study groups, such as Nomura Research Institute. Smaller companies build links with the universities, with the result that both Cambridge, Massachusetts and Cambridge, England have attracted a cluster of high-technology firms. Specialist consultancies have flourished, and, particularly in investment, there is a handful of well-known fund managers whose stock-in-trade is not principally information, but judgement. In the financial services industry, every sizeable securities firm produces reams of 'research', almost all of it material that is easily available – the only added value is the judgement that accompanies it. Good judgement will continue to be highly valued: successful financial analysts are, as a group, the best paid researchers in the world.

As well as the filters, there are also the manipulators. If the flow of information is so great that most users have little time to absorb it, there is great scope for people who are able to package information in an attractive way. The result is the growth of the public relations industry. Any breakfast TV show, certainly in the English-speaking world, will be packed with interviews with people selling products – these could be books or films. Newspapers and magazines are similarly full of packaged material. Sometimes the manipulators are also the filters. Business TV programmes are full of experts whose main job is to analyse information, but whose subsidiary role is to get publicity for their own research.

One effect of the information revolution, then, is to increase the number of people who process facts. Where will these people be located? Many of them will need to be reasonably near the people who buy their services because they will need to sell those services to them – the whole exchange of ideas seems to need some face-to-face contact. There is a string of semi-social functions, from conferences to visits to the opera, involved in the selling process. (Maybe in Japan they simply need to be near good golf courses!) This suggests that some form of central office location will need to be retained for a while yet for sales, marketing and senior management, but for other functions the magnet may well be a university town rather than the cluster of corporation head offices in a central business district: many university towns have generated a cluster of knowledge-intensive companies which use their skills. But people will not need to be in their offices or their laboratories *all the time*, particularly if many of them are not employees but self-employed people working on a contract or freelance basis. So in general, the impact of electronics on the information industry will be to move people away from the centre of cities. As a result, the glue holding a city together will increasingly become cultural and social, rather than economic. If this is right, then cities, originally social, administrative and trading centres rather than industrial ones, will tend to revert to their earlier functions. Cities which have developed a high intellectual and cultural base will prosper at the expense of those which have not.

If the boom in the quantity of general information is one change that will come from the rise in the capacity of electronic systems, the other is the increase in specific information that businesses will have about their own performance. Already management can know much more about each stage of the production or distribution process than it could even five years ago. One effect is to make it possible to fine-tune both production and distribution: as we have seen, the Japanese system of lean manufacturing depends on knowledge about each stage of production, and Marks & Spencer's fresh food on knowledge at each stage of distribution. Fine-tuning is useful in that it improves efficiency, but this does not in itself constitute a change in the structure of industry or commerce. More important in the future will be the knowledge that businesses can have about their customers. Building this knowledge has hardly begun. Indeed, the fact that direct mail is so ill-targeted as to be junk shows how little businesses know about the people to whom they are trying to sell things. The fact that it will soon be technically possible to hold on computer a more or less accurate profile of every family in the industrial world has enormous implications not just for commerce but also for public administration, and (as the enactment of data protection legislation around the world recognizes) for civil liberties.

The impact of cheap information will also affect the costs of setting up a new business. One obvious area where the entry cost has fallen sharply is in mail order – it has become possible for a new firm, with half a dozen employees and a PC, to buy sufficiently accurate mailing lists to be able to launch a range of products aimed at a small niche in the market. The information business itself has seen a fall in entry costs, thanks to the combination of new electronic products, cheaper printing technology and more accurate mailing lists, and this fall is also associated with decentralization of the workplace. There is no need for a mail order firm to be particularly close to its customers.

Working at home will become more usual as a result of the electronic revolution. Just as some businesses are able to use technology to move physically away from their customers, so too will some employees be able to move away from their employers. The telephone companies have been among the first to relocate their services from high-cost parts of the country to low-cost ones, for there is no reason why a service like directory enquiries should not be run from anywhere in the country, or, for that matter, anywhere in the world. Already British Telecom runs some of its directory enquiries from operators' homes, as well as from remoter areas of the country, so that a London enquirer can expect to talk to an operator in Shrewsbury or Enniskillen; expect other phone-based services, like banking, also to be done increasingly by people working at home.

Those who work at home will often, though not necessarily, also be working on contract rather than as employees. As we have seen, one social effect of the fragmentation of both manufacturing and the service industry will be a further loosening of the ties between worker and employer. The idea that a worker is likely to remain with a single company all his or her working career has already disappeared in North America and much of Europe and is weakening in Japan. Company towns with a single corporate employer will no longer exist. Whenever such a large employer either shuts down or cuts its labour force, its workers will look for jobs among much smaller companies in quite different segments of industry or commerce. Gradually institutions such as pension funds will have to adapt to this loosening of ties. Pensions will become attached to the individual, rather than being provided as an additional benefit by the employer.

The new pattern of work described by Charles Handy and others[5] is the trend towards 'portfolio' working: self-employed people working for two or more corporations on a contract or for a fee. This suits large corporations unsure of their labour needs, who prefer to buy in particular skills when they are required rather than have expensive people not fully stretched. It also suits many older workers who either do not want to work full-time, or who feel it more prudent to have more than one source of income – though many workers, particularly in the US, have been forced by employers to make a shift to temporary work from the security of a full-time salaried job. This move towards temporary employment would probably be taking place without the electronic revolution, but it has been greatly reinforced by technical change. Better communications have at last made it practicable for companies to do what they have wanted to do for a long time anyway: cut their permanent labour force.

This leads to a further question: to what extent will white-collar jobs cease to be office jobs at all? Has the electronic revolution made the towering office blocks in the central business district in every city in the world white elephants, built for a need which is disappearing at the very moment they are being built? Will the office, as Charles Handy suggests, become more like a club, where there is no personal space, merely functional space? Where workers would go not to do their regular work – they would do that from home – but for specific purposes such as meetings, briefings and the like? This would mean that a fraction of the office space that has been built would still be needed, which leaves open the possibility that, just as an earlier generation converted grand town houses into offices, the next one will turn offices into luxury apartments.

The best answer is to say that while some industries, in particular financial services, seem to need central locations and will do for the foreseeable future, there will be migration in other industries. All jobs with a high 'social' element – media, public relations, advertising, marketing, lobbying – will need to stay central simply because human beings need to be in rooms together for semi-social occasions. Generally, the numbers employed by such companies in city centres may be rather smaller than at present, for many 'back-office' jobs can be done out of town, but moving these tasks out of town carries costs, in that they may be more difficult to supervise. So the pattern may be for central locations to be retained for 'social' jobs and to provide the 'club' function for the other workers who would work mainly from home, but come in one day a week or a fortnight for meetings. It is possible that, while depopulating the city centre of its workforce, electronics will save it by turning it from what has in many US cities become a purely office environment into a semi-social one. The space released in the tower blocks from offices that were no longer needed would be converted into other uses – apartments, hotels, theatres – which would bring back 24-hour life to buildings now only used from 9 a.m. to 5 p.m. That would certainly be logical, for it is absurd to have a city's most expensive locations used for only one-third of the 24-hour day.

Those workers who are able to do most of their work from home will have much greater freedom to choose where they live, not only within countries, but also between them. Someone who needs to be in a London office only one day a fortnight can live in the country, or in Scotland, or in France, or even on a Caribbean island. The advance of electronics will enable many professionals to choose their residence on the basis of tax rates and lifestyle, rather than the strength of the local job market. This will weaken the hold countries have over their own nationals: governments will have to compete for inward migration of professionals, rather in the same way that they at present compete for inward investment from commercial companies. These international telecommuters may be quite small in numbers, but they will be commercially important because they are likely to be highly paid. Telecommuting gives people living in remote locations a way to enter the international marketplace.

For these people, the home will be the workplace, rather in the way that medieval tradespeople lived over the shop. Homes will tend to be larger, reversing the trend of the twentieth century for professional people to live in smaller homes than their great-grandparents in the nineteenth. Commuting will not disappear, but the pressure on urban transport will diminish as people will have more freedom to choose the hours they spend in the 'club' office. The pressure of the rush-hours will ease – again a logical development, for it is inherently inefficient to have immensely expensive transport systems used to capacity for only two periods of an hour and a half at each end of the day. It is even possible that electronics will make cities calmer and more pleasant places to live.

Finally, advances in electronic technology will change the relation-ship between countries. It will self-evidently change the nature of economic competition, for being good at mechanical technology will become, relatively speaking, less important than being good at elec-tronics. Since the value will be in software, not hardware, the real winners will be countries which are good at creating that. But elec-tronics will also open new economic opportunities to countries, creat-ing a new area of international trade – trade in white-collar clerical services.

Already many US companies have their computer software written in India, with Bangalore the particular centre for such work. This work is currently done by batch-processing, but the lower the cost of telecommunications the more likely this type of white-collar trade is to move on to an on-line basis. For example, it would be technically possible for a British bank, wanting to provide 24-hour telephone facilities, to provide nighttime cover from New Zealand. English-speaking people there could work local office hours on terminals identi-cal to those used on the day-shift in the north of England. Insomniac customers have no need to know where their phone calls are being handled, and it might well be cheaper to have people working day-shifts on one side of the world instead of night-shifts on the other. More than this, clerical jobs may migrate to low-cost areas, just as factory jobs have tended to do. Any labour-intensive screen-based function, like word processing, could be handled in countries where there is a ready supply of cheap well-educated labour, giving developing coun-tries a new area where they can compete with developed ones without running into trade barriers.

How societies will use their new technological power

For the second half of this century technical progress has been bound up with the production and consumption of consumer durables. Middle-class people throughout the industrial world have acquired more and more goods. One-car families have become two- or three-car families; those households with one TV set now have several; people with gramophones have acquired CD players, home computers and VCRs. These are not the only ways in which people have enjoyed technical progress: those who have acquired a large enough home and a reasonable array of consumer goods will tend to spend their increased wealth on foreign travel, more education and better health care, which themselves have benefited to some extent from changing technology. But some aspects of North American and European life have not been improved by advancing technology. Public safety is the most obvious example. Will that now change? Will technology be used to give people safer streets?

For technology to improve public safety, not only will known technology have to be applied more vigorously, but it may also have to be used to alter the way people behave. The social changes of the industrial revolution, which in many ways made society more brutal by herding people into insanitary and unhealthy cities, were followed by technical and organizational changes which humanized it again. Thus the new cities got proper sewage and fresh water; parks and public libraries were built; police forces were organized; postal systems were created; good street lighting helped cut crime.

Electronic technology has only just begun to be used to combat the rise in crime that most people are worried about. Pilot schemes to install video cameras to watch city centres have cut street crime dramatically. In Airdrie, Scotland, where such a scheme is in operation, reported crime has fallen by 75 per cent in the first eight months.[6] The video camera may become as effective a weapon in cutting crime as street lighting was, for both perform much the same purpose: they make people's actions visible to others.

Car theft could be eliminated by electronic immobilizers. Credit card crime is being cut radically by the schemes operating experimentally in the UK to etch the user's photograph on his or her cards. The personal telephone will certainly add to people's safety, just as the car telephone is already doing. It will become possible to put electronic tags on all convicted criminals, perhaps even as an alternative to prison sentences.

There are many other areas of public safety which can and will be improved by careful application of technology. Good road design can cut motor accidents. Fitting video cameras at city centre junctions and roads where speeding is common is an effective way of improving driving standards. Cars could be fitted with speed governors which, if electronically activated, could actually eliminate speeding as an offence. Technologies are being developed to stop cars being driven if their drivers show signs of being drunk.

That sort of advance is hardly contentious: few people are in favour of road accidents. Where the issue becomes more difficult is when civil liberties are threatened. The most contentious issue of all is the use of data bases. It is already theoretically possible to keep detailed files on everyone in the land; indeed, several credit-rating agencies can produce instant details of the borrowing and lending habits of everybody with a bank or building society account, a mortgage or a credit card, simply by typing a house number and post code into a computer terminal. Such data bases are not comprehensive – they have been created as commercial tools for credit-assessment and direct marketing – but they will undoubtedly be developed further, so that most people in the country will have all their personal details on somebody's file: educational qualifications, club memberships, honours and achievements, names of family members, speeding offences, records of criminal convictions.

Such detailed information is available at the moment, but it is expensive to gather. In the future, the level of detail which could at present be obtained only with the services of a detective agency could be made available for a modest fee to anyone with a phone line and a computer terminal. Already it is possible to pull up on a screen everything written on a subject or person in the world's main newspapers, but the service is too expensive at the moment for home use. Eventually, however, any home will have cheap access to these data bases.[7]

A thin line divides universal access to published information from state or other access to personal information which could be used as a means of social control. For example, a speeding fine could automatically be deducted from the culprit's bank account – with a police-officer's hand-held computer – an electronic version of the on-the-spot fines imposed on French autoroutes. If the speeder had insufficient funds the money could be deducted from future wages, or from state benefit. Technically all this is possible. If society wants to use technology to police the administration of public sector benefits more aggressively then it can do so. Countries will have to take a political choice whether to use technology in such ways.

Some societies may well feel that the potential loss of civil liberties is too great a price to pay for more social control. In that case state bodies, such as the police or the intelligence services, will be unable to use the full range of technology that is available. The private sector may then take over some of the functions previously carried out by the state, as is already happening with policing in North America and to some extent in Europe. The danger is that two-tier societies will be created, consisting of the more privileged members of society who are on the data bases, and the less privileged ones who are not. North America has gone some way down this route, as any foreign visitor without a credit card who has tried to rent a car will appreciate. There are other implications: people not on registers may lose the vote. Britain may have lost up to 3.4 million voters from its electoral register at the end of the 1980s,[8] as people sought to 'disappear' in case they had to pay the new form of individual local taxation, dubbed the 'poll tax'.

As it becomes easier to find out information about people, will they behave differently? Maybe drivers will become more cautious about getting speeding tickets, not so much because they will have the money lifted from their bank accounts, but more because they know the offence will appear on a permanent record available to all. Next time they apply for a mortgage, or a job interview, or even go to the doctor, their full life history might be revealed. It is impossible to guess how people will react to such technical possibilities. Some voters may well feel that some theoretical loss of civil liberties is a price worth paying if law-abiding citizens regain the practical freedom to walk safely in the streets after dark. Others may not.

Another technical possibility with potentially more far-reaching implications is the building of national DNA registers. When Francis Crick and James Watson first described the double helix which gave the clue to genetic transmission in Cambridge in 1953, they could not have envisaged that this could be the most powerful weapon against crime since fingerprinting. As with fingerprints, no two people carry the same genetic code: it therefore becomes possible to identify a person positively if any tissue at all is available – which in cases of crimes of violence it frequently is. The Federal Bureau of Investigation has started to build a DNA register, and Britain is considering it. Such a project would make it possible to identify many criminals who currently go unconvicted. An increase in the certainty of detection and conviction may well change behaviour. The potential benefits are enormous: nothing less than reversing the whole trend towards increased crime that is taking place throughout North America and Europe.

Whether societies are willing to pay the price is a social and political issue, not a technical one.

NINE

GOVERNMENT AND SOCIETY

Training governments to think like businesses

GOVERNMENTS IN developed economies perform two quite different tasks. They run an enormous business, providing services (and sometimes goods) for their citizens and charging for these either directly or through the tax system (this is, as it were, what governments do themselves), and they set policy in a wide variety of areas, partly through legislation, partly by executive action (this is, as it were, what governments tell other people to do). This chapter looks first at how governments provide services, how the areas in which they are involved will change, and how the way they perform their jobs will alter, and then examines ways in which the other main function, the setting of policy, is likely to change.

The size of the public sector in all the industrial nations is enormous, ranging in 1992 from 26.2 per cent of GDP in Japan to 59.1 per cent in Sweden.[1] Sweden is exceptional, but all the European nations tend to have higher ratios – typically around 40 to 45 per cent – than either the US or Japan. The European perception of the right size for the public sector differs from that of the other two main economic regions.

In Europe not all the 40 per cent reflects actual goods and services provided by the government. A large part of it, typically half, is really a giant recycling operation, where the state takes money from one group of people in taxation and then gives it to others (or sometimes to the same people) in the form of pensions and social-security payments. This recycling may have economic effects, for it generally means taking money from people in work and giving it to people who are not working, but, except in as far as government is running a compulsory insurance scheme, it is not providing a service as such. Strip away such spending (which is proportionately larger in Europe than elsewhere) and the size of the public sectors of the industrial countries look more similar.

The performance of the public sector as an industry therefore raises two rather different questions. The first, which applies when the public sector is producing goods and services, mainly concerns efficiency: does government provide police and defence at the cheapest cost in real resources, and if not, how else should they be provided? The question where social-security spending is concerned is about political choice: do voters want to take so much money away from one group of people and give it to others, and are they aware of the economic implications of so doing?

This is a good time to be examining the way government functions are changing and are likely to continue to change. From an historical perspective it looks as though the high-water mark of state intervention has just passed: in all developed countries the state has started to shed commercial functions (with the possible exception of the US, where the federal government carried out hardly any such tasks in the first place). Privatization of the nationalized industries, which began in Britain in the early 1980s, has swept the world, bringing considerable increases in efficiency in the companies concerned. State ownership of commercial businesses must rank as one of the most unsuccessful forms of corporate ownership ever developed, lasting less than fifty years, in contrast to partnerships, co-operatives and joint-stock companies, all of which have stood the test of several centuries.

Given the success of privatization, people naturally tend to assume that other state functions can be carried out more efficiently outside the public sector. Yet it is far from clear whether tasks such as the administration of social security can be hived off without damaging the interests of those in society least able to protect themselves, in particular the very young and the very old.

State-run services: the shrinking perimeter

Privatizing the nationalized industries has been easy. There is, in the joint-stock company, a tried mechanism for running industrial and commercial enterprises, which despite its many flaws seems to work better than any alternative. For the western European countries and Japan the process of privatization has been relatively painless, because the financial and legal structure existed, complete with institutional shareholders willing to guarantee the success of public flotation. Transforming management attitudes was not always so easy, but the experience of the 1980s showed that, in general, management performance improved as a result of the disciplines imposed by the financial markets. Privatization was more difficult in developing countries, for the model of the shareholder-owned corporation was less established, but again in most cases privatization improved performance. In eastern Europe, and more so in the former Soviet Union, the process is less certain. Neither the institutional structure nor the managerial culture ever existed. Even in the former East Germany, where the process has been supervised by people experienced in the market system from the west, the process has proved extremely difficult. In the other great Communist empire, China, privatization is still in its earliest stages, though as in Germany (but not the former Soviet Union) the skills are readily available from people of the same ethnic background – in Taiwan and Hong Kong.

The broad trend towards a global market economy, where the majority of large commercial enterprises are owned by shareholders through stock markets, seems certain to continue. The intellectual battle, and to a large extent the practical one, has been won – the state has proved itself not to be a very good owner or manager of commercial operations. But what of the rest of the services the public sector provides? How can their efficiency be improved? What functions should remain in the public sector? To answer these questions, it is helpful to distinguish three trends:

– Ideas of the appropriate size of the public sector will shift further, so that governments will be expected to do less, not more
– Instead, governments will increasingly be expected to achieve their aims by regulation, not provision
– What remains within the public sector will be much more subject to market discipline than at present

What is the core role of the state?

Taking as a model a European country like Britain or France in the early nineteenth century, before the state began to take on the provision of wider services, national defence, law and order and some large infrastructural projects would seem to constitute an irreducible minimum. All industrial states added communications, in the form of postal services, to the public sector during the course of the century, education towards the end of the century, and most added health care progressively from the end of the Second World War. (Note that although the state has usually taken responsibility for making sure that everyone had access to education and health care, it does not necessarily provide the services itself. To take two extremes in health care, in the UK the government not only finances health care but also provides more than 90 per cent of the 'output', while in the US the state provides none, and leaves some 30 per cent of the population uncovered by any insurance scheme. The programme of President Clinton aims to bring US health practice into line with that in other industrial countries by extending health insurance to all.)

As the process of increasing state involvement in services that began in the early nineteenth century is reversed, what will go, and what will stay? Clearly, people will continue to want these services, so the issue is not whether the services will continue to be provided, but rather whether the state will provide them directly or simply ensure that people have access to the services, and whether the services will be financed largely by the taxpayer, or by user charges which may themselves be financed in part by insurance.

One thing that will stay is defence. It is hard to imagine external defence being delegated to the private sector, except in the most marginal of ways such as more civilians in support roles. A few mercenary soldiers are employed to fight in civil wars but the numbers are tiny. The same, however, is not true of that most basic of public services, the police force. In practice, since the 1960s this role has been gradually taken over by the private sector, with the growth of security companies and body guards, both official and unofficial. In the US, the job of security guard is one of the fastest growing occupations, with even the lowest forecast projecting a further 24 per cent growth between 1990 and 2005 (the highest estimate being an increase of 40 per cent).[2]

This process has taken place by attrition. No government has made a specific decision to move out of some policing tasks, nor indeed have any moved out; the private sector has moved in. Partly as a result of the perceived failures of the police, partly as a result of other changes in society, private security firms have gradually been taking over much of the job of protecting ordinary civilians in their offices or shopping centres. As the gated communities of Los Angeles show, people are even moving some way back towards the medieval concept of a city, where the citizens live behind town walls patrolled by guards, and where access is possible only at controlled gates.

Quite aside from the official security guards employed by companies and people to protect their legitimate interests, there are the unofficial soldiers of the criminal syndicates. Again, this was not the result of any decision by the state to move out of army work, but the effect is the same: the private sector, this time the criminal private sector, has become relatively more important. Private armies, with highly sophisticated equipment, have grown up in many North American cities (and to a lesser extent in Europe and East Asia) to protect drug empires. Well-armed criminal gangs operated in the US during the era of Prohibition, but the size and scale of today's private armies is now vastly larger than almost anyone could have envisaged even twenty years ago. (One has to say almost anyone, for the growth of gangs of Uzi machine-gun-toting youths on inner city streets was in fact predicted by a Shell forecasting team. The ability to predict this was seen by Shell as one of the ways in which its scenario-building technique enables it to think the unthinkable.)[3] Sadly, the sheer volume of arms which is flooding on to the world market following the break-up of the Soviet Union is likely to increase the size and firepower of these private armies over the next twenty-five years.

If the order side of law and order is clearly being privatized, so too may the law be. The 1980s saw the growth of litigation in many countries, as the US practice of turning to the law for the resolution of civil disputes came to be imitated in the UK and elsewhere. Companies in particular became dissatisfied with the informal way in which disputes had been resolved in the past and sought legal rulings. For example, when TV-AM lost its franchise for breakfast television in London it sought judicial review for the franchise decision, unsuccessfully as it turned out. Meanwhile the flood of EC legislation encouraged EC citizens to challenge national decisions through the European courts.

Like many industries which have grown rapidly, the law has been bad at controlling its costs. Those costs are largely imposed by the process of litigation: the inefficiency of court procedure and the like. As a result, alongside this rising tide of litigation has come a rise in private arbitration, where both sides in a dispute will agree to a quasi-legal judgement decided on by an agreed mediator. As the costs and uncertainty of conventional legal procedures continue to climb, more businesses are likely to seek private solutions. Ultimately the national courts, or for EU members the European court, will have the final jurisdiction, but for many practical purposes law may come to be privatized. Indeed it may be the only way of containing the cost of law.

What of two other key functions of the state, infrastructure and communications? Here, nothing seems sacred. While the state remains the main provider of roads, the UK seems likely to experiment with privately-financed motorways, and the introduction of charges for publicly-built roads in Germany and Switzerland may pave the way to greater private-sector involvement. French autoroutes have long been privately-built and tolls charged to users. Both Germany and Britain have stated an intention to sell their rail networks. Telecommunications are rapidly being privatized all around the world, and postal services are being superseded for business use by couriers and the fax.

In education, which has been a public responsibility for more than a hundred years, there has already been a marked shift towards private provision as well as private funding in most industrial countries. While the state retains responsibility for basic schooling everywhere, spending on such schooling has fallen as a proportion of total educational spending with the growth of higher education and adult education. Higher and adult education is less likely to be the sole province of the state. Although in Britain the vast majority of higher educational establishments are mainly funded by the public purse, in other countries it is normal for private sector universities and institutes to compete with public sector ones: the most prestigious postgraduate business school in Europe, INSEAD, based in Fontainebleau, France, is a private institute. Even in Britain there is evidence of a modest shift away from reliance on the public funding of higher education, with the establishment of the private University of Buckingham, and the proposal by the London School of Economics to charge fees directly to students. Meanwhile, in Britain, the company sector is increasingly funding, and in some cases providing, adult education. Rover probably spends more than any other British company on educating its workforce, providing everything from remedial maths and English to funding its staff through PhDs.[4] Elsewhere the shift to the private sector has been more marked. In Japan the rise in the number of students going to *juku*, the evening cram-schools entirely paid for by parents, means that a greater proportion of the process of education is being both privately financed and privately provided. In the US, the structural shift towards emphasis on post-graduate training – largely privately funded – has meant that the private sector pays more of the total educational bill.

This change is, again, not the result of any specific, thought-through policy. Governments rarely say that they intend to require students to pay more of their total educational bill (when they do, students take to the streets – and their parents to ferocious letter-writing). But in practice that is what is happening – not because governments are consciously pulling back, but because they are not expanding in the fastest-growing areas of education, such as *juku*, language courses, management training, and post-graduate work.

Much the same process is likely to take place in health care. The US is still expanding the role of the state as a financier-of-last-resort, but elsewhere in the world, where the state role is long-established, the state is likely to be in retreat, both as a financier and especially as a provider. Again, as in education, there will be a structural shift in demand: demand for health care will come less from people who are ill than from people who are old, who will need long-term nursing care rather than treatment for acute medical conditions. Of course the demand for care of the sick, both from family doctors and in hospitals, will continue, but one effect of an ageing population is to increase the need for nursing care in the community and for old people's homes rather than for hospitals as such. Indeed improved medical procedures are cutting the average hospital stay so quickly, and enabling so many conditions to be treated in out-patient clinics, that the bright new hospitals which have been built around the industrial world may be white elephants which will never be used to capacity. Instead investment will have to be directed towards residential care of the very old.

Much of that care will be financed and provided by the private sector. The state in any developed country is not building sufficient places for the new generation of very old, nor does it find it easy to pay for nursing care, particularly where the elderly have sufficient funds to pay for this themselves. The result will be that while the commitment of the state to universal health care is unlikely to be weakened, in practice part of the rising bill for health care will be carried directly by individuals.

How far will the retreat from both state finance and state provision go? What ought to happen over the next generation is a much more rational, much less politicized debate about the appropriate role for the state. The result of this debate – what should be for the state and what for the private sector – will vary from country to country, if only because some central bureaucracies perform better than others, but it may well be that some core governmental functions are contracted out to the private sector. For example, tax collection is invariably the task of government in every developed country, but there is no necessary reason why it should be. A consortium of commercial banks might well contract to administer income tax, and a consortium of EU or national retailers might offer to collect Value Added Tax.

This sort of radical approach, which would have been unthinkable a decade ago, may not prove to be necessary. Both the UK and the US are seeking ways of improving the performance of the public sector. In the UK the process is 'top down': central government functions, including tax-collection, are being hived off to semi-independent agencies. This project, called the 'Next Steps' programme, was intended to revolutionize the central government bureaucracy in much the same way that privatization had revolutionized the public utilities. If Next Steps works it may well become a blueprint for reform with other governments, just as privatization has been imitated elsewhere. In the US the process is 'bottom up': various states and cities are conducting experiments to try to inject a business-style culture into public-sector activities.[5] If initiatives like these are successful then the public sector can rediscover much of its self-confidence, and eventually that will be recognized by voters. After all, the state can do some things right: both Japan and the UK, where the state has a large influence on the allocation of that spending, spend less than half what the US does on health in terms of a proportion of GNP, yet seem to achieve better overall health care.

If countries decide that they cannot face a radical restructuring of their public sector, then they must find other ways of improving their own performance within the existing organizational structure, or face the fact that what are now thought of as core functions will be hived off.

There is, of course, a third and altogether less attractive option: to accept poor quality public services for the people who cannot afford to buy their way out, while the better-off use their wealth to insulate themselves. This may happen, but it is not a way to stay rich. Countries which choose this option will find it hard to remain competitive in the next century. Their workforce will be worse educated, have poorer health and quite possibly greater social problems than the workforce of countries which maintain decent – and efficient – public services.

Will the voters pay?

Governments may find themselves contracting out more and more services, but the state will still be held responsible for their quality. The state will not wither away, as Karl Marx predicted, but its role and its regulatory functions will be redefined. Whether the state is providing a service or merely regulating it, the resources still have to be found to run that service. These can come either from taxation or from user charges.

One of the most important single questions facing governments is whether the industrial world has reached the practical limits of taxation. There are two reasons to suspect that it may have done so:

- Voters will not elect politicians who increase taxation, whatever they say in public opinion polls
- Governments which try to increase taxation beyond a certain point are likely to lose revenue, partly because of the impact of taxation on growth, partly because both business and rich individuals can migrate.

It is impossible to test either of these propositions conclusively. It is an observable fact that every important industrial country ended the 1980s with its top rate of income tax lower than at the beginning of the decade. Company tax rates have also tended to decline. But while top income-tax rates came down, the overall burden of taxation did not: the balance of taxation shifted from income to spending, with the fall in direct taxation offset by rises in indirect. This suggests that voters have rejected high top tax rates, not high taxation.

Very high taxes on income had become inefficient, as people found other ways of drawing income. Interestingly, in both the US and the UK the proportion of income-tax revenue from the top 20 per cent of earners went up, not down, despite the falls in tax rates. There are no published figures, but plenty of anecdotal evidence suggests that Britain, with relatively low taxation on income, has attracted large numbers of rich individuals from the rest of the industrial world, who have chosen to live under UK tax law. Similar conditions apply in the US. If, as suggested in the previous chapter, there is a sharp increase over the next twenty-five years in the proportion of professional workers who can choose their location freely, then competition between countries will ensure that taxes on income remain low.

But low income tax is not the same as low taxation in general. Countries such as France, which have high indirect taxes, have shown that it is possible to extract more revenue from taxing consumption than from taxing income without inducing excessive migration of businesses or individuals. (France is concerned about migration of jobs to the UK, but this seems to be the result of high social security charges, not high indirect taxes.) Within the European Union the policy of open borders limits the extent to which indirect tax rates can differ, but decisions on the level to which indirect tax rates can be driven is essentially a political rather than an economic issue. High indirect taxes will damage some export industries such as tourism, and they will encourage smuggling, but overall the economic effects of high consumption taxes are likely to be less damaging than those of high direct taxes.

Nevertheless, taxation levels will remain an issue, and a particularly important one as far as Europe is concerned. Europe is already a high tax zone – it has to fund significantly higher social security benefits. But as demographic changes increase the cost of those benefits, European countries, not just the members of the EU, have to ask themselves a tough question: will a shrinking group of working people want to carry on paying for a growing group of non-workers?

This question is sometimes put in these terms: can Europe afford its social security system? That is a misleading way of phrasing the question, for if voters are prepared to pay the tax levels necessary then there is no reason why it should not. But if the result is that most, maybe all, the benefits of increased productivity are absorbed by social security charges rather than showing through in pay packets, then workers may resent this. The great political tension of the next twenty-five years will not be so much between different ideologies about the way economies should be run, or between high earners and low earners, but between people who are working and people who are not working. European electorates have hardly begun to see the scale of the problem, and European politicians have hardly begun to seek solutions to it. If the US has problems in the quality of its social services, its public education, and its access to health care, Europe has the problem of financing them.

There is no easy way of squaring the circle, but what will in practice happen is that everything will give a little. The state everywhere – in Europe, North America and increasingly in East Asia, too – will retain overall responsibility for the quality of the public services. If there is a growing demand for the services which the state feels unable to meet it will seek participation from the private sector. This will come in the form of the introduction of user charges (for example for German motorways) and in some upward pressure on consumption taxes. But it will only be able to finance a basic, no-frills service, which will fail to meet the needs not just of the rich, but also of the middle-income groups. If people want more, they will buy what they need from the private sector, and the fact that they do want to buy the services will mean that they have an interest in pushing governments to control the quality of output. The result will be that while the state will do less, and the taxpayer pay for less, governments will be expected to regulate more.

The quality of regulation

It has begun to dawn on politicians throughout the industrial world that they can control the quality of services much more effectively and ensure much higher standards of accountability to the public if the state is not the provider but the regulator. If the state provides a service, politicians are, in theory at least, responsible for its quality and efficiency. As a result, they are forever being criticized for things that are beyond their control. The instinctive response of both Ronald Reagan and Margaret Thatcher during the 1980s was to distance themselves from the performance of the state bureaucracy: if things went wrong it was the fault of Washington or Whitehall, baronies that they themselves were trying to dismantle.

But while saying 'nothing to do with us' may be a useful political device, the fact remains that government is still responsible for the quality of the job. If it regulates badly, it can do as much damage as if it provides badly. In a competitive world, bad regulation puts a country at a serious economic disadvantage.

Governments do not think of themselves as competing against each other as regulators. They regard this role as axiomatic to the business of government. They are elected to pass laws and impose regulations, and to enforce those laws and police the regulations they rely on a mixture of the courts and various quasi-governmental agencies. They enact legislation in response to popular demand, be this for control over dangerous dogs (as in Britain), restrictions on advertising of alcohol (as in France), or control over pollution (everywhere, but especially in the US and Japan). Additional regulation is imposed at a European level by the European Commission. None of the bodies creating this regulation or legislation think particularly of the cost-effectiveness of what they are doing. They may respond, or not, to pressure from the groups who will have to foot the bill. But the compliance cost is not generally included in the calculation, or when it is, it is not attributed to the consumers of the service, who will ultimately have to pay for it.

Some extreme examples of regulations which have been imposed without any thought to their cost-effectiveness exist in US environmental legislation. For example, the Office of Management and Budget calculates that the cost of preventing a single early death by imposing a rule on wood preservatives would be $5.7 trillion, roughly equivalent to America's entire GNP. Paul Portney, an American economist, guesses that the cost of the 1990 Clean Air Act may be £29 billion to $36 billion a year, but the benefits would be worth between $6 billion and $25 billion.[6] There are plenty of other oddities. In Japan, regulation is used either to protect special interest groups, or to keep out imports. A good example of the first is the banning of self-service filling stations, ostensibly on the grounds of safety (it is too dangerous to allow unqualified motorists to fill cars with petrol), but in practice to protect small garage owners. A much-publicized example of the second was the banning of the import of foreign skiing equipment on the grounds that Japanese snow was different from snow elsewhere in the world.[7]

Frequently, ill-conceived regulation is simply the result of incompetence or the failure to rescind laws which were brought in for a specific purpose which no longer applies. Rent controls all over the world have restricted the availability of rented accommodation – not at all what the legislators had intended. British restrictions on pub opening hours were originally introduced during the First World War to discourage workers from socializing when they were needed for work in the munitions factories – hardly applicable now.

If, however, ill-conceived regulation carries economic costs, so too does lack of adequate regulation. Regulatory failure works both ways, and it is just as easy to list a string of examples of losses through under-regulation as it is to add up the costs of over-regulation. Indeed it is easier, for the costs of poor regulation are made evident by single newsworthy events, while the costs of excessive regulation are disguised

in higher-than-necessary prices. Poor regulation of financial institutions can have particularly spectacular results. Failure here allowed
the savings and loans institutions in the US to chalk up billions of
dollars of bad debts which ultimately were covered by the US taxpayer.
It allowed banks such as the Bank for Credit and Commerce International to collapse. Inadequate regulation of Lloyd's insurance market
in London led to grave losses for many of the 'names' who supply
its capital base; its future is in doubt as a result. The failure of the
former Soviet Union to regulate its nuclear power industry adequately
led to the catastrophe at Chernobyl, while poor environmental controls
have devastated the health of much of eastern Europe. Weak building
regulation meant that earthquakes such as that which hit Mexico City
in 1985 caused much greater loss of life than would otherwise have
been the case.

The whole pattern of government regulation since the industrial
revolution has been one of a disaster being greeted with a popular
outcry, followed by political intervention to try to stop it happening
again. The pattern has not changed, but the practice of regulation has,
for two reasons. First, regulation has become such an important part
of daily life in the industrial world that getting it right matters far more
than it used to. The numbers can be very big: it has been estimated that
the total cost of the savings and loans rescues in the US could be more
than $1,000 for every man, woman and child in the country.[8] Second,
because both businesses and people can migrate much more easily,
regulation does not just make people within one country feel a bit
richer or a bit poorer; countries can gain a genuine competitive
advantage if they get it right.

The negative economic effects of over-regulation of commercial
activities were widely recognized during the 1980s – airlines, telecommunications and financial services were being deregulated in the US
and UK, while less radical deregulation took place in continental
Europe and in Japan. The excesses which resulted are already leading
to calls for re-regulation, particularly in finance, while the long-
standing pressure for legislation over working conditions has continued
in continental Europe. Britain has been accused by its EU partners of
stealing jobs by allowing less rigorous regulation of working conditions: the new expression 'social dumping' has been coined to
describe migration of jobs to take advantage of less onerous regulatory
requirements. A similar pattern of job migration has emerged between
the US and Mexico, and between Japan and the newly-industrialized

countries of East Asia, although in both these cases differences in actual wage rates are probably more important than differences in the indirect cost of employing people as a result of labour regulations.

This process of job migration, with countries using regulation, or rather lack of it, as a way of attracting investment, will become a much more contentious issue over the next twenty-five years. Countries which give a high degree of protection to people in work will simply find that they have a much higher percentage of their labour force out of work. If it is expensive to shed labour, companies are much less likely to take it on in the first place. Since to change the situation will mean taking away rights which workers feel they have earned, they are liable to react badly. It is difficult for a generation of workers, brought up to think of unions protecting jobs, to grasp that they may instead be destroying them (although the trade union excesses in Britain in the 1970s and early 1980s have helped teach Britons of the dangers of too much trade union power). It is harder still for voters to see that legislation which purports to protect workers' rights may have the opposite effect. This will be a particularly difficult issue for continental Europe, which will have to reassess both its trade union legislation and its regulation of the workplace if it is not to find itself at a serious competitive disadvantage with the rest of the world.

There is one effective way of balancing the popular demand for greater regulation against the compliance costs that regulation imposes, and governments are likely to follow this. It is to sub-contract regulation to independent, single-function bodies which specialize in regulating a particular area. All the evidence is that good regulation is an extremely subtle, flexible business. It involves deals between the regulator and the regulated, where cost and thoroughness are traded-off against each other. It involves regulatory bodies in different countries co-operating with each other, for the greater the freedom of businesses to migrate, the greater the need for worldwide regulation. International banking provides perhaps the best example of how a worldwide regulatory system can be built, for the central banks of the main industrial countries operate a series of mutual agreements on bank capital requirements which, in theory, should prevent any one country securing an unfair comparative advantage or any bank escaping the net of international regulation. However, that BCCI did slip through shows just how difficult it is to regulate a wholly international industry.

There is one obvious advantage to governments in sub-contracted regulation. They are not themselves answerable for regulatory failure – the opprobrium for the BCCI crash was directed at the Bank of England and the other central banks, not the UK government – yet they retain ultimate control, for they can always introduce legislation altering the powers or constitution of the regulator. But the advantage is not just a question of saving politicians from embarrassment – the actual quality of regulation should improve. Regulators can specialize in particular industries and build up a cadre of staff who can then move into the industry and help it meet regulatory needs. The Securities and Exchange Commission, which orders share dealing in the US, is a good example of this special relationship between the industry and its regulator. They can do deals, intervening to reorganize management or force some course of action by using informal pressure, rather than formal legal powers. This combination of administrative convenience and practical advantage should ensure that the growing army of independent regulatory bodies will continue to flourish.

Can governments persuade?

Where regulation fails there is always persuasion. One of the features of late-twentieth-century life which governments have found hardest to tackle is activities or behaviour which are antisocial, but which are not so antisocial that they can be easily outlawed. Examples of these would include smoking and excessive drinking. Indeed, even when the law is used, for example against drugs, it is frequently ineffective. What has in practice emerged is a patchwork of laws, some of which are designed to discourage certain activities, and some of which actually prohibit activities. Of these laws, some are reasonably well observed, but others are ignored at least by a significant minority of the population.

This is extremely unsatisfactory. Governments have been moderately successful at discouraging smoking, for example by legislating against smoking in public places or at work, or, as in the case of Canada, by sharply increasing taxation on tobacco. They have been less successful at discouraging abuse of alcohol. Advertising controls have had very limited effects, and while increased taxation might curb overall levels of alcohol consumption, there is little evidence that it has any effect in cutting problem drinking. Campaigns against drunken driving, on the other hand, have been successful in that they have succeeded to some extent in cutting the number of drink-related road accidents. Where there has been universal failure has been in the control of drugs. Laws against soft drugs are ignored by a large proportion of young people in the industrial world, while serious drug abuse has continued to rise. A vast international industry has grown up, without any official supervision of quality standards, and with the gravest social side effects. Quite aside from the damage done by drugs themselves, the fact that the industry is illegal means that it is operated by criminal gangs which use violent means to protect their business. The law, at least in North America and much of Europe, has failed.

How governments respond to the fact that every day gun-fights take place between private armies in the streets of North American cities and, admittedly less frequently, European and Japanese cities, is one of the great practical issues that the industrial world faces. The combination of anti-drug legislation and an attack on the suppliers has clearly failed; while there is a clear profitable demand, the supplies will get through. Legalization of soft drugs would decriminalize a large part of the drugs trade, and if this were to happen soft drugs could be taxed so that the excess profits went towards the general revenues of the state, rather than being siphoned off into the hands of a few rich individuals, or wasted on the highly inefficient distribution chain. This solution, however, is not deemed a politically acceptable alternative by any government in the industrial world, though some countries like the Netherlands tacitly accept soft drug use.

Legalization would solve some of the problems associated with drug abuse, but probably at the cost of increasing overall drug consumption. The alternative approach to controlling drug abuse would be to cut demand. If people were not prepared to buy the product, there would be no profit in supplying it. How might governments alter the pattern of demand? Is it their proper role to do so? Can governments really influence social behaviour, such as drug-taking? Should they try and influence other aspects of human behaviour, like divorce?

This leads to one of the great issues which will preoccupy the governments of western democracies for at least the next twenty-five years: to what extent can, or should, the state use its influence to make people behave differently? This must to some extent involve moral judgements. A century or more ago it would have been quite normal for governments to make moral judgements about human behaviour. The indigent were classified into the deserving and undeserving and received, or did not receive, poor relief accordingly. Since the Second World War the governments of most industrial countries have become more reluctant to attempt to impose particular behavioural patterns on their citizens – this may in some measure be a reaction to the consequences of state-led and ultimately state-enforced communal behaviour in Germany and Japan in the 1930s and during the war itself.

From the perspective of the 1990s it seems that the state, pushed by the electorate, is starting to become less squeamish about trying to influence social behaviour; but there is, as yet, no great evidence of a sea-change towards a less liberal society. What is happening is a spotty, disorganized reassessment of the effect of a generation of liberal legislation, with different countries making very different value judgements about what is and what is not acceptable. Some countries, like Switzerland and Ireland, are still dismantling restrictive regulations; others, including the US and Germany, are probably starting to move in the opposite direction. To take one specific example, there has been a clear shift in attitudes to abortion, away from the prevailing permissive stance, in both these countries.

If one looks at the social attitudes of the 1990s from the very long viewpoint and compares them with, for example, those of a century ago, it is not so clear that western democracies are so much freer now than they were then. Indeed, there are some types of behaviour which were thought quite acceptable a hundred years ago which are actually illegal now. If a reasonably prosperous London man waiting for an underground train in the 1890s were magically transported a century forward, he would be astounded to learn that he was no longer allowed to light his pipe on the station platform. He would quickly discover how expensive it was to buy alcohol and be interested to know that the amount of alcohol consumed per head had halved over the century. If he tried to leave Britain he would quickly find he needed a passport. For men there are many restrictions on the way they live their daily lives now which did not exist a hundred years ago (whereas women, previously restricted by significant financial and social pressures, probably have more freedom in the 1990s than they did in the 1890s).

However, he would discover many freedoms, too. He might be surprised not just at what was allowed, but what was regarded as perfectly normal: the proportion of children born to unmarried parents, the number of marriages which ended in divorce, or (bearing in mind the fate of Oscar Wilde) the open portrayal of homosexuality in novels and plays.

The reason for making the point is simply that the laws of one generation look pretty odd to another. This is not the place to make a judgement about what western societies should now do, though it is worth observing that there seems to be a tug-of-war taking place. On the one hand people do not wish to return to the restrictions of the past, but on the other they are concerned about the costs of the freedoms which they have taken for themselves. The practical point from any government's point of view is how to use the mix of legislation, regulation and persuasion to encourage people to behave in such a way as to minimize those costs. Since both legislation and regulation seem frequently to work rather badly, expect, therefore, governments to seek the softer alternative: persuasion.

One way forward might be to make more explicit a new category of behaviour: a list of activities which, while not illegal, are frowned on. This has already begun in some countries – Britain is a good example: both drinking alcohol before driving and smoking are increasingly less acceptable. Other activities might include use of soft drugs, alcohol abuse, failure to complete education, becoming intentionally unemployed in order to claim state benefit. More contentious candidates would be divorce, or more contentious still, single parents. Broken homes do impose costs on society: 70 per cent of the juveniles in US state reform institutions were the children of one- or no-parent families.[9] Divorce imposes costs: Relate, the UK charity which seeks to keep relationships together, estimates that each divorce in Britain costs the taxpayer £10,500. The issue is not whether divorce or single parenthood should somehow be prohibited – to most people that would be absurd. It is rather whether it is right to ask people whose marriages stay together to pay money out of their earnings to those who do not. While the proportion of single parents or divorced people was small this was not a serious issue, for the transfer was tiny in relation to overall public spending. But these cross-subsidies now form a large part of the welfare budget of most western democracies. If governments, or voters, decide that this is not reasonable, then the government has to find ways of persuading people to change their behaviour.

There are powerful economic pressures on them to do so. While this issue has a moral dimension – how should governments persuade people to behave better? – it is also one of public finance. Governments which are able to encourage such changes in behaviour are likely to be much more successful in containing their spending and accordingly in holding tax rates down. Alternatively, they might sustain their tax levels and improve the quality of their service.

What levers to social change does a government have at its disposal? Here are some:

- Public relations. An oddity of western democracies is that PR is widely used for the political purpose of getting candidates elected, but less so for the task of governing once they are in office – it is used to make politicians look good, not to help them build support for worthwhile policies.
- Public education. Quite aside from improving general educational levels, which depends as much on demand as supply, little effort is made to educate voters about the real costs of the choices they make in their lives.
- Public disclosure. Unless the details of public finances are disclosed, the public, however numerate, is unable to identify the cost of its actions.

The market mechanism will to some extent help. Smoking, as noted earlier, is a good example of a legal but frowned-on activity. Because smokers suffer worse health than non-smokers they tend to pay higher life assurance rates. One way of persuading the more prudish societies of the west to legalize soft drugs would be to allow the market to penalize people who did use them: they might for example expect to pay higher car insurance rates (as do actors or journalists – supposedly 'unreliable' occupations). If convicted in the courts, soft-drug users might expect to be sentenced more severely than non-users. They might find it harder to borrow money from banks. All these would require public acceptance that an activity, while legal, should be discouraged: that society as a whole has a right to impose certain values on its members. This is easy for cohesive societies like Japan; much less so for pluralist societies like the US, or, to an increasing extent, western Europe.

This leads to a further question. Are societies which pay particular respect to the rights of the individual less efficient economic entities than those which impose a greater degree of social control? Is Japan inevitably going to beat the US in the economic race, as predicted by Konosuke Matsushita,[10] not so much because of any economic advantage as such as because of the very nature of its society – the ability of its people to work together for a common goal? If so, what can North America and Europe do to compete?

The problem with democracy

There is no reason why North America and Europe should not continue what has been an extraordinary economic success story. There is nothing in the western democratic process which makes these two mature industrial regions necessarily less efficient than the more recently-developed regions of East Asia. There simply is no clear link between democracy and the pace of economic development. While some forms of government clearly are destructive to sustained economic growth – Soviet-style Communism, for example – other very different ones all seem capable of delivering a good economic performance. Among the East Asian tigers, the authoritarian leaders of Singapore and the minimalist colonial rulers of Hong Kong have both succeeded in creating conditions where growth can flourish. Japan has a version of a western parliamentary democracy which is not so different from that of Italy; but Japan has a far more cohesive society than Italy.

It is important to recognize that cohesive societies have weaknesses. For instance, they make economic mistakes. The herd instinct of Japan's investment community, buying overpriced foreign assets, is one example; the concentration of its industrial exports on a narrow band of consumer goods, with all the dangers of protectionism, is another. Equally, from a purely economic point of view, individualism has many strengths: the vigour of the US economy, its ability to change its structure quickly, the ability to develop new technologies and then to apply that technology in innovative ways are due in no small measure to its individualistic culture. Yet it is difficult not to feel that to some extent, in rather different ways, both North America and western Europe have put themselves at an economic disadvantage by their quest for individual freedom. Maybe the real message is that all modern industrial societies have to find a way of striking a balance between individualism and social control, and that somehow the democratic process has to maintain that balance, making the costs and benefits clear.

If that process happens properly people can make a choice. They can choose between the rights of individuals to carry guns and the number of citizens who are killed by them. They can choose the crime level they are prepared to tolerate; they can choose how many marriages should end in divorce, how many children are brought up by single parents. At each stage, though, they need to be clear that there are trade-offs. Make divorce more difficult and therefore have fewer broken marriages and you will certainly have more unhappy ones. These are tough choices, and the problem with the democratic process is that it is difficult for politicians to present these in a way that electorates are prepared to accept. Thus within a matter of months over the period 1988–89, the would-be President Bush and Chancellor Kohl felt it necessary to claim that there need be no increase in taxation despite the clear need in both countries for this to happen. This unwillingness to confront choice, this feeling of the need to conceal the truth, cannot surely be the fault of individual politicians, for it is so universal. It must be a fault of the system. And that is really the key issue for the governments of the western industrial nations over the next generation. What is wrong?

I have a suggestion. The nature of politics is to claim that governments can solve problems – politicians feel they need to say that they can achieve goals – but the reality is that they have a very limited degree of influence over economic performance, and still less over human behaviour. They are free to make catastrophic mistakes, major wrong turns – one has only to look at the Soviet Union or Argentina to see the effects of a generation or more of extreme mismanagement – but their freedom on the positive side is much more circumscribed. Getting it right is a much more difficult and subtle process of small, incremental steps along the path to virtue. Great sweeping changes are taking place in the world which cumulatively are reducing governments' power. Governments are weaker because many other things have become stronger: financial markets, large corporations, the international media and entertainment industries, even some rich individuals, like Ross Perot or George Soros.[11]

Electorates have to be educated to the fact that governments are weak, not because the voters have deliberately elected weak governments or because politicians are frequently weak individuals, but because that is the nature of the world at the close of this century. How the different regions of the world are likely to react to this new reality will be one of the important features shaping their likely progress over the next generation.

III

THE WORLD IN 2020

TEN

NORTH AMERICA

Multicultural America

BY 2020 THE US WILL have moved much further away from its white, Anglo-Saxon roots. For the next twenty-five years the US will be the only developed country in the world which will continue to allow large-scale immigration – with the possible exception of Australia. During the 1980s it accepted more immigrants than in any other decade in its history; and some 90 per cent of all the immigrants from less developed countries to developed ones went to the US. The US will not yet have become a country where white people are nearly a minority, as is predicted for 2050 by the US Department of Commerce's Bureau of the Census, but it will have travelled far along the road towards becoming the truly multicultural society that it will be by the second half of the next century. As a result it will not only have begun to feel quite different from the US of today; it will also be quite different from the other mature industrial regions of the world, which will not have experienced either the benefits or the cost of such immigration.

The US will feel big and vibrant, but it will not, by the standards of western Europe or Japan, feel particularly rich. Many of its citizens will not feel at all rich by the standards of people elsewhere in the developed world, for the US economy will show many features of that of a developing country. It will, in a way, be the mirror-image of what will by then be the other great economy of the world, China. Much of China will still be a less-developed economy, but there will be large areas which have reached full industrial status, whereas most of the US will be the highly developed economy it is now, and parts will continue to be the richest regions of the entire world, but there will be quite large pockets where living standards, education levels, unemployment and public health will be more akin to those of a developing country than an industrial one.

It will also be operating in a quite different world. The end of the Soviet empire and the conversion of much of China to the market economic system has made the distinction between the First World, the 'western' industrial countries, and the Second World, the Communist countries, seem anachronistic. The development of a multicultural society and, more important, a multicultural economy in North America, together with the changes taking place in China, will mean that the division between the First and Third World will have become much more blurred.

What makes the US radically different is that it will be the only truly multicultural society in the industrial world – again, with the possible exception of Australia. Much of its immigrant population will enable the economy as a whole to continue growing rather more rapidly than in either Europe or Japan, but the inflow of relatively poorly educated, relatively unskilled workers will keep replenishing the pool of poor people.

The fact that the US will be quite different culturally from the rest of the 'rich' world raises a crucial and uncomfortable question: is a multicultural society inherently less efficient than a monocultural one? There are at least three reasons to expect that it is not. First, and most obvious, there are clearly many monocultural societies which run very inefficient economies. Second, many of the immigrants will bring energy, skills and ambition, and as such will be a force for revitalizing the region. Third, as comparative advantage in exporting shifts away from manufacturing to services and ideas, it may well be that the unique nature of the US people will itself become a greater asset than it is at present. The melting pot of America makes it a great generator of new ideas, and ideas are the raw material with which service industries make their new products.

Nevertheless, the multicultural nature of the US probably also makes it an expensive society to run. Ensuring fair play between different racial and cultural groups and preserving the rights of minorities are proper, necessary and admirable features of US society, but they add costs. These costs are evident in the medical and legal systems, which are not only more cumbersome and expensive than those of other industrial countries, but have to cope with additional burdens, particularly from new immigrants – a sad example is the growing problem of tuberculosis in New York. In an ideal world, such spending ought to make for a more efficient society, but in practice the resources are not always well spent. The tough question is whether the vast mass of ordinary middle-class people are prepared to have lower living standards in order to pay for living in a society which by its nature costs a lot to run.

Meanwhile, many members of the young generation of the poor seem to be locked into a cycle where they have neither the skills nor the attitude to work which makes them economically useful in an advanced post-industrial economy. It is very difficult to see how this cycle will be broken. The US, with its considerable human resources and its commitment to equality of opportunity, will strive to lift the skill levels of these people. It is important not to confuse the problems of the existing poor with those of the immigrant community. The vigour of many of the new immigrants will give a flexibility and drive to economic growth which other developed regions of the world will lack, but in the short term the continuing flow of immigration will in some ways be a drag on economic performance.

There will be many positive effects from continuing immigration. Most important, the ready supply of cheap, young labour will allow the US to keep a manufacturing base in areas where high labour costs will have priced them out of much of western Europe and Japan. There will, however, be quite large areas of the US, mostly in the inner cities, where the present cultural barriers to economic success will continue. High crime was cited in a 1989 study as the main reason why New York's small businesses were generating new jobs at only a third of the rate of the rest of the US.[1] It is very hard to see what forces might reverse this process which leaves crime as the only way in which young men are able to earn what they feel are acceptable wages. These parts of the US will continue to decline so that, were it not for an inflow of funds from the taxpayer, living standards would be little higher than those of what is now thought of as a Third World city. Of course there are parts of cities in Europe where a similar situation exists, where there is little or no mainstream economic activity – not even shops[2] – but the scale of the problem in the US is vastly greater and accordingly the cycle will be much more difficult to reverse.

Divisions by culture (not race, though the two may be difficult to distinguish) will have become much more marked than they are today. There are already large areas which are predominantly Spanish speaking. By 2020 not only will these areas be physically larger, but Spanish will be the standard language of the ordinary people of southern California, with English as the language of the elite. The border with

Mexico will still exist as a political fact, but it will have ceased to matter for economic purposes. North America will have become an integrated economic region. This would have happened even without the North American Free Trade Agreement signed in late 1993.

The US economy: its performance

The success of the US economy over the next generation will depend on the efficiency with which the country runs its whole society, not just its industrial sector. It is reasonable to expect US industry to perform rather well, for, as mentioned, it has both high productivity and a ready supply of labour. It will, however, continue to shed labour, as will the manufacturing sector in every 'industrial' country. Expect that by about 2010, though, this process of shedding of labour will be approaching its end, by which time manufacturing will probably employ little more than 10 per cent of the US labour force, maybe less.[3] America will at this point have more or less completed its process of de-industrialization, a position which other parts of the mature developed world, with the possible exception of the UK, will not yet have achieved. The US will continue to have on average the most productive manufacturing sector in the world, though its edge will have narrowed further.

US traded services – things like banking, retailing, distribution – will have increased their share of GNP still further. Both the pro-duction and the export of entertainment products and software will rise sharply, and new services will spring up and provide employment and generate wealth. It seems reasonable to expect that many of the existing service industries will continue to be as productive as any in the world, while the new industries will quickly learn to operate to world-class standards of efficiency too. So the whole traded services sector will continue to be the world leader in efficiency – except in two very important respects: where security costs add so much to total costs that the overall productivity of a US service is pulled below that of most other nations; and where the lavish use of labour is regarded as a luxury in itself. An example of the first would be shopping malls, which may have to spend even more than they do at present on security; an example of the second would be the growth of domestic service.

But if American industry and services will continue to be wonderfully efficient, why will the country feel, for many middle-class people, rather poor? The answer – touched on in Chapter 2 – lies largely in the rising cost of security, of professional services, and of government regulation. If a much larger proportion of Americans find themselves living in gated communities, or hiring personal body guards, or simply paying higher insurance premiums on their homes and cars, they will inevitably find they have less money to spend on other things. There is no sign of a decline in crime levels, and little of a retreat from extravagant court settlements. The costs of both might in the first instance appear to be covered by insurance, but ultimately these have to be carried by the whole community.

Nor is there much sign of a radical cut in the cost of providing health care or legal services: the best that can be hoped for is that both will be contained. And the cost of government regulation, though often invisible since it is 'paid' in the form of compliance costs, is still rising sharply.

For Americans to feel richer, there will have to be an overall rise in productivity in the economy. It is very hard to see any level of productivity increase in manufacturing or traded services which will compensate for these additional costs and leave a decent amount over to be deployed in higher living standards. Nor will the next generation of Americans be able to do what the present generation has done: compensate for the failure of real wages – and therefore family living standards – to rise by increasing female participation in the workforce. There may be some slight overall rise in real wages, but it will not be big. The prospect therefore is another full generation where there will, for many Americans, be no significant rise in their standard of living. A middle-class family in 2020 may have only slightly higher real living standards than one in 1970. If there is only one income, it may not be higher at all. It is even possible that ordinary US families will be no richer than their equivalents in western Europe and Japan, a situation which has not existed for more than a hundred years.

The US economy: its shape

If, in terms of its overall living standards, the US will become more like Europe and East Asia, the geographical nature of the economy will become more different. The communications revolution will enable more and more of the office jobs, which up to now have been carried out almost exclusively in city centres, to migrate to places which provide their workers with more attractive lifestyles, as elsewhere in the world. The difference in the US is that with the economic decline of the old city centres, and the growth of new communities grouped round shopping malls on their fringe, much of the US will be made up of edge cities, semi-urban agglomerations inhabited mainly but not exclusively by white professionals – as has been widely reported, most brilliantly in the book *Edge City* by Joel Garreau[4] – where many of the traditional functions of the city are provided by the private sector or not provided at all. This is a rejection both of the state as a provider of services and of the democratic political process. Physical protection will be provided by private security guards, communal decisions taken by residents associations, amenity societies, or even the developer, rather than by elected politicians. Even citizenship will sometimes be determined by the private sector: would-be residents will be vetted for suitability by householders' committees before being allowed to buy homes.

Edge cities, and the decline of inner urban areas, are a key feature which will distinguish the US from the rest of the world. Europeans and East Asians will still frequently commute into their city centres for their work and still look to them as places of entertainment and recreation. European cities (but not Japanese) will have areas of urban desolation, as they have today, but usually on new public sector housing estates on their fringes rather than downtown areas close to the central business district. Some cities in Europe (Liverpool in the UK, perhaps) will suffer some symptoms of the cycle of decline evident in many US cities, but there are several forces which will prevent the same degree of decline: higher land costs on the fringes, less pressure from immigration, a continued transfer of funds from the general taxpaying base to the core city, and better public transport systems. Indeed, since both Canada and Mexico have rather different financial and social conditions, 'Edge City' will remain principally a US phenomenon, rather than a North American one.

Efforts will be made to slow the process, but given the economic and social pressures on middle-class people to flee to the suburbs, it will be impossible to reverse. Better electronic communications will further make large cities redundant, for even people who do need to come into cities for their jobs will not need to do so very often. Friendships will increasingly be conducted by videophone and fax, with

occasional long visits, rather than by relatively frequent, often unsched-
uled, meetings. The result will be that the large urban areas of the US
will continue to lose both population and economic activity. What
then will happen to them?

There will be two main approaches. The more radical will be to
abandon parts of them, cutting off the services, putting a fence round
then and patrolling them to keep people out. This is a brutal economic
solution: the land value is not worth enough even to justify knocking
the buildings down. Parts of the inner city would become like Rome
during the Dark Ages, or many European medieval cities after the
Black Death, when large areas within city walls were abandoned for
three or more generations until population and economic activity
picked up enough to reoccupy the ground which had been allowed to
become wasteland. This has already been proposed in Detroit by the
City Ombudsman, Marie Farrell-Donaldson, who suggests fencing off
areas of the city, withdrawing all services, rehousing the residents, and
allowing the areas to return to nature.[5] Naturally there is opposition
to such a plan, but if it does happen, the US will have accepted that
parts of these cities at least have come to the end of their natural life
and will have no further function until social and economic conditions
change.

The less radical approach will be to muddle through. This will
mean accepting that many inner city areas will never pay their way on
conventional criteria and will continue to require a subsidy from the
rest of the community. This would be a piecemeal approach, involving
knocking down the areas of worst dereliction, patching up other areas
by encouraging self-help groups which can improve the local infrastructure, and, perhaps most importantly, encouraging new and vigorous immigrant groups to take over districts and turn them into
economically viable units. In theory it might even be possible that in
a few areas the middle classes can be persuaded to return to take
advantage of cheap housing and short commutes, providing that their
security can be guaranteed, that the basic amenities are provided and
that the housing stock is sufficiently attractive. But these areas will be
few and far between.

In practice, both these approaches are likely to be adopted. A few
inner city areas will be so bad that they will have to be abandoned;
others will be patched up. But from an economic point of view the
effect will be much the same. Quite large parts of the US economy
will leave the industrial world and revert to something akin to the

standards of the developing world. Geographically these areas will be quite small – a few miles across – but from an economic point of view their effect will be substantial. Unlike the residents of the parts of Third World cities with similar living standards, where the resources to make a substantial improvement in their conditions are generally not available, people living in the most deprived urban areas in the US will have to be supported by the rest of the country. There will have to be a continuing flow of subsidies from central government to keep people, as far as possible, at a level which gives them some basic human dignity.

But even this will be difficult. Already the health, education and living standards of some parts of the US are in practice at the levels of the richer developing countries rather than at those of the fully-developed world. According to the United Nations, on their Human Development Index the African-American population of the US ranks only just ahead of countries like Trinidad and the Bahamas, while Hispanics rank below them.[6] The UN sees the distinction in racial terms, but it is more helpful to see it in geographical and cultural terms. There are certain regions of the US (like inner city Detroit) which have lost their economic function – they are not even useful as farmland; and there are certain cultural attitudes which make it impossible for people who espouse those attitudes to contribute anything positive to the economy. Crime destroys wealth.

Is a dual economy sustainable socially? It is sustainable geographically, for unlike virtually all other highly developed countries, the US has room for the two types of economy to coexist; but the experience of dual economies elsewhere in the world is discouraging. The very large differences of income and wealth of the European nations a century ago led to enormous social tensions, which were only defused by the development of the welfare state and the involvement of government in large sections of economic life. There are large regional differences of income among many present-day nation states, but there is really only one country which has operated a truly dual economy in the sense that a developed and a less developed economy exist side-by-side in the same regions: South Africa.

The United States' neighbours

Whatever the politics of the North American Free Trade Agreement, the economies of Canada and Mexico will become more closely integrated with that of the US. The driving force for closer integration in both cases is migration both of people and of jobs, though the types of people (and jobs) doing the migrating is rather different. In the case of Canada the mobile are the skilled, in the case of Mexico the unskilled.

There is already a drift of brain intensive industries, like the media, financial services, communications, and in particular computer software, heading north up the Pacific coast. These jobs have been moving from California to what are perceived as 'nicer' places – places where middle-class people prefer to live – like Washington state. The move will carry on through Washington into British Columbia, particularly if western Canada adjusts its tax policies to attract such people. British Columbia has already been modestly successful as a financial services centre and could develop this type of business further. Immigration can play a part here: the property boom of the late 1980s and early 1990s in Vancouver was led by Hong Kong Chinese.[7] The border between the US and Canada has always been permeable and improved telecommunications will make it more so; but of course the movement can go both ways – unwise policies can drive business and people south as well as pulling them north.

To the east, Francophone Canada will continue to lose out as a result of its language policies whatever the political accommodation it reaches (or fails to reach) with the English-speaking provinces. Ontario will continue to be the chief beneficiary as business drifts out of Quebec, which it will do, not so much because of fears that the province will establish itself as an independent country, but more because of social factors, in particular the extent to which the Francophone education system creates a cultural barrier between Quebec and the rest of North America. It is perfectly possible that Quebec will form itself into a separate country by 2020, but its economy will remain as closely integrated as ever with the rest of North America.

Overall, Canada's economy is hitched to the US wagon, but while its economic performance deteriorated relative to the US during the 1980s, this performance – certainly of British Columbia and Ontario – may improve during the early part of the next century. The main reason for this will be the introduction of market reforms both by the business community and by federal and provincial governments. If this is reinforced by the development of Canada as an even more civilized and safe place to live, then there could be several decades when Canada pulls up and ahead of the US in terms of its living standards.

The US belt along the border with Mexico will continue to grow rapidly, fuelled by immigration from the south. This belt is already becoming the new industrial zone of the US, with the border – from an economic point of view – virtually disappearing. The integration of the two economies will continue, with the effect that the centre of gravity of Mexico will shift northwards. This will be accompanied by structural changes in the Mexican economy, such as the development of a modern financial services industry, and a high-technology communications industry. By 2020 economic growth in Mexico will have improved living standards to such an extent that the pressure to emigrate to the US will have disappeared. In fact, a city like Monterrey will have started to attract professional immigrants from the US.

Along with these economic changes will come cultural ones. Just as Spanish is used more and more in southern California and Florida, so English will come to be used increasingly in northern Mexico, because if Mexico can sustain its market reforms and provide stable administration, it will become less a typical Latin American country, more a Northern American one. The border will disappear not just as an economic barrier, but also as a cultural one. This will lead to a reassessment of the relationship between the US and Mexico. Mexico will always remain a junior partner in the relationship, but in relative terms its weight will increase, and as a result it will be taken more seriously by US politicians.

Gradually over the next generation the rest of Latin America will associate more closely with the US. If the move towards democracy and market-led economic decisions that took hold during the 1980s throughout Latin America is sustained, then the whole of North and South America will move together in both economic and cultural terms. It is perfectly possible, for example, that the North American Free Trade Agreement will have developed into an American Free Trade Agreement. Indeed if NAFTA is seen as a success, it is more or less inevitable that it will develop in this way.

This will transform South America, enabling countries which appeared in the early 1980s to be condemned to economic and political failure to hold their heads much higher in the world. It is quite possible that a country like Argentina will recover some of the ground that it has lost this century. It will not regain the living standards which, in relative terms, it had a hundred years ago – it is not going to be as rich as northern Europe or the US – but it could enjoy a period of considerable prosperity if only it can sustain a modicum of political stability. From a brutal economic point of view, it does not need to achieve a full western-style democracy, but what it does need is competent and corruption-free administration. Brazil, with its even greater resources, could have an extraordinary impact on the continent, given a decade of such government.

The economic damage wreaked by corruption is hard to overstate, and corruption seems endemic in the region. Building the institutions is not enough; corruption-free government requires deeper roots if it is to survive. In judging the future, two forces will pull against each other. On the one hand the fact that some Latin American countries seem to be establishing much higher levels of financial competence will inspire the others. A political (and ultimately economic) equivalent to the 'lead goose' phenomenon of the newly industrialized countries of East Asia could occur, with the more democratic and better administered countries acting as a spur to the others. On the other hand, to believe this one has to believe that a region which has, by and large, been badly governed will suddenly make a sea-change in the way it runs itself. It is quite difficult to see parallels in history where this has happened. Maybe the fact that Spain and Portugal have established functioning democracies will give Latin America role models; but this is uncharted territory.

The prize, though, is enormous. Latin America ought to be more successful than it has been for the whole of the post-war period. It ought not to be so easily outpaced by countries in East Asia. If it is able to establish greater self-discipline, then it will again become very attractive to world capital, as it was for much of the last century, and will accordingly be able to provide a much better life for its people. But whether it can sustain such self-discipline is far from clear.

Still the only superpower

North America will no longer be clearly the richest part of the globe, but the United States will remain the only superpower. For another generation its military strength, its cohesion as a nation and its sheer size will ensure that it will retain political leadership of the world. Neither of the other two developed regions – Europe or East Asia – will have this particular combination of strengths. Western Europe will lack its political cohesion, and will still be preoccupied with the integration of its fringe areas. Power in East Asia will be split between the two largest economies, Japan and China, while levels of development elsewhere will be uneven. The twenty-first century may turn out to be the age of Asia, but that will not yet be absolutely clear at the end of its second decade.

Meanwhile the intellectual leadership of the United States will remain. It will still be a magnet for the best brains in the world. This will have the paradoxical effect that continued leadership may depend on the work of foreigners at US universities and research establishments. The US will, however, continue to export its culture, its ideas, and its language. The dominant position of English as the world's universal language for both science and entertainment will be even more secure – even if its hold in the US may be weaker.

How will the US react to the fact that, though global leader, it is no longer the world's richest nation? Will it want to continue political leadership of the world? Perhaps for another generation it will be prepared to do so: it is hard to walk away from power. But by 2020 domestic support for its international leadership – and all that entails – will be wearing thin. If the US is not the richest country in the world, why should it pay for the security of countries which ought to be able to afford that for themselves? Because there is no other candidate for global military leadership it cannot but continue to play that role, but the physical support will be reduced: the US will have withdrawn all but token forces from Europe, and in East Asia forces will have been slimmed down to a fraction of the 1990s' levels. Europe will be expected to defend itself; so will Japan.

Instead the preoccupation of the US military will be defence of the US itself and control of international terrorism, which will rightly be perceived as more of a threat to world peace than the conventional armies of the major nation states. The US will naturally retain particular areas of special interest, for example in the Middle East and in Latin America, and it will retain an overall interest in stability in the rest of the world. It will be particularly concerned about the way in which the military power of the former Soviet Union is managed, a process which will not yet be complete by 2020. But direct threats to US interests will diminish, and it will be reluctant to intervene in trouble hot-spots unless it feels its own interests are directly at stake. The US will not have reverted to isolationism, but it will have accepted that it cannot solve the world's problems on its own.

A further sign of the US retreat from global leadership will be the weakening of its financial support for multinational agencies. As a result bodies such as the International Monetary Fund, the World Bank and in particular the United Nations will fade in importance. Their functions will increasingly be passed to the private sector – the financial markets supplanting the IMF, international banks and fund managers rendering the World Bank redundant, and a combination of charities and countries under a series of bilateral deals carrying out many functions of the UN. The bodies will still exist, such is the durability of bureaucracies, but as US funding for them diminishes, so their roles will shrink.

Much will depend on the level of support for the Federal Government from the US citizenry. Since the 1960s the executive has been particularly weak – much weaker than the executive of most European nation states or even, in some respects, of Japan.[8] The United States has the great advantage over the European states that it is not involved in a great debate about the relationship between its nationhood and the economic zone to which it belongs – it is not in the position of having to cede power to a wider group of countries, and cope with the cumbersome bureaucracy involved in this process. But it has the disadvantage of operating a cumbersome bureaucracy in the first place. The US democratic system is not only an expensive way to run a country; it is also one which makes it difficult for the executive to carry through decisions. This would not matter if there were general approval for the system; but while within the US there is very little pressure for a change in the system as such, ordinary citizens are walking away from it. In national elections a much higher proportion of the US electorate fails to vote than in Europe or Japan. Around 55 per cent voted in the US presidential election of November 1992, compared with 77.7 per cent in the UK general election of April 1992, and 73.3 per cent in the Japanese general election of February 1990.[9] And at a local level, the voters are literally driving away from traditional structures by leaving the old cities for the new private sector mall-based societies on their fringe.

If there is little faith in national politicians or the process by which they reach office, there is unlikely to be much support for the role of running a world police force. This is a natural enough response, but one which should give serious worry to the rest of the world. The US has been a benign and honourable leader of the western alliance. The thinner the internal support for its world leadership role the more dangerous the world will become.

Some tough choices

The US will have to make some tough choices about its domestic affairs. It will start from the realization which will gradually seep into the US citizens' minds that it is no longer the richest country in the world. People will begin to wonder why. They might wonder too why so many US assets are foreign-owned (a legacy from the big borrowings of the 1980s, 1990s and the early 2000s – it will be some years into the next century before the US external deficit is back in balance). One response might be protectionism, and some such measures will surely be invoked. Another and ultimately more damaging response might be pressure to confiscate foreign-owned assets. But neither line of attack would solve the actual problem, for this lies within the US itself: it is the high cost of operating the whole society.

Specific problems fall into three main groups: problems of bureaucracy, problems of security, and what might be called, for want of a better expression, 'problems of lifestyle'.

Problems of bureaucracy include the extent to which pressure groups are able to impose their views on, or extract funds from, the majority; the size of awards that juries are able to impose on 'soft touches' like insurance companies, banks and large corporations; the cost of regulation; the propensity to litigate; the courts' sensitivity to the rights of the criminal; the cost of elections, and so on.

Problems of security, aside from the problems of crime itself, include the acceptance of anti-social behaviour; the extent of drug abuse; the lack of gun controls.

Problems of lifestyle are enormously broad. They range from the failure to push for higher educational standards (or even common standards in the use of language) to the low savings levels, the high divorce rate, or the large proportion of children born to single mothers.

It is important to be clear that these are not all problems of the poorer segments of US society, though many are. Some of them are problems at the very top: some people might want to include problems of ethics in the business and professional communities. It is important to be clear, too, that many of these items cited as problems are also freedoms. However, they are freedoms which make America poorer than it need be, and ordinary Americans will become increasingly aware of these costs and frustrated at a society which imposes them.

Eventually this frustration will break though. It is building at the moment, but for the time being the barriers which preserve the existing value system are too strong. These barriers include the power of professional bodies such as the medical and legal establishments, of the National Rifle Association, of the Hollywood moguls, even of the liberal press – as President Clinton has highlighted.[10] At some stage, most probably in the second decade of the next century, there will be one of those great radical shifts in US political attitudes which take place from time to time, a shift akin to the New Deal of Franklin D. Roosevelt. This could happen in a benign way within the existing political system, with a new president catching a mood which emphasized citizens' duties rather than their rights, and in particular their obligations to each other. An absolutely crucial element in these obligations would be the rebuilding of the family unit as a means of bringing up children. Or it might happen in a destructive way, as suggested by Alistair Cooke (see page 45) – there could well be a return to McCarthyism where the 'deviant' behaviour is not Communism but a failure to espouse family values. But this will not be so much a politically-driven revolution – governments will become less powerful, not more. If America returns to a form of McCarthyism it will be because most Americans want it. The change in values will start at the bottom and move up; it will not be imposed from the top down.

It will be tough on the American people, brought up on myths of their country's special place in the world, to have to rethink not only that place, but also their own place in American society. America will not go back to the smug self-confidence of the 1950s. It is much more likely that it will go back to the rough, rapidly-changing society of the early 1900s. For perhaps fifteen or twenty years there will be a great tug-of-war between two established US traditions: the robust individual self-reliance that created US capitalism and helped make it the richest country in the world; and the much newer tendency for people to refuse to take responsibility for the consequences of their own actions and instead blame the state, big business, insurance companies, anyone who can be sued, or simply the fact that they are in some way 'disadvantaged'.

The most alarming aspect of this denial of individual responsibility occurs in some universities where it is not possible even to discuss the extent to which social problems might be the result of individuals being stupid, selfish, lazy or wicked rather than caused by some external force. A book written by the tennis star Arthur Ashe, published just after his tragic AIDS-related death in 1993,[11] asks black Americans to look at their own behaviour and take responsibility for it. The statistic he quotes, that one in four black men between the age of eighteen and thirty is either in jail or out on parole, is particularly devastating. But the US problem should not be seen solely or even principally in racial terms, for the refusal to take responsibility is evident, though in different ways, in the other racial communities. The abuse of the law – suing on what to non-Americans would seem absurd grounds, or just padding insurance claims – is much more a vice of upper-income-group whites than poor blacks, and is just as destructive to national wealth. Like crime, it redistributes wealth in an arbitrary way, and imposes large additional costs as it does so.

This will all change. Anyone who knows and loves the US cannot but be hopeful of its ability both to confront these domestic problems and to redefine its place in the world. There is a richness, breadth and energy to US society which has in the past enabled it to make great changes in its social direction. At some time ordinary Americans will decide that they do not want to live in a country where half the marriages end in divorce, or where feature films can show a hundred or more acts of violence in less than two hours. There are signs that deep down the pressures are building which will lead to the great earthquake of a change in values – the calls for gun control, the attempt by President Clinton to reform health care, the Arthur Ashe book. The US must bear in mind, in assessing these pressures, that the longer the earthquake is delayed, the greater will be the shock when it comes.

ELEVEN

EUROPE

An association, not a superstate

THINK BACK TO medieval Europe. It was a clear cultural unit, unified by the Roman Church, with a common language – for the literate – of Latin. There was a substantial level of regional trade, but the region was not yet a series of nation states. There were a few countries which already had clear cultural identity, like England and a substantial part of France, but in the main Europe was a series of small kingdoms and principalities, some of which were linked by a vernacular language like German, Italian or Spanish, some of which were not. The degree of economic development varied widely, but in some respects the elements of Europe were more similar then than they are now: the domestic architecture was broadly similar across northern Europe; the church gave a central authority, albeit an uncertain and often weak one; gold provided a common currency; bankers from northern Italy were starting to provide Continent-wide financial services (though only for the very rich, a rather limited clientele). There was even for a while – in the Crusades – a single foreign policy and a common military taskforce, something which Europe cannot begin to agree upon now.

Of course the clock will not go back, but Europe's future – unlike North America's – will be shaped by its past, so the medieval model is not a bad one for helping to understand Europe's future.

The best-documented evidence of the very limited extent to which the political map of Europe has changed is Italy. Robert Putnam studied the level of economic development and civic performance in modern Italy and compared it with Italy in the thirteenth century.[1] He concluded that regional government in the twentieth century works best in regions where it also worked best seven centuries earlier: in the regions of northern Italy with a tradition of a 'civic community' – co-operation, tolerance, trust, and active citizen participation – as opposed to those of the south which have an autocratic tradition.

There are other examples of the power of Europe's political heritage and the problems it now causes. The troubles of the former Yugoslavia go back to the break-up of the Byzantine empire by the Turks. The troubled relationship between Britain and Ireland dates back to the medieval conquest of Ireland and the subsequent movement of Scottish Protestants to Ulster.

If one starts from the medieval model, it becomes much easier to see how the European Union might develop. The great debate is whether it should widen or deepen: whether it should accept more members, or whether the existing members should move towards ever-closer political union. The reality is that, for a while, it will do both, but eventually it will reach a point where it becomes impossible to proceed further. Geography and economics dictate that it cannot remain an exclusive body; other nations of the European economic zone and cultural tradition will inevitably join in closer association with the core members of the EU. It is quite arbitrary that Denmark should be a member and Norway not: the countries of the European Free Trade Area will become members of the EU by the early years of the next century. The countries of central and eastern Europe will subsequently join, for once their economies become closely integrated into the market economy of western Europe, the commercial pressures from both sides will make it very difficult for them to be excluded.

By 2020 this process of enlargement should be more or less complete. The borderline cases would be Russia and Turkey. History suggests that Russia will be in and Turkey out. Russia has long been poised between rich, developed Europe and the great Asian hinterland, with successive Tsars seeking to look west, but relying on the resources of the great land-mass to enable them to do so. If Russia does succeed in converting itself to a market economy on the western European model (and this process will take at least twenty years), then it will have followed its historical pattern of having a burst of 'copycat' activity, when it seeks to learn from its western neighbours, buying their skills and supplying them with raw materials to pay for them. Turkey, on the other hand, has not for many centuries been part of the European economic system. For many years it was the ancient enemy, the country which conquered much of eastern and central Europe and which reached the gates of Vienna in 1683. More recently, it was the 'sick man of Europe'. Its influence in Europe will depend on how well it runs its economy, and how solid a member it remains of whatever succeeds the NATO alliance, but its future is unlikely to be more than a buffer state between the EU and the increasingly turbulent Middle East. It is very important for Europe to retain such a buffer state, and accordingly the European nations will seek to support and preserve it, but they will not welcome it into the EU itself. The cultural and religious differences are too great.

So the EU will widen, but it will, by 2020, be approaching its natural limits. How far will it deepen during this time? A bit, but not a lot. A look at the political pressures that would be caused by further deepening in economics, in finance, and in foreign policy explains why.

Economic specialization may carry on a little further, but long before 2020 will have reached its political limits. Economic nationalism is too strong. Specializing inevitably involves ceding control of large areas of economic activity. Even in motors, one of the most integrated of all European industries, further consolidation will be difficult. In 1993 the shareholders of Volvo rejected the proposed merger with Renault. Italy will protect its car producers despite the fact that it has little comparative advantage in that area, if necessary by barriers against (for example) British-built Japanese-designed cars. Trade within the EU in services will increase, but will reach cultural limits: British people will not want to place their money in German banks, or vice versa. The one thing which might encourage a higher degree of economic integration would be were Europe to become a single financial entity, in particular by establishing a single European currency. But again the evidence would seem to suggest that the political cohesion required for voters to agree to abandon national control of currencies will be hard to attain.

The currency issue is tremendously important, for it is the point at which economics and politics meet. A national currency is not just a symbol of nationhood; it is one of the key practical ways in which a government can control and unify a state. On purely economic grounds there is a strong case for seeking a common European currency as the Maastricht treaty recognizes. Yet as countries as diverse as Singapore and Japan have demonstrated, it is perfectly possible to achieve rapid economic growth without one's currency being part of any larger bloc. In any case, the upheaval in the European Exchange Rate Mechanism in the eighteen months after the treaty was signed showed how difficult it will be in practice to establish a single currency for Europe. Indeed this upheaval has rendered the Maastricht timetable for achieving a single currency by 1997, or 1999 at the latest, quite unrealistic.

Nevertheless, the pressures, more political than economic, for a single European currency will continue.

So between now and 2020 there will be a series of efforts to impose such a currency. It is quite possible that some form of EU currency, based on an enlarged Deutschmark zone, will be introduced. It is even possible that France might join such a zone. But it is equally possible that, if France were to do so, she might subsequently leave. For example, picture the following scenario: such a common currency is introduced around 2005. There follow a few years when the main European nations use it, but a combination of a series of weak governments in France and the pressures of a worldwide recession in 2015–17 lead to a break-up of the European currency zone in 2018. An alternative scenario might be that social and political upheavals in Germany in the period between 2010 and 2020 lead to very rapid inflation in Germany and the end of the perception of the mark as the anchor currency of Europe. Instead, sterling would become Europe's strongest currency and in the period between 2020 and 2030 the other EU countries would seek to anchor to it. Both scenarios, of course, are pure surmise. The simple point is that even if a common European currency were achieved in the early part of the next century, it might not last.

It is equally possible that the European nations will decide that they do not need a common currency, for improved technology will surmount most of the practical barriers that different currencies create. At a personal level, where the sums are relatively small, it is easy to see how things might develop. Electronic tills could quote goods in any currency. If electronic funds transfer becomes the normal method of making payments, even for small items, then there would be no need for travellers to carry foreign currency. For commercial transactions, where even small swings in exchange rates have a large impact on the profitability or otherwise of a contract, it is harder to see automated transfers becoming acceptable, but there are other changes taking place in the world of finance, referred to in Chapter 7, which may make the whole issue less contentious. If interest rates and inflation come down worldwide, then the pressures for changes in European exchange rates will diminish. There could be a single European reference currency, like gold in the nineteenth century, to which the various national currencies would be pegged. In a low-inflation (or zero inflation) world there would be hardly any need to change these pegs. If, however, a country did decide to move its exchange rate, it would be free to do so without the disturbance of leaving the European currency zone.

Whether European integration reaches a common currency or not will be a crucial test of the degree to which it can deepen. On balance, the internal economic tensions are such that it is unlikely that a European currency, if it exists at all, will have more than a core of members whose economies are most closely linked to Germany: it would be a greater Deutschmark zone. But there may well be some quite sophisticated system of linkages between the various European currencies which would work much better than the 1980s Exchange Rate Mechanism. Some countries will be core members of this system, others fringe ones.

Even that degree of harmony will be hard to attain in foreign policy. Europe has for a thousand years been spectacularly unsuccessful at developing not just a common foreign policy, but even a *modus vivendi* for the different peoples who share the Continent. The twentieth century has, on the harmony scale, been the least successful of all. The memory of the catastrophes of this century should certainly be strong enough to enable western Europe to live at peace with itself for another generation at least, but it is unreasonable to expect nations with very different histories to agree on policies towards the rest of the world. National self-interest differs too much.

The first decade of the next century will be spent adjusting to the collapse of the Soviet empire. That process will continue to be extremely dangerous, for it is quite unrealistic to expect tensions which have been suppressed for at least two generations (in some cases much longer) to disappear overnight. The best that can be hoped is that western Europe will not make too many decisions which damage its long-term economic potential, or any decisions which disrupt the rest of the Continent – it is overwhelmingly in western Europe's self-interest that the rest of the Continent should be prosperous and stable. As for central and eastern Europe, it has to learn the same lessons as the west: that stability is an essential but insufficient condition for prosperity, and that building a modern market economy is a slow and complex task.

If this line of argument is right, it is possible to sketch the outlines of Europe a generation from now, accepting, naturally, that the detail will inevitably be inaccurate.

The EU will have become a wider association but a more layered one: there will be several different classes of membership. Germany and France will continue their close association, though this will have stopped short of having a durable common currency. The Benelux group will join them, but this association will not extend to a common foreign policy, and deals will have to be done on an *ad hoc* basis as particular issues arise. Outside this core will be a group of countries which will be economically integrated, but which will opt out of some of the core decisions. These will include Italy (if it remains a single country), Spain, Portugal, Ireland, the Nordic countries (possibly including Finland), Austria and probably Britain and Greece. Outside this group will be a further ring of states which will be part of a European trading zone, but which will prefer a looser association. These will include Switzerland, Poland, the Czech and Slovak republics, the Baltic states and, conceivably, Britain and Greece. For Britain and Greece to leave the EU might seem almost inconceivable. But if Europe ceases to be a successful economic entity, Britain might see its self-interest in focusing on non-EU markets. As for Greece, as eastern Europe develops it might build up its relationships with that area rather than remain a junior member of the EU. Countries like Ukraine, Belorus and Russia itself will have negotiated trading relationships with most of the western states and returned to their traditional role as suppliers of raw materials to a more sophisticated west. There will, however, be a difference in the relationship from the past: Russia will also be exporting skills, in particular in service economy areas like computer programming or engineering design, because it will be able to supply brain power more cheaply than the west.

This will not be the final constitutional form of Europe. In fact there will be no final form. The most important difference between the Europe of the 1990s and that of 2020 is that people will have realized that Europe is not progressing towards some goal of greater unity, and that the closeness of the association of European states ebbs and flows over the centuries. The second half of the twentieth century happened to see a voluntary movement towards closer association in the west, balanced by a similar but involuntary, or externally imposed, movement in the east. With the break-up of the eastern association, the nature of the western one will inevitably change, with countries east and west looking more to their national self-interest rather than their position as members of a bloc. In some respects that national self-interest will encourage closer links; but in some it will not. Nation states themselves may conclude that they no longer wish to continue in a particular relationship, as did the Czech and Slovak peoples. Italy, one of the newest of the European nation states, may split into two.

Europe is already a jigsaw: it will become a much more complicated one. Just how individual countries might fit into this jigsaw will be discussed in the next sections of this chapter.

Britain and Ireland

From a purely economic point of view it is easy to see that the next twenty-five years will be a period of modest success for Britain. It has three substantial advantages over the rest of Europe: it is ageing less quickly than any other large European country; it has made the structural adjustment out of mid-technology manufacturing industry more quickly than the rest of Europe; and it has closer relationships with both North America and East Asia than its continental partners.

This last point may become very important if European economic performance lags, for Britain is in the unusual position of being able to hedge its bets: if Europe stagnates, it can work on building up its trading relationships with North America, Japan and China. If the European economy becomes more inward-looking and overly protectionist, it is even conceivable that a country like Britain, with other economic opportunities, may see some economic advantage in trying to distance itself from the European economy and focus instead on the rest of the world. Britain would need to maintain a free trade arrangement with the core community, but would not necessarily need its present close association. Negotiating such an arrangement might, however, prove very difficult.

It is quite possible that these structural advantages will mean that real income per head in Britain will be slightly higher than that of France, Germany or Italy by 2020 instead of slightly lower as it is at present. The less successful the continental European economy, the more likely it is that the UK will outstrip it. If, however, Europe as a region is able to make similar structural changes as the UK, then the UK's relative position will not improve so much.

Not everyone in Britain will share this modest success. Its educational system still pays too little attention to the less academic section of the community, even with current initiatives to improve the situation, which will make the system a little more like that of other European countries. While its emphasis on creativity and individuality will probably be more appropriate for the early twenty-first-century economy than it was for the late twentieth-century one, it also tends to increase inequalities. Not everyone can be a fashion designer or a pop star, and those who do not have the talents to benefit from such an education will find themselves confined to low-skill service industry jobs. Even if educational levels were raised sharply there would still be a generation of poorly educated people who will not be able to share fully in economic growth. Many countries suffer to some extent from the educational attitudes of the 1970s and 1980s, but Britain suffers more seriously than most.

This uneven performance will lead to greater social tensions. The successful British will be among the most successful in the world, and the less successful will resent this. This resentment will show in a number of ways, and will help lead to important political changes within the UK.

One will be for greater political autonomy for regions which feel left behind. The process of centralization evident for most of the post-war period (and partly a legacy of wartime controls) will go into reverse. Regions will see that it is not in their long-term interest to devote time to lobbying Westminster, but more effective to promote regional advantage directly to potential investors and residents. Some regions will be better at this than others, with the result that cities which are physically quite close together – Leeds and Sheffield, for example – will have very different economic performance, as indeed these two already have. The possibilities of electronic communications – enabling workers to live in pleasant surroundings while 'telecommuting' to less desirable areas – will mean that regions which can create an attractive environment will be able to move up in the economic ranking quite quickly. On the other hand, the decline of the less successful regions could become very serious: Liverpool is not yet in the position of Detroit, losing more than half its population, but its hold on its economic base is clearly precarious. Greater local autonomy may be seen to be in Westminster's interests, too, if it encourages a sense of civic responsibility and self-reliance.

If the English regions get more autonomy, Wales can also expect an even greater degree of say in how it organizes its affairs. It will, for most purposes, still be administered in parallel with England, but a greater cultural self-confidence may lead to calls for a greater degree of political independence, stopping just short of a full political break.

Scotland may well have chosen to go a stage further. It may well have become independent from the Westminster parliament by 2020, no longer sending representatives to it, but electing members to a Scottish parliament. All it needs for such a break to occur is a government in England which sees an electoral advantage in encouraging this. Without the Scottish Labour MPs there could be no prospect of a Labour government in England. At some stage during the next twenty-five years it is at least an evens chance that a set of circumstances will arise which leads to the setting up of a Scottish Parliament.

One possible catalyst for an independent Scotland would be Northern Ireland uniting with the south. Eventually Ireland will be reunified. The timing of this will depend on the rate of population shift within Northern Ireland. On present trends, by 2020 Roman Catholics will be a clear majority in the north. This trend is most unlikely to be reversed; if anything, it will speed up, as the Protestant community feels it is losing critical mass and its younger members increasingly look to building their lives in Britain instead. At some stage, probably during the second decade of the next century, there will no longer be majority support in Northern Ireland for maintaining its links with Britain, and Britain will see that it is not to its advantage to try and preserve the link either.

If the gradual emigration of Protestants from the North becomes an exodus, this could have important consequences for Scotland, where many will go, because the Northern Irish immigrants to Scotland will feel bruised by England, and will reinforce existing pressures for independence there. Again, the majority in England will see it as an advantage were Scotland to have a more separate identity. In terms of social attitudes, Scotland and England are probably more different now than at any stage since the Industrial Revolution. As for the Republic of Ireland, it has run a successful democracy and made considerable economic progress during its first seventy years as a state controlling more than three-quarters of the land area, and there is little reason to believe that it could not adapt to running the remaining part. It would need to adapt – to become a more secular state – but it is already in the middle of a social revolution which will eventually transform it into a modern European democracy. Long before 2020 the south will be ready for the north.

Were Ireland to be reunited it would become possible for Britain to build a better relationship with the republic. The great contribution that Ireland can make to the British Isles is that, alone in Europe, it has a ready supply of young, well-educated people. Many of these work in the UK and will continue to do so, thereby helping give the two countries (maybe three countries, conceivably four if Wales also seeks a separate identity) economic viability. The solution to the Irish problem will make England a calmer place, and not just for the obvious reasons that its cities will no longer be bombed. If the tensions between England, Ireland and Scotland were eased, England would have rounded off a 300-year experiment with colonialism, a period of its history which began with the unification of the Scottish and English parliaments in 1706, passed through the takeover of Ireland, the building of a network of commercial interests around the world and then of a colonial empire. England would be back to being England, and would feel much more comfortable with the idea that it was responsible for the fate of its own people, not of others.

Of course it will be a different England. The heritage of the past is visible in every street with the growth of its new immigrant population from the commonwealth. By western European standards, England has managed quite well to live in harmony with new immigrants, and this immigration has certainly made the country a more interesting place. A generation from now, with no further immigration on a significant scale, and, unlike the US, a growing proportion of cross-racial partnerships, Britain should feel more comfortable with its minority ethnic groups, unlike much of the rest of Europe.

Will these changes to the UK as an administrative entity lead to abolition of the monarchy? That seems unlikely by 2020, for modest economic success and some reforms of the monarchy itself should have made it more acceptable to the British people. Indeed the monarchy may have found a new function in unifying England and Scotland, allowing a close association of the two countries despite the fact that they come to be governed by separate parliaments. It that were to happen, the relationship between Scotland and England would have returned to that which existed during the seventeenth century. The monarchy would have found a role.

Western Europe

The key relationship in western Europe is between the two large countries at its core, Germany and France.

The German people will find the last years of this century and the early years of next very difficult. Germany's economy has to make three difficult transitions. It has to reduce the size of its manufacturing and expand its service industries; it has to lift the performance of the former East Germany; and it has to encourage its workforce to accept longer working hours and cuts in state benefits. It addition to these economic pressures there will be a social pressure. The German people have to cope with a flood of immigrants, something which, historically, Germany has never been good at accepting.

All recent experience of the response of the German authorities and industrialists to these pressures suggests that they will approach these economic difficulties in an ordered, logical way and eventually will overcome them. Manufacturing industry will be slimmed down, with companies pushing their products up-market yet again; new know-ledge-intensive niches will be found in the middle-technology manu-facturing sectors in which German industry excels. There will be some development both of the broad middle range of private sector service industries like retailing and financial services, and Germany will be able to improve its telecommunications industry once it has been fully deregulated. Eventually, too, German industry will be able to reap the benefits of the rapid economic growth which will be taking place to the east. But all this will take time, and Germany has to complete this restructuring against a background of the oldest population in Europe. For a decade, perhaps two, there will be no significant rise in German living standards. By 2010 they will be somewhat below those of Britain, France and northern Italy, and it will only be recovering slowly by 2020. It will be very difficult to explain the reasons for this to the German people and to get them to accept it. As in the US, the political and business leaders have to explain that if the country is to continue to enjoy an exceptionally high standard of living, it must make changes in the way it organizes both its economy and the way people live their daily lives.

It would be quite wrong to underestimate the strength of the post-war democracy which West Germany has established, the order and discipline of the workforce, the depth of German education, the atten-tion to quality at a string of different levels, even the sheer size of the economy, the largest in Europe. But however confident one is that Germany will overcome its social and economic difficulties, it is impor-tant to realize that the German economy has a very difficult period ahead of it. It will not, a generation from now, be the powerhouse it appears to be today.

This will have important consequences for Europe. The most immediate will be for the close trading partners of Germany, the Benelux countries. The economies of Belgium, the Netherlands and Luxembourg (like those of the French regions abutting Germany) are so closely integrated into the German economy that Germany's problems will feed through directly into their prosperity. But the Benelux countries will be protected from Germany's difficulties in a number of ways. Belgium and Luxembourg both benefit from having large parts of the EU bureaucracy stationed on their territory and paid for by taxpayers in other countries – the EU bureaucracy will survive, despite efforts to contain it. The position of the Netherlands is more interesting. It does not benefit much from direct payments from the EU; its particular characteristic is that it exports an enormous proportion of its output – around 55 per cent. This international orientation shows in a large financial services sector, and, for a relatively small country, it is unusual in having three very large multinational corporations – Philips, and the Dutch sides of Unilever and Shell. Much of its future turns on two things: the ability to find new markets if Germany falters, and the success of those three giant companies.

Germany's problems will also be inflicted on the EU itself. It will be difficult to persuade German voters that they should continue to be the paymaster for the EU; certainly there will be great pressure from Germany not to increase the size of the community's budget. The Common Agricultural Policy, which eats up three-quarters of the EU budget and which gravely distorts European agricultural production, will by 2020 have substantially withered away. This will make membership a less attractive proposition for the Mediterranean countries, Ireland and to some extent France. The scaling down of the CAP is, however, essential if eastern European countries are to use their comparative advantage as cheap producers of agricultural products. But the most important influence on the EU from Germany will be its sluggish growth. This will encourage France and Italy to look elsewhere for markets for their industrial goods and for their service industries. Throughout its formative years the EU never had to cope with a chronically weak German economy. Persistent weakness in Germany might be the force which prises the EU apart.

For France the next quarter-century will be a tantalizing time. In many ways the country is well placed to become again the dominant economy of Europe. It has great strength both in some corners of high-technology and in highly-crafted products which the rest of the world wishes to buy. Given reasonable political stability it can deliver steady growth in a low-inflation environment. On the debit side, however, it has a record of bouts of political instability, and it is not hard to see what might trigger another such bout: the pressures from immigration from north Africa. The fascinating question is whether the centralized, planned French economy will deliver a better performance than a market-driven economy like the US or, to a lesser extent, the UK.

Strong central government direction has meant that France, more than most other large industrial countries, has its eggs in very few baskets. Most obviously it has poured resources into the Ile-de-France region – greater Paris – rejecting regional centres of potential economic growth. Large cities with very high densities can be made to work by spending a lot on infrastructure, but they may be less efficient producers of goods and services than less dense agglomerations like the south-east of England or greater Los Angeles. For France to be successful, Paris has to come right. If its economy falters, France has a serious problem.

If one looks at French industry, the country has made judgements which need to come right. One is investment in nuclear power: France is more dependent on nuclear power than any other nation. If, for some reason, the world has to retreat from this source of energy, France will be more severely damaged than anywhere else. It is also heavily dependent on a few industrial sectors, mostly in middle-technology, some in high-technology, to be motors of growth for the rest. It has been poor at attracting Japanese investment, to the detriment of its consumer electronics industry, and slow at building a modern financial services industry. Most worryingly, the instinct of many French industrialists when confronted by foreign competition is to call for protectionism. (French agriculture also has that response, but that is more understandable for farmers always seek protection.) The best of the French economy is wonderful, but there are curious gaps and weaknesses – for instance in financial services, telecommunications and air transport – which are the result of its centralized decision-taking.

On balance, provided France remains stable politically, it can expect to continue to have high living standards and an enviable lifestyle a generation from now. The potential problems are social and political as much as economic. The social tensions stem from France's concern about immigration, compounded by the costs of running the French social security system. Immigrants, however unfairly, are likely to be blamed for those costs. French unemployment will persist at high levels through to the end of the century and beyond, because of the inflexibility of the labour market. These two forces are likely to lead to an erosion of confidence in the elite, and an attack on the way political decisions are taken. The Fifth Republic has been running for thirty years, rather longer than most systems of government that France has adopted since the Revolution. It seems highly likely that at some time in the early years of the next century there will be another political shock which will result in a Sixth Republic being formed. It would be logical for France to move to a system which gave fewer powers to the president and more to parliament, but as with any such constitutional change this will only take place after a period of instability. It is impossible to be precise about timing, but by 2020 this unsettled period should have passed, French politics will have calmed down, and reasonable economic prosperity will have returned. But, at some time, expect the *pavé* of the Paris streets to be ripped up by rioters, as they were in the events of 1968.

Italy is the most fragile of the middle-sized European states, yet in some ways it has the most competitive economy. The fragility shows in the levels of organized crime and of corruption, in the lowest birth rate in Europe which may indicate a deeper social malaise, and above all in the contrasts between the rich north and the poor south. These tensions will increase, partly because of the ageing of the population, which will increase demands on social security, and partly because of immigrant pressure. The Italian state is a recent enough creation for its future to be in serious doubt. As Robert Putnam's study[2] shows, the influence of history on Italian civic development is very strong, and it is quite realistic to see the north seceding from the south. Some form of a central Italian state may persist, but it would be one in which the provisions of a normal unified state – such as common taxes and common social security benefits – would no longer apply. If the country splits, the big transfer of wealth from north to south will cease for there will no longer be sufficient political support in the north to sustain it.

Shorn of the south, northern Italy could again become the most successful economic region of Europe, as it was six hundred years ago. Already on some measures it is the richest, but its advantages will become even more evident in the future, for it produces goods and services which cannot be imitated elsewhere. It is the best place in the world for producing high quality craft-based goods with a very large proportion of the added value coming from design. Even if some of the production moves overseas, which is already happening, the value will still be added in Italy. As the world, albeit slowly, becomes richer and as people seek individuality in the services and products they buy, so the comparative advantage of this high-skill region will increase. If its resources are no longer sapped by the rest of Italy, this could happen rapidly.

Splitting the country might work to the advantage of the south, too. It would, in the short-term, suffer from a decline in the scale of transfer payments, but in the medium term it might gain from the dynamic effects of having control over its own destiny. Maybe, as Putnam suggests, the south needs a different form of government – more autocratic, less 'civic' – than the north.

Spain and Portugal will experience a further period of 'catching up' with the rest of Europe. The economies of Spain and, to an even greater extent, Portugal are still in the early stages of a climb to northern European income levels. There are several reasons to believe that they will continue on this climb for another generation at least: they still have relatively low labour costs (though the level of employment in Spain is kept high by an inflexible labour market); the fall in the birth rate is relatively recent, so the adverse effect of demography on the size of the workforce will not be apparent until well into the next century; both economies have a strong service industry tradition; and both are improving public education.

For Portugal, the issues are essentially economic: how can it turn the potential disadvantage of being on the periphery of Europe into an advantage? It will be helped, as it seeks to do so, by the mobility of individuals and by improved telecommunications. For Spain, which in the early 1990s had Europe's highest unemployment rates, the key issues will be social and political rather than economic. Spain is in the 'right' sectors – a mixture of low-cost manufacturing and middle-market service industry. The task is to improve the quality of both sectors, and that will undoubtedly happen. Once labour market rigidities are attacked, growth will be faster and unemployment reduced, and it is really a question of whether these changes are made in the last part of this century or the early years of next. It is harder to see how Spain will cope with its internal pressures, including Basque nationalism. Tensions between Catalonia and Madrid will continue to be just tensions, but the Basques may well have attained a greater

degree of nationhood. As with other regional independence movements elsewhere in Europe, whether the Basques succeed in their aims
will depend on whether the majority sees it to be to its own advantage
to allow them to do so.

The future prosperity of both Spain and Portugal does at least lie
in their own hands. This is not so in the other EU Mediterranean
state, Greece. What happens in Greece depends on what happens on
its borders. Writing in the early 1990s it is important not to be mesmer-
ized by the civil war in the former Yugoslavia, for an accommodation
will have been reached by the turn of the century and by 2020 the
entire Balkan region will be a modestly prosperous series of mini-states.
However, between now and 2020 there will be a series of upheavals,
certainly involving large population movements, possibly involving
further civil war. This will be very disruptive to the neighbouring
Greek economy, heavily dependent as it is on tourism. It is difficult to
see how the economy can be more closely integrated into the western
European system while turmoil persists to the north. Naturally – as
long as peace in the region prevails – Greece retains its attractions as
a tourist destination, and it will continue to attract some subsidies
from the EU. Like Portugal, it can hope that improved telecommunications will enable it to offset some of the disadvantages it suffers from
its fringe location, but it is not going to grow rapidly enough to close
the gap in income per head between Greece and northern Europe.
Greece will remain relatively underdeveloped.

The Nordic countries were not, with the exception of Denmark,
members of the EC in the early 1990s, but they will join the EU, as
will Austria, before 2000.[3] The key economic issues for these countries
vary: for Norway the trend of the oil price is the dominant force on
the economy; for Finland it has been the opportunities and problems
of the former Soviet Union and its allies; for Sweden (and to some
extent Denmark) the principal problem is the urgent need to cut the
size of an overly-ambitious welfare state. The common difficulty these
countries face is that they have created a system of social welfare that
they do not seem to be able to afford. There is a curious irony that
countries which have among the highest per capita GDP in the world
also suffer an exodus of skilled people seeking to escape their tax
rates: Denmark loses 0.4 per cent of its own nationals each year from
emigration.[4] If that does not sound much, consider that, at that rate,
by 2020 the equivalent of one in ten of Denmark's nationals would
have left the country. As skilled labour becomes more mobile, the

whole Nordic world could face a serious drain of its most talented people unless it is able to find ways of rolling back the state sector. EU membership will make it even easier for people to leave.

That, to a large extent, will be western Europe's problem. It will, with the exception of Japan, have the highest proportion of old people anywhere in the world. Its people will still have relatively high tax rates despite pressures to contain these. Its young will be well-educated and mobile. If they feel they are denied economic opportunities in Europe, either because the economy is underperforming or because they do not get sufficient value from their governments, they may seek to leave. The borderless EU gives them the freedom to do so. That leads to the most important question of all facing western Europe: once European integration reaches the stage where it cannot proceed any further, will the process simply plateau, or will it go into retreat? On the timescale of this book, a plateau is more likely. But it would be wrong to write off the possibility that some members of the EU will find that it is no longer to their advantage to remain core members and that it might be a better deal simply to negotiate a free trade agreement with their neighbours and stand back from everything else. The most likely candidate for this role is, of course, Britain. This may well happen. The glue is probably strong enough to hold it together at present, but after 2020, as the contrast between the performance of Britain and the rest of Europe becomes more striking, the EU may come unstuck.

The eastern hinterland

The future of some parts of the eastern hinterland is easy to see. It is quite clear that countries like Hungary and the Czech republic will become prosperous members of the European economy within a generation, as they were before the First World War. There are larger doubts about the pace at which Poland or Slovakia can reach present western European income levels, and still larger ones about the Baltic states, Latvia, Lithuania and Estonia. But the debate is about the speed of change, not the direction of it. Things will get better. By 2020 these countries will, to a greater or lesser extent, be sharing in the wealth of Europe. They will be functioning parliamentary democracies, living at peace with each other, having by then learnt the skills of developed market economies. There is, within the folk memory, an idea of how such economies work, and how the democratic process operates, and this will help.

To say this is not to pretend that the next twenty-five years will be easy. There are specific problems of geography, such as the minority Russian populations in the Baltic states, or the Russian military outpost in Kaliningrad. There will have to be, in all probability, quite large population movements, though there is no reason why these should not take place in a peaceful and ordered way, and enormous structural problems within the eastern European economy have yet to be addressed. These will be difficult and dangerous years, but at least it is possible to see where the region is going.

That is not so clear in the case of Russia itself, or the new nations of Belorus and Moldova, or even the Ukraine. These countries have virtually no folk-knowledge of either a market economy or a democratic system. Belorus has never been an independent country, and the Ukraine has only a short experience of this. It is difficult to see these countries, or Russia itself, becoming a 'normal' parliamentary democracy, but then from a purely economic point of view these countries do not need to do so. As many Asian nations have shown, there is little linkage between democracy and economic growth – certainly in the early stages of the take-off. Western Europe needs successful economies to its east which can supply it with raw materials and with which it can trade. It does not need identikit parliamentary democracies. The practical questions are whether these countries will live peacefully with each other (which is by no means clear), what help they will need to cope with their environmental problems, and at what stage they will start to contribute positively to the European economy.

Writing in 1993, with the region's economy in a state of collapse, there is a great temptation to conclude that the collapse will continue, and that the region will remain an economic disaster for a generation. That is wrong. The technical skills of Russia remain as strong as ever; they merely need to be redirected. The human resources are enormous; they have merely been misapplied. There is now growing evidence that commercial skills are being rebuilt, with signs of an effort by many in the business community to give service, to attract customers, to supply needs. It may even eventually prove the case that Russia was right to allow political change to run ahead of economic change, unlike China, for once economic restructuring is secure, Russia will have a legitimate government, supported by the broad mass of the people, something which China will find it very hard to develop. The popular view that China has made the change to the market economy more effectively than Russia may be right on a ten-year view. But on a 25-year view, it is quite possible that Russia's method of transition, for all its flaws, will seem more secure than China's.

It is always worth recalling the rapid progress of the Russian economy in the first decade of this century. The human, physical and organizational resources for a Russian economic take-off are there, and at some stage during the next quarter-century they will ensure that that will happen. A sensible guess – it can be no more – is that the period between 2010 and 2020 will see Russia again become an economic giant.

There remains the question of the Balkans. The chilling lesson of the Yugoslav civil war is that history repeats itself: the atrocities committed by all sides and the extent to which civilian populations are targeted along with the military forces mirror the experience of the Balkan wars just prior to the First World War.[5] The best assessment, perhaps, is to recognize that the conditions for these countries to live together in reasonable harmony will not exist for the foreseeable future. Since, in addition, several nations, including Greece, have territorial claims on Macedonia, there is always a danger of the conflict spreading beyond civil war into international war. From a purely economic point of view, the region will not be sufficiently stable for it to be more than modestly prosperous a generation from now. Eventually new borders will be established, but these are unlikely to be accepted by all the players, and will need external policing by other European nations. In practical terms the region is unlikely to bring anything positive to Europe's economy; it is much more likely to be a drain on resources and a source of continuing concern.

The first half of the twentieth century was Europe's catastrophe. The second half has, in its way, been Europe's triumph. If the period from 1945 to 1990, when the Berlin Wall came down, saw the reconstruction of western Europe, the period from 1990 to 2020 will see the reconstruction of central and eastern Europe. This second half of the process of reconstruction will be less easy than the first, for the countries of eastern Europe have in every sense further to travel. It is unreasonable either to expect a smooth path, or to believe that the process will be complete by 2020. All the newly-emerging nations of eastern Europe (and maybe some of the older ones) will not yet have become rich market economies, with extensive social security systems, populated by prosperous professionals with weekend cottages and BMWs. But there will have been progress. Europe is still moving forward, even if both halves of it have a great deal to learn.

TWELVE

EAST ASIA

The contest for the leadership of Asia

THE FIRST QUARTER of the next century in East Asia will see a
contest for influence between Japan and China, fought on the battle-
ground of economic growth. Eventually China will emerge as the
dominant power: the size of its population and land area will ensure
that. But this will only have started to become clear by 2020, for China
has too many political hurdles over which it must jump for its
economic progress to be easy or smooth. For the next century to
become 'Asia's century', in the way that the nineteenth was Europe's
and the twentieth has been North America's, these two countries will
have to form a relationship which enables both them and the newly
industrialized nations of the region to prosper. In purely economic
terms, as discussed earlier, the two giants should be natural partners.
Both may be ancient cultures, with a vigorous and hard-working population, but in every other respect they are different: one has technology,
the other resources; one a diminishing elderly population, the other a
relatively young growing one; one is a close ally of the world's only
superpower, the other is viewed with grave suspicion by the democratic
world. Potentially both are very useful to each other, yet because of
historic suspicions between the Chinese and Japanese, it will be
extremely difficult for them to manage their relationship, however
much it might seem in their mutual self-interest to do so.

The next two sections discuss how the two giants might develop,
but first it is worth making some more general observations about the
region, for the next quarter-century will give East Asia an extraordinarily bumpy ride. On the one hand it is, and will continue for a while
yet to be, the fastest growing region of the globe. On the other, the
motors of that growth, principally the building up of light industries
which export a fair proportion of their output to Europe and North

America, will not be so powerful in the future as they have been in the past. The policy of using such exports as a motor of growth worked for tiny city states like Singapore and Hong Kong, and staunch US allies like Japan and Korea, but it will not work for a giant like China. Nor, increasingly, will it work for a Japan which is seen by the US and much of western Europe (though not Britain) as a dangerous predator rather than a slightly idiosyncratic friend.

The run of growth in East Asia has great momentum. A good performance in one country stimulates activity in its neighbours. Some countries with great human potential, like Vietnam, are only just starting their economic take-off, while others have sufficiently cheap wages that they can expect labour costs alone to give them sufficient comparative advantage for some years yet. The higher-cost countries have invested sufficiently in the education of their workforce (and have a workforce which is prepared to study hard and save) to compete at similar income levels to Europe and America. But there are two powerful reasons to be wary of projecting that Japan will be massively richer in terms of income per head than Europe or North America in 2020, or that East Asia will quickly become the dominant economy of the world. The first is that the region's economic power is narrowly based; the second that the west can copy, too.

It is a constant struggle to make money out of producing goods which become cheaper almost every month. The prices of the consumer electronic goods in which East Asian producers excel keep falling. To maintain sales, products have to be made more and more complicated: more and more features have to be added to justify the price. Once a product line becomes mature – as, for example, have colour TVs – the profit goes away. Fortunately, electronics is moving ahead so fast that new products, or genuine advances to existing ones, seem assured for another decade at least. But if the actual manufacture becomes a smaller and smaller part of the total cost of a product, then the size of the profit attributed to the manufacturing country will steadily diminish. Any Asian economy dependent on selling to the west will find it tougher.

This leads to the second point: the west will learn. For much of the post-war period, East Asian countries have achieved growth by copying products made in Europe or North America. Shop in Hong Kong, Bangkok or Seoul and you will quickly see imitations, down to every detail, of the glamorous products of the west. Now Japan has long moved away from such practices and is itself the world leader in manufacturing technology. Knowledge is a two-way street: both the US and the UK have learned much from Japan's lean manufacturing techniques, and continental Europe will learn, too. Japan, like every other nation, faces the dilemma that the more productive its manufacturing industry becomes, the smaller the proportion of the country's workforce is employed.

To carry on growing beyond a certain point these countries have to become as good at producing exportable services as they are at producing exportable goods. They have to stop drawing from the pool of scientific knowledge of the west and learn to contribute to it. They have to develop individualistic, creative talents alongside their established virtues of hard work and application. It is not at all clear that they will be able to make this transformation. Catching up is easier than pulling ahead, copying easier than creating.

Nevertheless, no-one should underestimate the capacity of the region to adapt. Its nimble economies are able to dart in and out of activities in a way which is extremely difficult to replicate in Europe, or even in North America. If these countries' established markets cut back – for example – on imports of electronic goods, East Asia will find other things to do. It may have to.

Japan – the greatest commercial empire on earth

It is impossible not to be impressed by Japan. People who visit the country regularly will see a Tokyo which is visibly cleaner, smarter and more stylish each time they go. The factories are more modern, the workers better educated, the restaurants more sophisticated. It would be easy simply to extrapolate from this obvious progress and say that by 2020 the Japanese economy will have made yet another leap forward, so that by then it will have clearly outpaced all other developed countries to become the richest and most sophisticated society on earth.

Easy, but wrong. Japan will continue to develop both its economy and, more important, its view of its role in the world, but progress will be much slower and in many ways more difficult. There are at least three great challenges which the Japanese people will have to meet:

- How to cope with the ageing of its population, a process which
    will inevitably hold down both economic growth and the
    living standards of its workers
- How to move further out of manufacturing and towards
    becoming a more skilled manager of an enormous external
    commercial and financial empire
- How to become a regional world leader, responsible for its own
    national security and able to provide wise and mature
    guidance to other smaller and technically less advanced nations

No country has ever had to make the change from being the youngest
of the large nations to being the oldest in two generations, so Japan
will have to teach itself as it goes. It can deny that there is a problem,
arguing that the elderly Japanese, with their health and education, will
not be like the elderly of other nations, that they will be more productive, more adaptable. There may be something in that. It is true
that Japan has great scope to use labour more efficiently in its service
industries, by applying some of the ideas developed in manufacturing
to areas like retailing, finance and public administration. It also, by
comparison with any other industrial country, under-uses the women
of its workforce, which, looked at positively, gives it the opportunity
to make quite radical improvements to living standards.

However, while the ageing process, properly managed, need not be
an economic disaster, it will change the character of the country. It
will want to become a more leisurely society, changing less dramatically
and growing more slowly. It will reject the endless – and often spurious
– product development, where manufacturers bring out new and supposedly improved products which cost more but do not in reality
perform any better than the ones they replace. Many people may seek
to return to their cultural roots, rejecting or at least questioning
western materialism. Interest in religion will rise, as will interest in
the Japanese past. This will show in minor details, such as the more
frequent use of traditional costume, rather than any major political
shift of policy, such as a return to isolationism. Japan's self-interest
will keep it looking outwards to the world, but it will look outwards
with some fear, for there will be neighbours which eye Japan's wealth,
social discipline and sense of order with envy. Those neighbours, of
course, include China.

This need to look outwards will be much reinforced by the structure
of Japanese foreign earnings. Physical exports will tend to decline as

a proportion of GDP over the next twenty-five years, as they have in the past ten. Instead Japan will rely on revenues from the profits of overseas subsidiaries and from its international portfolio of investments. Japan will move from being an invisible importer to becoming an invisible exporter, relying on profit, interest and dividends for a substantial part of her foreign revenues. By 2020 the current account surpluses of the 1980s and 1990s will probably have been eliminated, but it is reasonable to expect a current account surplus to last well into the first decade of the next century. The foreign assets acquired during this period will have a profound influence on Japan's whole outlook on the world. It will become much more like Britain in the late-nineteenth century than the Japan of the post-war period. Thus foreign policy will be directed to protecting the value of those investments, preserving the income stream from them, and seeking new investment opportunities, rather than preserving access for physical exports.

The size of this empire will be enormous. Japan will control, for example, three-quarters of the British motor industry (which will, incidentally, by 2010 be the second largest in Europe after Germany). It will own most of the prime office accommodation in the city centres of America. It will have expanded its chains of hotels around the world, with the effect that it will be quite difficult to stay in a large hotel without being in one owned by the Japanese. And it will have a significant portfolio of investments in most large European and American corporations, which will as a matter of prudence almost invariably have a Japanese representative on their board of directors. Japanese attitudes to business will shape commercial behaviour throughout the world.

If Japan becomes truly ingenious with its money, it could become the main source of venture capital for the would-be entrepreneurs of Europe and America. These people will go to Japanese sources of finance because they will feel they are more likely to achieve a long-term partnership with Japanese fund managers than they would with their own national institutions. It could, therefore, through its financial might, gain access to entrepreneurial and intellectual skills which it might lack.

In one sense demographic change will fit in with this structural change in the way Japan earns its way in the world. The country will become much more of a contractor rather than a manufacturer, using its experience and intelligence (skills of the old) rather than its manufacturing expertise (skills of the young). It will be a difficult transformation, nonetheless, for running a worldwide commercial empire will need a sense of history and a feeling for the way in which other peoples think. It is not at all clear that the Japanese educational system, for all its excellence at what it is trying to do, has prepared sufficient people for this role. Indeed it would be hard to think of an educational system less suited to these new needs.

As a result, Japan will make mistakes in managing its commercial empire. It will make unwise investments, naturally, but more seriously it will find itself the object of envy in countries poorer than itself. For the rest of the world to cope with an image of Japan as a financial as well as an economic superpower Japan will have to act with great sensitivity. If it is not careful in the way it deploys its wealth it will find its assets being stolen under the guise of nationalism. This has happened many times in the past: British and French assets were nationalized with only limited compensation as their former colonies achieved independence, while Latin American countries used the excuse of nationalist needs to justify defaulting on their bank credits during the 1980s.

Many of Japan's investments will be in North America and Europe, but gradually the balance will shift towards Asia. This will be mainly because, for the first few years of the next century at least, this region is likely to continue to grow more rapidly than elsewhere and will therefore offer better investment opportunities. But unlike North America and Europe, where Japan is dealing with countries of broadly similar development and international status, in Asia Japan is dealing with a diverse patchwork of countries, of vastly different size and with very different political systems.

This has political and, indeed, military implications. Japan cannot assume that the US will continue to maintain substantial forces in the East Asian region; it will inevitably come to take on a larger defence role itself, and will gradually become an important military force. Instead of the region's security being guaranteed by a benign US, its security will be determined by the relationship between its two great powers, Japan and China.

This will make the East Asian region feel deeply uncomfortable. Memories of Japanese military expansionism linger, and Japan's diffi-culty in coming to terms with its history will add to foreign suspicions. Unlike Germany, which has accepted the reality of past horrors and come to terms with its history, Japan finds it hard even to teach its children about the circumstances of its involvement in the Second World War, or of its treatment of East Asian neighbours during periods of occupation.[1] There is a flaw in Japan's perception of its role in the world – essentially an inability to see itself as others see it – akin to the arrogance with which Britain saw its place in the world at the end of the nineteenth century, or US arrogance in the years following the Second World War.

Japan has, in the last quarter of this century, become the second most important power in the world, but it does not behave as though it is. It does not take the lead in international politics that its economic might justifies, or show the restraint (in commercial matters) needed to prevent such power being resented by allies and competitors.

If there is one quality which Japan seems to lack (as argued in Chapter 4), it is judgement. When the decision is how to produce the best luxury car or a new camcorder, Japanese leaders can lean on their skills of imitation and refinement, and the dedication and talent of the country's workforce, to produce something which is better than can be made anywhere else in the world. But that does not require a sense of history, still less someone who can ask: 'Is this really sensible?'. A few people in Japan are able to lean against the countervailing orthodoxy, and think in a contra-cyclical way, but not many have the vision to run a vast commercial empire, or even to appreciate that Japan has already become, in terms of its external assets, the largest empire on earth. This is power which, if applied properly, could bring enormous benefits to the world. From a British perspective, it has enabled a rebuilding of the motor industry: Japanese commercial power has turned a country from manufacturing disaster to modest triumph. Large parts of East Asia are in desperate need of such skills.

Japan could make a similar contribution to its neighbours and to Siberian Russia. It could teach China energy conservation and waste management, for after making many mistakes Japan has better energy use and environmental controls than any other similar industrial country. It has so much to teach, not just in industry or technology, but in social behaviour. To have the lowest crime rate in the world is an extraordinary achievement, particularly since there is no evidence in the country's past history that the Japanese are particularly law-abiding by nature.[2]

Looking ahead, Japanese society will be pulled in two directions. There will be a temptation to retreat into a comfortable but protected lifestyle. Japan would continue to exclude foreigners and gradually export the less pleasant jobs abroad. The country would depend increasingly on its investment income, secure in its self-image of being different from the rest of the world – rather like Edwardian Britain. But there will also be a desire, founded on a slightly different perception of national interest, to go out and teach the world – to enjoy the leadership role. Japan would use its financial power to help other countries learn some of the lessons it has taught itself during the last forty-five years. It is greatly in Japan's self-interest that it should choose the latter course. The more it tries to teach, the more it will itself learn about other societies. And it needs to learn if only to protect its commercial empire from the envy and greed of others. Which way will it jump?

The reality, most probably, is that it will move in both directions at the same time. It will to some extent take on a larger leadership role in the world, and particularly in Asia. As a new generation of young Japanese takes control of the economy, and more and more of this young elite travels abroad, simple logic dictates that Japan will want to have a greater say in the way the world is organized. But the people who have worked hard to rebuild the country will also increasingly want to enjoy the wealth they have created. Much of the rest of the world may become more dangerous, and the calm and order of Japan will seem very attractive. There have been many periods of the country's past history when it has retreated into a life of ordered luxury. At some stage in the future it will surely do so again.

Perhaps the most likely pattern will be that for the next fifteen years or so, say to 2010, Japan will continue to push outwards, extending its commercial empire, and increasingly playing a more active part in world politics. Then at some stage towards the end of the first quarter of the century, maybe about 2020, the other side of the Japanese nature will come to the fore. It will not turn its back on the world, but it will become less interested in it. It will become even more confident that its own way of organizing society is the best, with some reason. Maybe the change will take place suddenly, provoked by some external event, perhaps in China, perhaps in the US; or maybe there will be a gradual, inexorable shift in the country's focus as it becomes an old and deeply conservative society. Maybe it will lose its interest in the rest of the world, and its capacity to learn from it. Maybe it will simply reject western materialism, realizing that people are not any happier because they have four televisions instead of only three.

Two things are quite certain. The first is that Japan's astonishing economic performance still has some momentum in it: growth will slacken, but it will not disappear. The second is that this burst of energy will not continue for ever. Sometime quite soon the tempo will change, and the country will end its great post-war run, and head off in a different direction.

China: the giant wakes

It is difficult to see any set of circumstances where – measured in a sensible way – China will not be well on its way to becoming the world's largest economy by 2020. But it will be a very different China, for it is equally difficult to see the country remaining a centralized political entity. With growth will come increasing divergences of economic development, and these divergences will weaken the glue which holds this giant country together. Parts of China, a generation from now, will be richer than Europe or North America today. (Some parts, Hong Kong perhaps, will be richer than Europe and North America will be then.) But there will be a vast rural hinterland where economic development has not reached take-off, where, in economic terms, nothing significant has happened. It is very difficult to see how such a diverse entity can operate as a single political unit. The further Chinese people get from Beijing, both ideologically and physically, the richer they become.

So China needs to split. Or rather, if it is to fulfil its economic potential, it has to give so much autonomy to its regions that, to all intents and purposes, it will cease to operate as a unitary state. Greater China, encompassing not just Hong Kong and Taiwan, but also the external Chinese community elsewhere in the world, will have an enormous financial and cultural impact on the world during the next century, but what is now the People's Republic will, in all probability, turn into a loose federation. This will of course include Hong Kong, but may very well also include Taiwan. Indeed the only way of including Taiwan, making a success of Hong Kong, and reaping benefits from the external Chinese community is to develop China into an association of semi-independent states. The glue holding this association together will be economics. Just as Europe has used what was originally a free trade area to pull together very different nation states, so China will use a free trade area to hold together a set of states which would otherwise fly apart. China will be the EU in reverse.

Of course anyone has to admit that this sort of association may be impossible to operate. China in any case has rapidly to manage complex political change: generation change, as the old leaders die; ideological change, as the remnants of Communism are dumped; and regional change, as the financial power of the new industrialized zones (and the regions around them) leads to demands for increased political autonomy. Rapid economic growth of some regions is already leading to large population movements, as the poor flow to the rich areas in search of jobs. It is always difficult to envisage the full consequences of very large population movements, but it is fairly clear that this movement will increase the power and autonomy of the new economic zones. Accommodating these zones will be very difficult.

China also has to accommodate Hong Kong. One should not under-estimate its ability to make a mess of this transition. There are enough instances in China's history of political ideology wrecking hitherto sound economies to be wary. There is also sufficient history of a war-lord culture to produce both a concern in Beijing that the country might fragment, and a potential for civil war.

China's handling of Hong Kong after 1997 will be a litmus test for its ability to live with its new booming regions. Self-interest – the need to raise hard currency to pay for essential imports – should dictate that Hong Kong's economy is protected, even enhanced. But countries do not always act in their own self-interest, and assimilating Hong Kong's particularly robust form of capitalism into what is still nom-inally a Communist state will not be easy. Hong Kong's natural role is to be the financial capital of the southern Chinese industrial region, just as Shanghai should be the financial capital of its own economic hinterland. (Ultimately Shanghai should outpace Hong Kong, which it regards as an upstart.[3]) But Hong Kong under Chinese rule may turn out to be an economic disaster. Great cities can go into serious decline if they lose their prime economic function. Hong Kong's anomalous position as culturally and economically part of China, but legally and administratively a British colony, may turn out to be a uniquely favourable historical accident, never to be repeated.

It is very easy to extrapolate from China's economic growth in the 1980s and argue that China will pass the US in size somewhere during the first decade of the next century,[4] but it is much more likely that growth will slow, that China will make mistakes in economic policy, and that the country will run into difficulty in boosting its exports, the motor of growth for the rest of the region. It is inconceivable that North America and Europe will give the same freedom of access to their markets to China as they have, for example, to Japan. Further, the goods that China produces will depend crucially on its cheap labour; and these are the type of product the price of which tends to go down. Developing high value-added exports will be a long and difficult path, and North America, Europe and Japan will not be idle. China will have to rely on internal rather than export-led growth to a much greater extent than Japan, or the 'tigers'.

As a result, it will be well into the second decade before China does indeed pass the US in economic might. Though the process will be slower than many enthusiasts for China claim, it will eventually happen. The only thing which can stop it is China disintegrating in an unpleasant and dangerous way. That is not impossible – indeed it may very well happen; but it is not inevitable either. The most dangerous period for China will be in about fifteen years' time, when the prosperity of its new industrial regions is assured and their citizens start to demand the freedoms of the overseas Chinese community. Providing the country can loosen its hold on its most vibrant regions in time, turning itself peacefully into a federation, then it will become the economic leader of Asia, a region which will by then have become at least an equal partner to Europe and North America. But it will be a race against time, for the expectations of the new rich will be high. Handled badly, the country could face chaos, famine and war.

Whatever happens to its economic progress, China will not achieve political superpower status by 2020. Like Europe, it will be too divided. The Chinese are an old and proud people, and there will be too many internal tensions and rivalries for them to impose their will on the region, still less on the world. Maybe that is a good thing. The rest of the world will be frightened of China during the next century. The less united it is, the happier the world will feel.

The 'tigers' old and new

How long before the tigers lose their claws? The four newly industrialized countries of East Asia which are usually grouped together – South Korea, Taiwan, Hong Kong and Singapore – have little in common beyond their experience of rapid economic growth. Here they have helped each other, and will do so increasingly in the future, for they can expect to do a rising proportion of business with each other, rather than relying on markets in North America and Europe. But while economic success in one country will continue to encourage better performance in another, and the region as a whole will continue to prosper, economic growth will tend to slow, and politics will become the main factor determining the relative performance of the various countries.

Korea will be just Korea, for it is very hard to see anything other than unification of north and south by 2020. By then the two countries will not only be one, but will have made considerable progress in joining their economies together. The obvious parallel, noted in Chapter 4, is Germany, but it is an imperfect parallel, for there are several reasons to expect that the path to unity will be easier, and several that it will be harder.

Reasons why it might be easier include:

- Korea has seen what went wrong in Germany and will learn from its experience
- North Korea has not created the dependency culture of East Germany
- The relative economic success of South Korea is even more striking than that of West Germany

Reasons why it might be harder include:

- The timing of the merger will not be set by a grand external event, such as the crumbling of the Soviet empire, but will be provoked by unrest within North Korea
- North Korea has considerable military forces, including, probably, some form of nuclear weapons
- The North Korean people have been less exposed to ideas from the west than East Germans, who were able to watch western TV
- South Korea does not have the resources to bring northern living standards up to southern levels in the space of five years as is being attempted in Germany (its population is only twice as large as the north, whereas in Germany the ratio is more than three to one.)

The process of unification will therefore have to be very different. It will have to be a willing act of co-operation between the two sides, rather than a takeover of one by the other, and that act of union will have to be triggered by some political upheaval in the north, which itself could be gravely damaging to the stability of both countries. The south, by virtue of its economic success and larger population, will be the dominant partner, but it will have to teach the market system, rather than impose it. There will not be large transfers of wealth from south to north. Integration will be both a slower process and a less complete one: it will take at least a generation from the moment of practical union for the two countries to operate as one economic entity, and the political attitudes of the north will have a considerable influence on the south in a way which has not really happened in Germany. One of the lessons the south has learnt from Germany is that unity would in the short-term work to its disadvantage, and that therefore full union should not be offered until the north has made some progress towards establishing a market economy.

It should also be acknowledged that unity could lead to economic disaster. In the case of Germany it is clear that the country, despite its social and economic difficulties, will remain a prosperous western European state, for the depth of resources to make Germany an efficient economy do exist in the west. In Korea's case, the economic base is much more fragile: heavy debts, a narrow export base, no areas of outstanding excellence. All it has, and has in abundance, is hard working, well-educated and relatively cheap labour. Unlike the German economy, the Korean has little fat to trim. In that sense, Germany can afford to make mistakes in unification, while Korea cannot. The timing for the start of the unity process cannot be more than a best guess: perhaps some time between 2000 and 2010. The north's movement towards market economics could start very soon, particularly if it becomes clear that Vietnam is making a successful transition from a planned economy to a market one.

So the most likely picture of Korea in 2020 will be for a unified country, with the south helping the north go through a period of rapid economic change, possibly including the reconstruction which will be necessary following a civil war. The south will remain a separate economy which will retain many of its present strengths and weaknesses: it will remain strong in middle technology goods and will be a useful sub-contractor for Japan, but will be unable to make much headway in upmarket products or in services. It will not be regarded as a particular threat to North America or Europe, despite acquiring the north's technology for making nuclear weapons: it will be too preoccupied

with internal concerns. But it is much easier to see the answer to the
'what will happen?' question than the 'when?'.

Taiwan will also eventually find itself in association with mainland
China, but, as argued earlier, by the time real links are established it
will be a very different China. Taiwan's economy is inherently more
robust than Korea's – more broadly based, with less emphasis on central planning and less reliance on external sources of finance. But by
2020, whatever association it reaches with China, growth will have
slowed right down. The next stage of economic development in Taiwan requires not only large-scale investment in infrastructure, but a
shift into higher value-added products. This will not be easy.

Politics are enormously important. If the US and the EU adopt a
more protectionist approach to East Asia in general, Taiwan will be
forced to look to mainland China for markets. The easiest way for
the two countries to rebuild their relationship is through the gradual
development of economic ties. By 2020 it is quite likely that Taiwan
will be part of a Chinese economic zone, trading freely with what may
by then be a series of administratively distinct republics, while retaining
its own governmental autonomy.

If politics dominates prospects for Taiwan, in the case of Hong
Kong they are everything. Consider the two extremes. Hong Kong
could be the glittering financial capital of China, the New York of the
twenty-first century;[5] or it could be a sleepy little city of faded gran-
deur, with its once-shiny bank towers and office blocks converted into
shabby flats. That is China's choice.

Singapore is fascinating, because it is the most perfect example anywhere in the world of a disciplined, ordered city state which has made
a virtue out of having no resources. By education, application and
discipline (and some arrogance) it has become an example to the world.
But in itself it does not matter to the world economy, for it is tiny. It
is Monaco writ large, not China writ small. If it were suddenly swal-
lowed up by the sea it would be a tragedy, but there would be no
lasting impact on the region's prosperity. It is, however, important as
an example. What makes the next generation so interesting is that if
any country in East Asia can match Japan and succeed in pulling not
just alongside but actually ahead of Europe and North America, it is
Singapore.

Singapore's achievements are so remarkable that it is hard not to
continue to be optimistic. As an entrepôt centre it could be damaged
by instability in the region, for anything which damages trade will

damage Singapore. By the same token the region's general improved economic performance will benefit entrepôt centres. Thus its skills in communications and financial services will benefit from the growth in local securities markets. Its airport and indeed its port facilities will continue to benefit from the growth in regional trade. The fact that it is a new self-reliant country means it is not hampered by notions of nationality, so that it can cut through old jealousies. Above all, it provides an extremely accessible entry-point for North American and European businesses seeking an East Asian presence.

The most likely portrait of Singapore for 2020 would show it still to be a prosperous little island, but one that people are a little less impressed by. Its population will be smaller and older, a function of its low fertility rate, compounded by emigration. Other centres will have sprung up to rival it. As the whole region develops it will need pockets of calm competence like Singapore, but other places will be able to provide this, too. More than anywhere else in East Asia, Singapore will show that it is easy to imitate the west in technology, hard to pass it in overall economic competence. Meanwhile, other much larger places will have taken on the torch of growth.

These will be the new tigers. They will certainly include Indonesia, whose sheer size and natural resources will have turned it into the largest economy in the region after China and Japan. They will also include Malaysia, helped partly by its proximity to Singapore. But the most important focal point for growth will be the crescent of countries to the north – Vietnam, Cambodia, Laos, Thailand and Burma (as it may well again be called). Given honest and competent government committed to the market system, this whole region can achieve economic take-off and reach, by 2020, income levels akin to Taiwan today. Government does not need to be democratic; it simply needs to be competent. Not all countries will be able to provide this and progress will be uneven. Thailand shows some sort of model; Vietnam will soon show another. The example of China will have an important impact on the region: if it disintegrates into war-lordism, this will have a powerful disincentive effect on other regimes; if it succeeds in retaining some form of central control and some national order, then it becomes a model. The region will, however, have to reach its own destiny; no country in the west will be motivated to help. The whole region will increasingly be on its own.

Australia and New Zealand: going Asian

As Asia moves apart from North America and Europe, the two 'Anglo' countries to the south will have little choice but to look north. They are in the early stages of a redirection which takes them away not just from their British heritage – they started on that path when Britain joined the Common Market in 1973, with the official repudiation of the 'White Australia' policy – but from being part of the western economic system. It will be evident by 2020 that Australia is gradually becoming an ethnic Asian society, for already most immigration comes from Asia: in 1990–91, over 50 per cent of immigrants to the country as a whole were from Asian countries. Australia is deliberately targeting the most skilled potential immigrants,[6] and so is using immigration to improve its stock of human capital. This works: witness the thirty-five immigrants amongst the richest 200 individuals in the country referred to in Chapter 7. For Australia and New Zealand, the combination of their location and their ability to absorb immigrants is enormously advantageous, for it helps bolt their economies on to what will eventually become the world's largest economic region. Gus Hooke, an Australian economist, predicts that by 2050 Asia (excluding Japan) will account for 57 per cent of the world economy.[7] Even if that is over-optimistic, Australia and New Zealand will benefit, for one simple reason: almost alone in the entire region, these countries have a long history of being able to deliver political stability.

So it is easy to see an Australia in 2020 well on the way to becoming an ethnic Asian society, starting to pull back ahead of Europe and North America in its living standards. The language and culture of Australia will still retain their Anglo-Saxon roots, but psychologically the country will have moved still further away from Britain. The vast bulk of its international trade will be with East Asian countries. It will, naturally, have become a republic.

For New Zealand the picture is slightly different, for, being more isolated, it will find it harder to earn its way in the world. From the perspective of the 1990s it is fascinating, not as a resource-rich country, but as an innovative one in social and economic policy: in particular rolling back welfare commitments and establishing an independent central bank charged with attaining price stability. If success in competition between countries means to a large extent getting government right (as this book argues), then the New Zealand experiments of the

1980s matter enormously. If they are perceived as successes they will be imitated widely elsewhere; if they fail, western governments will have to seek other ways of adapting their policies.

In short, Australia and New Zealand are likely to be winners from the East Asia boom. If the region continues to be enormously successful they will benefit because they are part of the region. If the region falters it will be because of political uncertainties, not economic potential, and in this case they will shine as islands of calm. In the short term it might be difficult to cope with large numbers of immigrants, and upheaval in their newly-established markets would damage growth, but in the long term both Australia and, in a slightly different way, New Zealand, have a golden future ahead of them.

The relationship with the west

This, perhaps, is the entire region's great challenge. It has done brilliantly – unevenly, to be sure, but brilliantly nonetheless – but this progress has only been possible because the west has been prepared to take its goods, and in many cases provide it with external security. Western countries have taken its goods because of a combination of historical ties (Singapore, Hong Kong) and military self-interest (Japan, Korea). The west is not going to continue that game. It will increasingly introduce protectionist measures and demand greater access to Asian markets. It will be motivated solely, and quite possibly brutally, by self-interest. It perceives that it owes no moral debts. The comparative advantage of the region as a producer of low-cost manufactured consumer items, mostly electronic, will remain, but it will shift within the region to the low-wage economies, in particular China. The leaders will find that they have to compete head on with the west in very high technology and in service industries. Japan will manage to retain sufficient corners of exporting to continue to prosper, though its international trade may continue to shrink as a proportion of the whole economy. Other countries will find it tougher. The more successful they are, the more concerned the west will become and the harder they will find it to export. The region will have to look inward for growth, not outward.

To say that is not to advocate a policy of protectionism by North America and Europe. Nor is it to assert that creeping protectionism will destroy the open economic relationships that East Asia has, by

and large, enjoyed with the industrial world. It is simply to acknowledge that the faster East Asia grows, the less the west will welcome
that growth. While the region will not become a political competitor
to the United States for the foreseeable future, its two giants, China
and Japan, will feel by 2020 that they can look the US in the eye, and
they will want their role respected. They will also be shaping the world
order. Asian leaders will expect to have a voice on global issues like
the environment and human rights. Asian ideas, which at the moment
hardly feature, may start to influence the west. Asian money certainly
will, unless ... unless, somewhere out there in the future, there is
some catastrophe at which we can only guess.

THIRTEEN

THE PRIZE

The economic case for good behaviour

I HAVE SOUGHT TO portray the way the world might develop over the next generation. Details of the picture will inevitably be wrong. It would be absurd to suggest otherwise, for not only will some things happen which are by their very nature unpredictable – natural disasters, for example – but the timing and scale of change is extremely uncertain. One might, for example, have foreseen that the Soviet Union's empire in eastern Europe would collapse, like others before it, but it would have been much harder to guess when, or to foresee that the loss of this empire would lead so swiftly to the break-up of the Soviet Union itself.

Yet it has been possible to paint this picture because there are some things we do know about the future, and others for which history may offer a guide. We know, with a fair degree of confidence, roughly how many people there will be in the world in 2020, where they will be living and how old they will be. The only thing which would destroy that confidence would be some catastrophe, such as the uncontrolled spread of the AIDS epidemic or a nuclear war. We also know that the rise in population will put serious pressure on world resources, but we can be reasonably confident that these pressures, for one more generation at least, will be manageable, partly because of advances in technology. We can see now, in outline at least, these advances. Such are the lags between the invention of a technology and its adoption into popular use, that we can be reasonably sure that the everyday technologies of 2020 already exist in some form or other. And it is not too difficult to see the way in which demography, resources and technology will interact to put pressures on governments, companies – indeed society as a whole.

We know something, too, about the changing nature of economic advantage. The central argument here is that economic success is essential to continued political influence, a truth that has become more evident after the collapse of the Soviet Union than it was before. Many people still see economic strength as lying in the old manufacturing industries rather than the new service ones. They see the shrinking portion of manufacturing in the GNP of countries like the United States and Britain as a sign of weakness rather than of strength. But providing countries are able to make new exportable products to pay for their necessary imports, it matters little whether these are goods or services, though it is, in fact, probably easier to maintain a comparative advantage in producing services than in producing manufactured goods. Of course one should not push the argument to caricature – even the most successful producers of service exports need some manufacturing, just as successful manufacturing nations retain some agriculture; and it is possible that countries can change their economic structure too quickly, for example by allowing their traditional activities to be run down before they have had time to build up new ones. In general, however, the more nimble countries are at shifting between different economic activities, and thereby making the most of their own particular economic advantages, the more likely they are to prosper.

But this is not enough. One of the central themes of this book is that while being efficient at different types of economic activity is a necessary condition for wider prosperity and influence, it is insufficient. Enduring prosperity requires societies which are stable, ordered and honest. Countries can manage a burst of growth based on the exploitation of cheap labour and natural resources, and stomach a fair degree of corruption while they do so. But as the experience of a country like Argentina shows, it is hard to maintain prosperity amidst chaos. However, these values of stability, order and honesty are not absolutes. Even the most stable of countries will periodically experience a political earthquake. Canada, for example, may well break into two. Even the most ordered will suffer major loss of life from traffic accidents: proportionate to its population, Germany kills almost twice as many people on its roads as Britain. Even the most honest will experience examples of theft or corruption: Japan has its problems with gangster wars and political scandals.

Stability and order (though maybe not dishonesty) may sometimes conflict with another increasingly important quality in economic competition: creativity. If people are going to be creative – invent new medicines, make exciting new movies – they will probably need to work against a background of some disorder, for creating something new involves doing something differently from the way it has been done before. But while order without creativity will result in a boring but reasonably prosperous country, creativity without order is likely to result in misery for all. The most interesting and successful societies will combine both.

How they achieve such a happy blend is far from clear. 'Top-down' imposition of order by the state, even in a democracy, carries costs and may be ineffective. In anything other than the short term, command societies are no more likely to prosper than command economies, and if the 1980s made one thing absolutely clear, it was that the command economy was a catastrophic system of industrial and commercial organization. Yet 'bottom-up' generation of order is hard to achieve in a liberal society. There is a powerful economic case (quite aside from the many social arguments) for wanting to try to persuade citizens to behave in an orderly way – not to rob people in the street, have children they cannot look after, waste the time of the courts by suing on absurd pretexts, drive dangerously, take drugs, fiddle their taxes or claim social security benefits to which they are not entitled – because as it becomes tougher to increase the productivity of a country simply by improving its manufacturing industries, the standard of living of the next generation in the developed world will depend very much on whether the present generation behaves with civic responsibility. For this to happen, ordinary people have to want to sustain the balance between order and individualism which leads to societies which are both efficient and humane. Put bluntly, if countries wish to carry on becoming richer, their people will have to learn to behave better.

That is not to say that people will have to conform to some new version of a Victorian morality code, but it does mean accepting limits to individual freedoms, or rather a redefinition of what those freedoms are and should be. To take a simple example, if citizens are required always to carry identification which can be electronically checked in order to reduce crime, then the freedom of some individuals has been limited. But if the result is that more people can walk the streets safely at night then the freedom of others has been enhanced.

That is the sort of choice that people must make. They will express their choice partly through the ballot box, but if electorates are divided, which they inevitably will be, there may not be a lot that politicians can do. Politicians have a duty to explain the choice: that it will be hard to increase living standards over the next generation unless people are prepared to accept in the first instance a greater degree of self-discipline, and on occasion a greater degree of external discipline too.

Raising living standards will be most difficult for the advanced industrial countries. The newly-industrialized nations, the next generation of advanced countries, can expect to increase living standards by doing the things which those higher up the ladder of development have done before them: essentially relying on the big productivity gains which can be made as a country industrializes. Nothing succeeds like success. The fact that living standards are increasing rapidly enables countries to make mistakes in economic management and yet continue to grow, as has been happening in China in the first part of the 1990s. Rapid growth allows governments to limit human freedoms in ways that would be unacceptable in richer countries. It is not just that the about-to-become-rich are prepared to accept poor working conditions and meagre political rights which would seem very unattractive to the already-rich, though this is certainly the case. It is more that the spur of growth itself reinforces a sense of self-discipline, which in turn encourages further growth. But for the advanced industrial world it is much harder to establish such a virtuous circle. Growth in productivity will continue, but it will be slow, and the rewards from it unevenly spread. More and more of the productivity gains which can still be made are liable to be absorbed elsewhere in the economy and fail to show through in ordinary people's lifestyles.

Western-style democracies are bad at coping with a period when living standards do not rise. They utterly failed to cope with such a period during the 1930s, and while it is implicit in this book that a return to the conditions of the 1930s would be most unlikely, it is quite possible that living standards in western Europe, North America and Japan will be only a little higher in 2020 than they were in 1990. Demography alone will tend to curb the rise in living standards. So too will pressure on resources. If in addition we are unable to increase service industry productivity as fast as we have manufacturing, then boosting living standards will be tough indeed. It is not at all clear that democracies will cope well with this down-scaling of expectations.

This leads to a further danger: that the retreat from the liberal individualism which has dominated most of the post-Second-World-War period will become a rout. Some retreat is already taking place. In Britain the right to strike has been curbed considerably since the 1979 election of a Conservative government. (That provides a good example of conflicting freedoms: if the freedom to withdraw labour has been restricted, the freedom of ordinary people to go about their business without being inconvenienced by industrial unrest has been enhanced. On balance there is a plus for society.) Pressure on public spending is starting to cut welfare benefits right across Europe. As such pressure increases, as it will, shortage of public sector funds may impose other restrictions on people's behaviour, for example the freedom to reject jobs on offer and still claim unemployment benefit. Already in the early 1990s there were moves in several European countries to cut the level of unemployment benefits.

What has not, as yet, happened on any widespread scale in the advanced industrial world is the introduction of restrictive social laws. Practice varies greatly from country to country and, in the US, from state to state, but in general there has been little rolling back of the tide of liberal legislation of the 1945–90 period, such as the laws which made divorce progressively easier, which gave similar rights to the children of parents who were not married as to those who were, and which made homosexual acts legal. There has been rising concern over abortion in the US, but there has been nothing in western Europe, North America or Japan akin to the fundamentalist revolution sweeping across the Muslim world.

However, there may indeed be a fundamentalist revolution in the west. This may not take the form of Christian fundamentalism – it is more likely in fact to be driven by secular populism – but it could have the same effect: aggressive assertion by the majority of its values which are then imposed on the various minorities. Such a process could be benign: a grass-roots movement where ordinary people revived their faith in the Protestant ethic of honesty, hard work and family values.[1] But it could be destructive: one or more populist leaders encouraging the persecution of 'deviants', meaning anyone who did not conform to the majority's idea of proper behaviour.

The most helpful guide to the way societies behave under pressure is their past. Those who have watched the break-up of the Soviet Union's empire (or for that matter the troubles in Northern Ireland) cannot but be aware of the long shadow of history. So where judgements have to be made about the choices that countries will make in meeting social pressures, the best guide is history. This has led to several conclusions expressed in earlier chapters.

For example, one very important conclusion concerns the United States. It is that the forces of rugged individualism, humanity and decency of the United States will reassert themselves and check the tendency for policies to be driven by different interest groups at war with each other. If the US does reimpose majority values, it will do so in a spirit of decency and humanity. The United States has to come to terms with an inability to increase living standards for the majority of its people until and unless its citizens behave in a more ordered way. But it will do so.

As far as Europe is concerned, a thousand years of history suggest that it will never become a single national entity. And so European integration will reach a point from which it cannot advance further, for the pull of nationalism is too strong. Within Europe, countries with a relatively stable past (like England) will retain such stability, while those with a more turbulent history (like Italy) will continue to have periods of turmoil. Regionalism will grow as smaller states and regions seek to assert their identities. If, from an economic point of view, Europe has to encourage integration – attacking its high costs, its commercial rigidities and getting better value from its social spending – then from a political point of view it has to appreciate the natural limits to integration.

Another conclusion based on history concerns China. The whole East Asian region has to build greater political stability and learn to lead, not just to imitate. The relative fortunes of each part of it will depend on the vigour with which they attack these tasks, though the sheer size of China's population will gradually move the global balance of influence to the east. Yet while China will undoubtedly play a much greater role in the world in 2020 than it did in 1990, the coming generation of economic development will not proceed in a straight line. China has shown great capacity in the past to make mistakes, and it is likely to continue to do so.

There is a common thread which binds the future of all three regions, and binds it more obviously than would have seemed possible at the beginning of the 1980s. It is that all the countries which aspire to be economic successes have embraced the same financial and economic system: market capitalism. Countries as different as the US and China, Switzerland and Singapore, Norway and Vietnam are playing the same game by the same rules. The western system of economic organization has won. But as the whole world converts to the market economy, the west will find itself faced by much greater economic competition than it has before. The established market economies will continue to dominate the world economy for a few more years, but they will find their lead diminishing if they fail to learn not just to be still more effic... producers, but to run honourable and ordered societies.

What might go wrong

The future as described so far is, in the main, a reasonably comfortable one. The different regions, the different countries, have some tough choices to make. The dramatic changes of the late 1980s and early 1990s have created a more complex world. The end of the Cold War has destroyed the uneasy balance between First and Second World, while great social and economic changes have blown away the concept of the Third World as a clear geographic identity. The Third World has moved to parts of Los Angeles and the First World to Singapore. But these changes are probably manageable. This book has assumed that there will be no collective 'nervous breakdown'[2] such as struck the German people in the 1930s, no domination of a giant nation by a wicked emperor such as Joseph Stalin. This section briefly considers some things that might undermine such assumptions.

One obvious danger is that of a great natural or environmental disaster. At some stage in the next twenty-five years it is highly likely that such a disaster will occur. For example, one has only to look back over the last hundred years to see the probability of a destructive volcanic eruption or a great earthquake. What happens matters less than where it happens. Two places are particularly vulnerable: Tokyo and Los Angeles. Rationally it was ludicrous to build the world's largest urban agglomeration and America's second largest on seismic fault lines. An earthquake in either city might have more than local effects for at least four reasons: the financial interdependence of countries; the impact of a breakdown of sophisticated technology on the environment; increased environmental stress on the world; and the growing fissures within societies.

While we have plenty of experience of natural disasters, we have no idea whether the many skyscrapers built in the last twenty years will withstand the shock of an earthquake, still less whether their computer and communications systems are robust enough to cope without destroying records which will be very difficult to reconstruct. A severe earthquake in Tokyo or Los Angeles could put great pressure on the world's insurance industry. Quite apart from financial considerations new technologies may be unexpectedly vulnerable: we have no experience of the effect of a giant earthquake on nuclear power stations. What can safely be said is that the next great earthquake in Japan or California will have a greater economic impact world-wide than shocks of the past.

It is impossible to assess the effects of two or three things going wrong at the same time; better simply to acknowledge that the total will equal more than the sum of the parts. For example, some volcanic explosion which reduced the amount of light reaching the earth for a couple of growing seasons, combined with a quite separate crop failure against a background of continued rapid population growth could be disastrous.

More likely is a combination of the third and fourth dangers: natural disaster combining with social tension. While a cohesive society can be pulled together by adversity, a divisive one may be pulled apart. The riots in Los Angeles in 1992 gave the US a glimpse of the thin line between civil order and chaos: were a natural disaster to strike an already tense US city, and were that disaster to be seriously mishandled by the authorities, then a social explosion could result. The face of a city like Los Angeles could be changed for ever.

Underlying this is the reality of nuclear proliferation. The world has become a more dangerous place, both because of the inevitability of accidents, and because of the possibility of nuclear warfare. To date the most disastrous event has been the accident at Chernobyl, an incident which – aside from its effect on the health of some ten million people – has damaged political relations between Russia and the Ukraine, with consequences yet to be seen. With more than four hundred nuclear power stations and many other nuclear installations around the world,[3] it is inevitable that at some stage over the next generation there will be further accidents, some of which may be more serious than Chernobyl. The obvious area for concern is the safety of other reactors in the former Soviet Union of similar design (several of the former Soviet Union's nuclear plants are built on seismic fault lines) but given that some lessons must have been learnt, the more serious worries should perhaps be over the combination of a nuclear accident with something else: a natural disaster, say, or a terrorist attack. What everyone should realize is that other nuclear disasters will happen; the issues are not whether, but how serious and when.

And nuclear conflict? Our assumption here is that there will be no general nuclear conflict in the foreseeable future. That surely is the

only possible working assumption one can make. However, the possibility of some modest nuclear bomb (modest, at least, by the standards
of the trade) being detonated is surely quite high. Guessing where or
how is pointless. Several unstable countries have or are close to having
nuclear capacity, including Iraq and North Korea, but all past history
suggests that the catastrophe will not occur where it is most expected.
It would be comforting to believe that, faced with such a threat, the
industrial world would uncover it and combine to avert catastrophe:
the nuclear site would, in the jargon of the US military, be 'visited'
and the weapons destroyed before they could be unleashed. But perhaps this is unrealistic in an age where the technology is fifty years
old and is relatively easy to acquire. The break-up of the Soviet Union
and the probable lack of control over the dismantling of its nuclear
armoury has made nuclear proliferation more difficult to contain.

A quite different kind of threat comes from ethnic disharmony. The
rise of hostility towards ethnic and religious minorities is one of the
most disturbing features of the late twentieth century. There are many
flash points. The break-up of the Soviet empire, and the conflict in
the former Yugoslavia will be very difficult, maybe impossible, to manage in a peaceful way. The national borders of central and eastern
Europe cut across ethnic groups. The memories of past conflicts are
too strong, and current antagonisms too great, for there to be any easy
transition to the sort of relative calm that exists between the nations
of western Europe.

Tension in central and eastern Europe will lead to large flows of
cross-border migration which will add to the strains that the recession
in western Europe has put on tolerance towards the immigrant population. The pressure for further immigration, particularly from North
Africa, will increase. Europe has the world's oldest and almost the
world's richest population; Africa has the world's youngest and poorest.
All Europe will inevitably tighten immigration controls, and it may be
possible, by doing so, to reassure its citizens. Some countries within
Europe – Britain for example – have a reasonably secure tradition of
welcoming immigrants and integrating them into the community, but
Britain has virtually stopped immigration, and the Britain of 2020 will
in ethnic terms not be so different from the Britain of 1990 – certainly
not as different as 1990 was from 1960. Given a further generation of
integration, Britain may well become more harmonious, but it is difficult to see a similar harmony extending across continental Europe.
Germany, which has accepted far more foreigners than Britain, has

had great difficulty assimilating them. Yet that is the task it has to carry out. It is deeply distasteful, but not impossible, that people living in Europe who are not white will in some way be expelled: that the 'ethnic cleansing' of the former Yugoslavia will become a common phenomenon in other parts of Europe.

There are other flash points. It is hard to see change in southern Africa taking a peaceful course. The best hope will be for another two decades of difficult transition, with the continuing gradual return of people of European stock to Europe and a competent and courageous black government working hard to resolve the underlying tensions between different ethnic groups. The worst fear is the unbearable prospect of racial and tribal war there and elsewhere. Parts of Asia have scope for equally nasty inter-racial conflicts. In India the tensions are principally religious: it is perfectly possible that India may divide again, for it is not at all clear that the glue holding together the world's largest democracy is strong enough to last for another generation.

In the US, old tensions between white and black Americans will be joined by new tensions between immigrant groups such as the Koreans on the one hand and other disadvantaged but longer-established min-orities on the other, in particular the African-Americans. Managing a peaceful transition from a US which is dominated by white European culture to one which is truly multiracial, and very different from Europe, will be the greatest single challenge the US will face in the coming generation. Failure would destroy the American dream, but the transition will test the tolerance and adaptability of the nation more sternly than perhaps any other change in its remarkable history.

Yet another kind of threat comes from the killer virus. Quite a lot is now known about AIDS. By 2020 there may or may not be a 'cure' as such – probably not – but a combination of education and changes in personal behaviour – which are already evident, but will become much more established – will have contained its effects in the industrial world. The developed world is likely to take a more censorious attitude towards sexual promiscuity and drug abuse. In some parts of the poorer world, however, it is difficult to have much confidence that the disease is containable. Africa is desperately vulnerable; parts of Asia and South America at serious risk. At some stage AIDS will cease to make further inroads into the population, but in parts of Africa this point of stability may be a long way off. It is at least conceivable that AIDS will be, in Africa, akin to the Black Death in Europe, or – worse – the introduction of European diseases to the American continent in the early 1500s.

The most worrying thought of all, though, is not that AIDS in its present form will continue to spread, but that the virus which causes it will mutate into something which is more easily transmitted. Nature's creation of a 'new' disease, just at the moment when humankind thought it was well on the way to eliminating many of the 'old' diseases, carries an awesome message: if AIDS, caused by a virus which is difficult to transmit, can suddenly burst on the world, are there other viruses out there which could follow it with even more devastating consequences? Consider the position of medical knowledge in the 1960s. The first heart transplant had been conducted; antibiotics were wonderfully effective against most bacteria; incremental progress was being made against diseases like cancer. Further medical progress seemed inevitable: it was just a matter of time and resources. It never struck people, in their wildest nightmares, that a new disease like AIDS could sweep across the world. Now, while it is reasonable to suppose that considerable progress will have been made against AIDS in its present forms, there is no guarantee that the virus will not change its form again and again, maybe to return in even more devastating guise. The reappearance in the west of diseases like tuberculosis which were thought to have been permanently eradicated should give pause for thought. We should not be so arrogant as to assume that throwing resources at a problem will solve it.

What might go right

All these thoughts are dispiriting, for they suggest that the unexpected will inevitably make matters worse: that the potential surprises are all on the downside. That is misleading, for if many of the possibilities are negative, many of the probabilities are positive. As a result the next twenty-five years could turn out to be better for the whole world than most people would imagine.

For a start, it is probable that most countries will be far better governed than at any previous period of history. Indeed, if countries are weighted by population, this may already by true. While the quality of governance in most western democracies may not seem noticeably higher than it was in, say, the 1950s, this is not where the progress is being made. The real advances are in Russia, China, Latin America, parts of Africa. The good governments may be no better, but there are far fewer really dreadful ones. Put at its worst, the world's main governments are likely to make fewer really big mistakes over the next twenty-five years than they have in the past twenty-five. Put positively, better governments worldwide ought to produce better results for the world as a whole.

Not only are most countries becoming better governed, their people are becoming better educated too. This progress may be less apparent in Europe and North America, where there is some justified concern about falling standards. But any modest fall, if indeed it exists, is offset by the rise in educational standards in the rest of the world. This has taken place at every level. Proportionately, more people are literate than ever before, more are completing primary and secondary education than ever before, the universities have more undergraduates than ever before, and there are more people engaged in post-graduate work. There are more adults in some form of education than at any other time in human history. Most people don't appreciate what an astonishing achievement this is, or think through its likely effects. If each generation is better educated than its parents, surely the next generation is likely to make better judgements than the last.

Next, the triumph of the market system over central planning means that the world economy will be far better run than at any time before. This is not to pretend that uncontrolled capitalism (or even the controlled capitalism of western democracies) makes all the right decisions, but it makes far fewer really big mistakes over the allocation of scarce resources than any alternative system. World growth will no longer be dragged down by Communist misallocation of resources. Eventually, the performance of western democracies should also improve, as the role of the markets in making big investment decisions increases.

The world also has far better technology and communications than ever before. These interact. If something works in one place, be this a new strain of rice, a new drug, or even a new set of government policies, the news of this success is spread around the world in a few moments. Technology is advancing all the while: each year, even each day, advances are made somewhere in the world which will ultimately make the lives of many people materially better. Technology can be used not just to enable people in the developed world to drive about in larger cars; it can also be used to encourage them to drive in smaller ones or, by using telecommunications instead, not to travel at all. For both the developed and the less developed worlds it can be used to tackle problems of environmental degradation, and in particular it can be used to improve the lot of the poor without the drain on natural resources the process of industrialization has imposed in the past. With advanced communications, ideas, be they good, bad or indifferent, do get into the marketplace much more quickly than ever before. Communications not only makes possible the transfer of knowledge about new discoveries or new products. It also transfers knowledge about human behaviour. This is an important discipline on governments. If they are aware that they can't hide their actions from the world community, they must also be aware that there is a price to be paid for, for example, breaches of human rights. The events of Tiananmen Square may have cost Beijing the Olympics.

Finally, the world is healthier. Most people live longer, are better fed, and generally have better health than at any previous stage of human history.

Being better educated, better informed and healthier does not necessarily mean being wiser, but on objective measures of human resources, the stock of capital of our species is higher than ever before, and rising.

Anyone carrying out a similar exercise a century ago would have probably assumed that the great wave of Victorian prosperity would have continued well into the twentieth century. They would have been horribly wrong. The first half of this century was a catastrophe, with nations and people behaving with unspeakable stupidity and brutality. The second half, though, has been something of a triumph. Things really have turned out far better than anyone looking at the world in 1950 could have reasonably expected. I believe that this general progress will continue. We know which economic system works best. We know which forms of government are, over the medium-term, most likely to work best. The dominant nations of the world know that by co-operating they can improve opportunities for all. Yet those whom the marketing people call 'opinion formers' are not so arrogant as to assume that they always know best. The fact that there are such intractable problems – of crime, drugs, family break-up, poverty, and, in some parts of the world, hunger, danger and despair – should keep us humble. Provided we retain that humility, there is no reason why the world in 2020 should not be a still better place.

The world beyond 2020

It is possible to envisage a world which will not be dramatically different from today in just one more generation's time – the forces that
threaten global stability can probably be contained for at least one
more generation, but not for much longer. I am reasonably confident
about the prospect for the next thirty years, but much less so for the
period beyond that. If the world seems dangerous now, it will seem
much more so by 2020.

For the moment there remains just one superpower, the United
States, a benign democracy which whatever its flaws is deeply committed to democracy and individual liberty. Yet if the US does not deal
with the high cost of running its diverse and complex society, by 2020
its days as the only superpower will be drawing to a close. Its chief
rival for dominance will probably be China. Unless the Americans of
the next generation are better educated and show greater self-discipline
than their Chinese contemporaries, economic might, and hence world
leadership, will gradually but inevitably shift to China. But the China
to which it shifts will very different from the China of today. It will
probably have become an even more decentralized entity where the
core political institutions have relatively little control over the periphery. The result would inevitably be a less secure world.

Some reduction of US influence over the next generation may be
inevitable, but the American people can choose to what extent this
happens. Over the next thirty years they will have to make a series of
decisions. Some of these are financial: in particular they have to decide
to save more, for this will determine whether the country remains a
net debtor or again becomes a net creditor. Other decisions concern
education. Still others concern public order, attitudes to drugs, attitudes to the family. These choices will frequently involve some sacrifice
of short-term gratification for long-term prosperity.

Different choices face other developed countries. While the US has
remained the leader of the western alliance they have been able to
shelter under its protection. As US dominance declines, they must
decide whether and how they should take greater responsibility for
world stability. The diverse nations of western Europe have to decide
whether they can achieve a sufficient level of agreement to act together
as a force in world politics. This means putting aside ancient jealousies.
They also have to decide how to adapt their economies to a world

where, along with Japan, they will have the oldest population. Japan has both to learn how to manage its global commercial empire, and to decide whether it wishes to have a greater political voice in its region. That means coming to terms with its own military history and acknowledging the suspicion in which it is held in much of South-East Asia. If western Europe and Japan fail to acknowledge these greater responsibilities, then the world in the second quarter of the next century becomes a much more dangerous place.

The world can just about feed its growing population without putting an unbearable strain on its resources, but as population continues to grow it will become progressively harder to do so from about 2020 onwards. The message that smaller families are vital must be spread to all countries where there is rapid population growth if there is not to be an explosion of famine and misery. The fact that virtually all the increase is taking place in the presently poor countries will put enormous strains on the relationship between rich and poor. The rich need to help the poor tackle the problem of population growth, but that requires a level of trust and understanding between the two worlds that does not exist. Some of the influence of the industrial world on population growth, for example that of the Roman Catholic Church, is actually perverse. Adding another 90 million people to humankind every year that passes will increase the population pressures of the middle of the next century.

Even without rapid population growth the pressure on all natural resources will increase. The intensity of the pressure naturally varies: for example the supply of fresh water is harder to allocate than that of fossil fuels. Even where resources are plentiful it costs to use them up. The world's fossil fuels will last for several generations more, but the costs in terms of climate change will start to become apparent. Water needs to be treated as precious immediately, for shortages will become grave in some parts of the world within one generation. A culture of frugality – treating all natural resources as scarce – needs to be developed now if those resources are not to be even more scarce in the future. Decisions made by this generation will determine whether the world is safe and hospitable for the next.

What happens between now and 2020 will be of enormous importance for the future of humankind. This is the core issue for what is at present the developed world, and it will soon become the core issue for the new cast of countries which will join it. If we as individuals make sensible and humane decisions in the way we live our daily lives, then the societies in which we live will become more sensible and humane. More than this, the developed world will become a better model for those other countries which will achieve developed status. If on the other hand we are lazy, corrupt and greedy, then the rich world will not just lose influence; it will, in any meaningful sense of the word, become less rich. This is an issue for all people, not just for politicians. The more we can understand about the way the world is changing in the run-up to 2020, the greater the chance we have of securing its future in the years beyond.

A Note on Sources

The factual core of the analysis of how the world economy is changing is based on the general work of the Organisation for Economic Co-operation and Development in Paris (OECD), from which most figures are drawn. The work of the long-range forecasting group there, co-ordinated by Barrie Stevens, was particularly helpful, and the summary of some of its views, published in a booklet, *Long-Term Prospects for the World Economy*, in 1992, is an excellent starting point for anyone seeking to understand the process of global economic change. The long-range forecasting group maintains a database which tracks the work carried on elsewhere on future world economic development and kindly searched it for me. It was interesting to see what other people were looking at – the range was quite extraordinary, the quality (as far as one can judge) very uneven. A second group of people at the OECD have also been enormously helpful: those working on social policy. I have been influenced by the ideas of two people in particular: Donald Hirsch for his judgements on the way attitudes on the role of the state in social policy have been changing, and Chris Brooks for his insight into the relationship between economic change and the development of cities. I am also grateful to Henry Ergas for his thoughts on the link between technology and economic growth.

Other general sources of ideas on the nature of long-range fore-casting come from Shell, which developed scenario-building as a way of trying to understand the future. This work is described by Peter Schwartz in his book *The Art of the Long View*. I am grateful to DeAnne Julius, then chief economist for Shell International, now for British Airways, for guidance on Shell's approach.

Ideas on the development of the main regions of the world have come over twenty-five years of conversations, readings and visits that it would be impossible to list in detail. But I am aware of several debts to people whose views I have found particularly convincing, and whose judgements I have much respect for. In North America these include two economists working in financial service organizations, Rimmer de

Vries at J.P. Morgan in New York and David Hale of Kemper Financial
Services in Chicago. They also include Felix Rohatyn, of Lazard
Frères, for his robust defence of the best of American liberalism, and
Michael Kinsey, former editor of *The New Republic*, for his perceptions
of the process of social change in America. I also (though I have
never met him) have been influenced by the debunking spirit of P.J.
O'Rourke.

For Britain and continental Europe particular economists whose
judgement I have come to admire include Alan Budd, now chief economic adviser to the Treasury, Mervyn King at the Bank of England,
John Atkin at Citibank, John Kay and his colleagues at London Economics and Lord Desai at the London School of Economics. I have
also been impressed by the work on change in the European economy
of Jonathan Hoffman and his colleagues at CS First Boston. I have a
long-standing debt to William Clarke, formerly head of British Invisibles, who first taught me of the importance of service industries.

For Asia, the range of sources include several visits to Japan. There
I owe the greatest debt to Tadashi Nakamae, of Nakamae International
Economic Research, an economist of rare individuality and judgement.
I have also benefited by meeting many people from the Japanese business community, including Masatoshi Ito, founder of the retail group
Ito-Yokado, whose judgement on the relationship between social and
economic change I much respect. Tsutomu Hata, currently foreign
minister, has been very helpful in clarifying my views on the long-term
foreign policy objectives of Japan.

Elsewhere, I am grateful to Freddy Orchard and his colleagues at
the Government of Singapore Investment Corporation for teaching
me about the success of Singapore. For China (which, unlike much of
the rest of East Asia, I have not visited) I have borrowed judgements
from the Fairbank Center for East Asian Research at Harvard University, from its chairman John Guth and from Professor Ezra Vogel; and
from Sir Alec Cairncross, my father-in-law, chairman of the Centre for
Modern Chinese Studies in Oxford.

For demography, factual information has come mainly from UN
sources; for resources and the environment, largely from the excellent
World Resources Institute in Washington. For judgements I have been
influenced by John Ermisch of Glasgow University and by my wife,
Frances Cairncross, of *The Economist* and author of *Costing the Earth*.
Information about technology has come, more than from anywhere
else, simply from the range of journals which follow it, and from my

own observations over the last generation of what technology seems to satisfy consumer needs and what does not. For the role of government, living in Britain through the 1980s was itself an education, as Britain pioneered the process of privatization which was to sweep the world. But I should also acknowledge a debt to Sir Peter Kemp, the British civil servant behind the Next Steps programme of reform of Government.

Two final points. The first is that the list above only scratches the surface of the contacts and friendships which are in one way or another reflected in the book – some of the specific references which follow really refer to much more substantial assistance. The second is that the usual disclaimer applies more absolutely in this book than most: none of the mistakes of fact or judgement should be attributed to people who have helped me – they are entirely my own.

Notes and Sources

CHAPTER ONE: WHAT MAKES
COUNTRIES GROW

1. By convention, the term 'East
   Asia' (sometimes 'Asia-Pacific')
   economies normally includes four
   North East Asian economies –
   Japan, the Republic of Korea,
   Taiwan and Hong Kong – and six
   South-East Asian economies –
   Brunei, Indonesia, the
   Philippines, Singapore, Thailand
   and Malaysia. The People's
   Republic of China is not always
   included in the term, but for the
   purposes of this book it will be.
2. Gross Domestic Product (GDP) is
   the economist's normal measure of
   a country's output of goods and
   services, and has been used
   generally through this book. Gross
   National Product (GNP), which is
   used occasionally, includes income
   earned from the country's assets
   abroad and excludes payments to
   other countries from assets that
   they own in the country in
   question. For practical purposes
   either measure is accurate enough,
   subject to the problems discussed
   later in this chapter.
3. Study of growth became a newly
   fashionable field in economics
   during the 1980s, with investment
   in human capital being seen as the
   key to economic growth. A World
   Bank paper in 1993 (*The East
   Asian Miracle: Economic Growth and*

Public Policy, Oxford University
Press for the World Bank,
September 1993) argued that
education and investment both
played a substantial role in
generating East Asian countries'
prosperity.
4. The best study bringing out the
   common features of East Asian
   growth is the paper produced by
   the World Bank group, *The East
   Asian Miracle*, as above.
5. Paper by Larry Summers, then
   chief economic adviser at the
   World Bank, 1993. Details were
   published in the World Bank's
   *International Economic Insights
   May/June 1992*.
6. *Statistical Abstract of the United
   States, 1920*, IMF, OECD, 1988,
   quoted in the *Economist Book of
   Vital World Statistics*, Hutchinson,
   1990.
7. Department of Statistics, Ministry
   of Trade and Industry, Singapore.
8. *The Economist Book of Vital World
   Statistics*, Hutchinson, 1990, 1988
   figures.
9. A brilliant study of the shift of
   manufacturing from the 'old'
   industrial countries to the 'new'
   ones, and the growth of services
   within the 'old' industrial
   countries, which won the annual
   Amex Bank Review awards in
   1993, is called *Is Manufacturing Still
   Special in The New World Order?*,

by Richard Brown and DeAnne Julius.

10. OECD National Accounts; note: US, 1987 figures; UK, 1988; Germany, Japan, 1990; France, 1991.

11. Governments do see it as their responsibility, witness the programme announced by the British government in 1993 to reduce obesity and discourage smoking.

12. A method of calculating exchange rates which equalizes as far as possible the prices for goods and services in each country.

13. Calculated from OECD figures, 1970 and 1988, quoted in *The Economist Book of Vital World Statistics*, Hutchinson, 1990.

14. A thorough discussion of the problems this creates was published by Demos: *The Patenting Deficit*, Amitai Etzioni, 1993.

CHAPTER TWO: NORTH AMERICA: THE GIANT IN RETREAT

1. The fact that agreement was reached on creating the North American Free Trade Area at the end of 1993 will explicity create a single economic identity.

2. Figures are US GNP as a percentage of the total GNP of the OECD countries.

3. United Nations National Accounts statistics, calculated by the Berkeley Roundtable on the International Economy, quoted by John Zysman in 'US power, trade and technology', an article in *International Affairs*, 67, I, 1991.

4. OECD, with purchasing power parities calculated by Citibank, N.A.

5. *British Invisibles Annual Report 1992*, quoting IMF data. Note that the OECD, calculating on a different basis, puts the figure rather lower than this at 20 per cent, but both sources agree on the rising trend.

6. *Structural Shifts in Major OECD Countries: Annual Review, 1992*, OECD.

7. *St Petersburg Times*, 15 June 1993.

8. The roots of McDonald's go back to the 1950s, but it was only in the 1970s and 80s that their massive overseas expansion took place.

9. US Social Security Administration figures, *Statistical Abstract of the United States 1992*, published by the US Bureau of the Census.

10. Speech to Davos Symposium, Switzerland, 1993.

11. Study by Edward Wolff, New York University, quoted in *The Economist*, 13 February 1993.

12. US Department of Justice: *Report to the Nation on Crime and Justice* and *FBI Uniform Crime Reports*, 1990.

13. OECD, 1986 figures.

14. US Bureau of Labor Statistics, *Employment and Earnings*, January 1991.

15. *Report to the Nation on Crime and Justice*, US Dept. of Justice, 2nd ed., 1988, quoting estimates by *Security World* magazine.

16. Burglary was the one major category of crime in the US that fell during the 1980s. *Uniform Crime Reports*, FBI, 1991.

17. *Report to the Nation on Crime and Justice*, as above, quoting research by Research Triangle Institute, 1983.

18. *Statistical Abstract of the United States, 1992*, as above.

19. In the UK the charity Relate calculates that each divorce costs the taxpayer at least £10,000.

20. Quoted in *The Economist*, 10 October 1992.
21. S. Fuess and H. van den Berg, University of Nebraska, quoted in *The Economist*, 10 October 1992.
22. Japan Federation of Bar Associations, 1992.
23. S. McGee, University of Texas, in *The Economist*, 10 October 1992.
24. T. Hopkins, Rochester Institute of Technology, quoted in *The Economist*, 10 October 1992.
25. OECD Health Data; *OECD Health Systems: Facts and Trends 1960–91*, OECD, 1993 (1991 data – latest figures).
26. OECD Health Data; *OECD Health Systems: Facts and Trends 1960–91*, OECD 1993.
27. Taken from OECD figures in the table above.
28. Quoted in the *Chicago Tribune*, 3 September, 1989.
29. *World Economic Outlook*, IMF, October 1993.
30. 1990 figures, *Advertising Statistics Yearbook*, Advertising Association, 1992.
31. Education at a Glance, OECD Indicators, HMSO.
32. A broadly similar pattern, with Chinese students at the top and Caribbean students at the bottom, seems to be developing in the UK, according to an analysis of Islington schools' GCSE results: *Evening Standard*, London, 4 March 1993.
33. National Science Foundation, quoted in *Newsweek*, 22 February 1993.
34. The *Financial Times*, 5 October 1991.
35. John Cleland's novel *Fanny Hill* was only ruled not obscene by the Supreme Court in 1966.

CHAPTER THREE: EUROPE: THE BABBLE OF MANY TONGUES

1. OECD, *Tourism Policy and International Tourism in OECD countries*, 1993 (1991 data).
2. EC figures, quoted in *US Industrial Outlook 1993*, US Dept of Commerce.
3. Scrip Yearbook, 1991.
4. OECD, *Tourism Policy*, as above.
5. Eurostat, The Statistical Office of the EU, 1991.
6. CERN is an interesting example of European co-operation which includes non-EU countries, and is located in a non-member state. Europe can co-operate without the help of the EU.
7. *The Economist*, 13 February 1993.
8. *The Making of Managers: A report on Management Education, Training and Development in the USA, West Germany, France, Japan and the UK*, by C. Handy and others, Manpower Services Commission, National Economic Development Council, British Institute of Management.
9. The figure of four years assumes a Bachelor's degree after three years, and a subsequent one-year Master's degree. There is no Bachelor's degree in Germany – the first recognized degree is a Master's.
10. Formerly Director of the London School of Economics, member of the founding committee and later Professor of Social Science at the University of Konstanz, and now Warden of St Antony's College, Oxford. See Dahrendorf's essay, 'Did the Sixties swing too far?' in *The Legacy of the Golden Age: The 1960s and Their Economic Consequences*, ed. Frances Cairncross and Alec Cairncross, pub. Routledge, 1992.

11. OECD, 1991 figures, in *OECD in Figures: Supplement to The OECD Observer*, No. 182, June-July 1993.
12. See for example the work of Nicholas Bosanquet, *Social Market Foundation*, in progress.
13. *Statistical Abstract of the United States 1920*, table 462.
14. See the work of Professor Paul Krugman at MIT, e.g. *Geography and Trade*, MIT Press, 1991.
15. *Wall Street Journal Europe*, 1 February 1993.
16. See the paper by Richard Brown and DeAnne Julius, *Is Manufacturing Still Special in the New World Order?*, referred to earlier.

CHAPTER FOUR: EAST ASIA: THE FRAGILE BOOM CONTINUES

1. Institute for the Information Industry, 1991 figures.
2. International Civil Aviation Authority, 1990.
3. This famous speech was made by Matsushita in 1979 and was widely quoted in May 1989 shortly after his death.
4. MITI figures, quoted in *Asahi Shimbun Japan Almanac 1993*, Asahi Shimbun Publishing Co., 1992.
5. *Education at a Glance*, OECD Indicators, HMSO, and National Institute of Economic and Social Research Report, series no 5: *Educational Provision, Educational Attainment and the Needs of Industry: A Review of Research for Germany, France, Japan, the USA and Britain*, by Andy Green and Hilary Steedman, Institute of Education, University of London and NIESR, 1993.
6. International Assessment of Education Progress, 1992, 'Learning Mathematics' and 'Learning Science'.
7. The *Independent*, 4 June 1991.
8. *The Making of Managers: A report on Management Education, Training and Development in the USA, West Germany, France, Japan and the UK*, C. Handy and others, Manpower Services Commission, National Economic Development Council, British Institute of Management, 1987.
9. *How Chinese Managers Learn*, Malcolm Warner, Macmillan, 1992
10. The China-Europe Management Institute (CEMI), established in 1984 as a co-operative venture between the European Commission and the Chinese government, accepts some forty young managers on to its two-year MBA programme, which is taught in English in Beijing by top European academics, and includes a four-month period of training in blue-chip European companies. Since 1990 CEMI has also been providing short courses in Chinese for senior executives, training some 200 managers per year – still a drop in the ocean, but nevertheless a commitment to learn western management techniques.
11. Derived from Bulletin of Labour Statistics 1992–4, International Labour Organisation, Geneva.
12. Taijun Tomobe, Buddhist monk at the Myokeiji temple in Yamanashi prefecture, quoted in *The Economist*, 9 August 1988.
13. Quoted in the *Financial Times*, 29 March 1993.
14. The term 'tigers' is common shorthand for the South-East Asian NICs – notwithstanding the fact

that rapid industrial development has sadly helped restrict the tigers' range.

15. Ministry of Agriculture, Forestry and Fisheries, Japan, 1990 figures, quoted in *Asahi Shimbun Japan Almanac 1993*, Asahi Shimbun Publishing Co., 1992.

16. OECD, Main Science and Technology Indicators, 1992.

17. ASEAN was formed by Thailand, Malaysia, Singapore, the Philippines and Indonesia in 1967. Brunei joined in 1984. A sharp analysis of the future direction of ASEAN was given in *The Economist*, 1 February 1992.

CHAPTER FIVE: DEMOGRAPHY

1. Office of Population Censuses and Surveys: *Registrar General's Quarterly Return for England and Wales*, quarter ended 31st December 1951; UK Census, 1991.

2. *World Population Prospects: The 1992 Revision*, UN, 1992.

3. Demographers use the concept of the 'total fertility rate', the number of children that are born on average to each woman during her life, rather than the simple concept of a 'birth rate', the number of children that are born each year as a proportion of the total population, to show the trends in population growth.

4. Calculated from UN estimates.

5. OECD, *Ageing Populations*, 1989, and Ministry of Welfare, *White Paper on Welfare*, 1988, in *Long-Term Prospects for the World Economy*, OECD, 1992.

6. UN, *Demographic Yearbook*; Council of Europe, *Recent Demographic Developments in the Member States* in *OECD Long-term Prospects for the World Economy*, 1992.

7. *Japan in the Year 2010*, Economic Planning Agency, Tokyo, 1992.

8. Nearly half of the men aged between fifty-five and sixty-four in the industrial countries have moved out of the labour market. In the 1980s non-employment rates for men in this age group averaged 42.5 per cent and were as high as 60 per cent in some countries. *Employment Outlook*, July 1992, OECD.

9. It is too early for this pattern to show up in the figures, but retirement by the mid-fifties has become increasingly common, for example in many financial service companies in the City of London.

10. In the US, Medicare spends six times as much for recipients in the last year of their life as it does for its average members. *Health Expenditure for Older Americans 1990–2040*, Alan M. Garber and Victor R. Fuchs, Stanford University, and the National Bureau of Economic Research Inc., 1993.

11. *Is the Rise in UK Inequality Different?*, Paul Gregg and Stephen Machin, National Institute for Economic and Social Research, London.

12. See for example the work of John Ermisch, Bonar-Macfie Professor of Political Economy, University of Glasgow.

13. The most accessible summary of the wealth of work in this area is contained in *The Parenting Deficit* by Amitai Etzioni, a paper published by Demos, London, 1993.

14. See *The Parenting Deficit*, Amitai Etzioni, Demos, 1993.

15. 21 per cent are joint registrations, and 8 per cent are a single parent registering the birth; UK Office of Population Censuses and Surveys, 1990 figures.

16. *Population Projections of the United States, by Age, Sex, Race and Hispanic Origin: 1991 to 2050*, US Department of Commerce, 1992.

17. Since 1973 Australia has implemented a global non-discriminatory immigration policy, followed in 1987 by the creation of the Office of Multicultural Affairs – part of the Department of the Prime Minister and Cabinet – who launched the 'National Agenda for a Multicultural Australia' in 1989 in recognition of the commitment to a multicultural society.

18. Malthus's *Essay on Population* was first published anonymously in 1798. He outlined the theory that population growth would always tend to outrun the food supply.

CHAPTER SIX: RESOURCES AND THE ENVIRONMENT

1. See previous note.

2. Quoted in *Population Change and Economic Development*, World Bank and Oxford University Press.

3. See, for example, *World Resources 1988–89*, World Resources Institute, Washington DC, 1988.

4. *World Resources 1987*, World Resources Institute.

5. *The Dammed: Rivers, Dams and the Coming World Water Crisis*, Fred Pearce, The Bodley Head, 1992.

6. *Water – The International Crisis*, Robin Clarke, Earthscan, 1991.

7. *Water – The International Crisis*, as above

8. *World Development Report 1992*, World Bank.

9. Pearce, *The Dammed*, as above.

10. *BP Statistical Review of World Energy, 1987*.

11. The *Independent*, 17 April 1993.

12. An estimate from Professor Donald Steadman of Denver University, quoted in the *Observer*, 21 November 1993.

13. *Toward an Environmental Strategy for Asia*, Carter Brandon and Ramesh Ramankutty, World Bank, Washington, 1993.

14. *International Herald Tribune*, 5 May 1993.

15. *International Herald Tribune*, 5 May 1993.

CHAPTER SEVEN: TRADE AND FINANCE

1. Each year the Bank of England surveys the changes in the net external asset position of the main industrial countries and publishes its results in its *Quarterly Bulletin*. These figures are taken from the *Quarterly Bulletin*, November 1993. Current account figures collated by the OECD.

2. *Bank of England Quarterly Bulletin*, November 1993.

3. Data taken from national sources and the IMF *International Financial Statistics Publication*. Taken from *Bank of England Quarterly Bulletin*, November 1993.

4. Tokai Bank, 1989. The probability of such an earthquake is widely accepted. For a descriptive account of its possible consequences, see *Sixty Seconds That Will Change the World* by Peter Hadfield, Sidgwick & Jackson, 1991.

5. *Liberalisation, Foreign Investment and Economic Growth*, DeAnne

Julius, Shell Selected Paper, 1993.

6. *Euromoney*, May 1987, 'The Corporate List'.
7. *Size Analysis of UK Businesses*, Central Statistical Office, 1993.
8. *Multicultural Australia*, prepared by the Overseas Information Branch of the Dept of Foreign Affairs and Trade, Australia, May 1991.
9. See for example 'The Fall of Big Business', *The Economist*, 17 April 1993.
10. Distillers company records.

CHAPTER EIGHT: TECHNOLOGY

1. *The Economist*, 22 December 1990.
2. *The Economist*, 22 December 1990.
3. To give homeworkers the sensation of being together in an office, BT allows them to use their networks to chat to each other free for electronic coffee breaks.
4. Pierre Wack originally developed forecasting techniques at Shell in the early 1970s. Peter Schwartz learned about forecasting from him and has since written a book, *The Art of the Long View*, Century Business, 1993.
5. *The Age of Unreason*, Charles Handy, Business Books Ltd, 1989.
6. *Glasgow Herald*, 29 July 1993. The idea of using video cameras came about because local youths wanted to be captured on film in their youth club so that they wouldn't be accused of offences committed in the neighbourhood!
7. Profiles, owned by the *Financial Times*, is the main UK on-line service of this nature.
8. Office of Population Censuses and Surveys, quoted in the *Independent*, 17 June 1993.

CHAPTER NINE: GOVERNMENT AND SOCIETY

1. *OECD National Accounts*, 1993 (1990 figures for both countries).
2. US Bureau of Labor Statistics, *Monthly Labor Review*, November 1991.
3. *The Art of the Long View*, Peter Schwartz.
4. Sir Graham Day, former chairman of British Aerospace, Rover's parent company, in a speech to the University of the South Bank, London, November 1993.
5. See *Reinventing Government: How the Entrepreneurial Spirit is Transforming the Public Sector*, David Osborne and Ted Gaebler, Addison-Wesley, Reading, Mass.
6. *The Economist*, 8 August 1992.
7. The author heard senior Japanese industrialists still defending the line that Japanese snow was different from that of the rest of the world at a conference at the London School of Economics as recently as 1992. They stressed that though the actual snow might be similar to that of other countries, the conditions in Japan were different, because of more crowded pistes and different skiing techniques!
8. Calculated from estimates from the Resolution Trust, the US Federal body charged with the rescue.
9. According to a study of the Bureau of Justice Statistics, quoted in *The Parenting Deficit*, Amitai Etzioni, Demos, London, 1993.
10. See page 75.
11. George Soros, the US-based Hungarian investment manager, was credited with causing the ejection of sterling from the European Exchange Rate Mechanism in September 1992.

Even if one rejects that judgement, his support for investment in eastern Europe would give him as much influence in that region as any of the fledgling governments.

CHAPTER TEN: NORTH AMERICA

1. Quoted in *Systems of Survival: A Dialogue on the Moral Foundations of Commerce and Politics*, Jane Jacobs, Random House, 1993.
2. OECD study, forthcoming.
3. See for example the paper by Richard Brown and DeAnne Julius referred to earlier, *Is Manufacturing Still Special in the New World Order?*
4. *Edge City – Life on the New Frontier*, Joel Garreau, Doubleday, 1991.
5. The *Independent*, 31 May 1993.
6. *Human Development Report 1993*, UN.
7. *The Economist*, 26 June 1993.
8. It is not absolutely clear why this should have happened, but the weakening of the power of the president and his cabinet has something to do with the growth in power of the various special interest lobbies and the declining power of the two main political parties interacting with what was already a fragmented political system. Environmental organizations have several times the income of the main political parties in the US. Greenpeace alone had an estimated income of $50 million in 1993. *The Gazette*, Montreal, 31 July 1993.
9. *Keesing's Record of World Events*, Longman, 1990 and 1992.
10. President Clinton attacked the 'knee-jerk liberal press' in an interview with *Rolling Stone*, quoted in *The Economist*, 4 December 1993.

11. *Days of Grace*, Arthur Ashe, Heinemann, 1993.

CHAPTER ELEVEN: EUROPE

1. *Making Democracy Work: Civil Traditions in Modern Italy*, Robert Putnam, with Robert Leonardi and Raffaella Nanetti, Princeton University Press, 1993.
2. *Making Democracy Work*, as above.
3. It is conceivable that opposition in Norway to EU membership will prevent entry.
4. 'The Future of International Labor Migration', John Salt, *International Migration Review*, Vol. xxvi, No 4, 1993.
5. 'The Balkan Crisis: 1913 and 1993', George F. Kennan, *New York Review of Books*, Vol. XL, No 13 July, 1993, makes a fascinating comparison between the Balkan wars and the Yugoslav conflict and draws some sober conclusions for the future.

CHAPTER TWELVE: EAST ASIA

1. The shortcomings of Japanese education in attributing blame for the wartime experience is recognized by many of the more thoughful senior Japanese, and acknowledged privately. The best documented analysis is in *The Enigma of Japanese Power*, Karel van Wolferen, Alfred A. Knopf, 1989.
2. Karel van Wolferen (as above) explains low Japanese crime in terms of the indoctrination of people's obligation towards the rest of society from a very early age.
3. The best recent study of Shanghai is *Shanghai* by Harriet Sergeant, Jonathan Cape, 1991.

4. See for example *Global Prospects and the Developing Countries 1993*, World Bank, Washington DC.

5. Anthony Sampson wrote a brilliant essay on the parallels between Hong Kong and New York for the Hong Kong and Shanghai Bank.

6. *Australia Briefs: Immigration*, Dept of Foreign Affairs, Australia, January 1993.

7. *Asian Wall Street Journal Weekly*, 17 May 1993.

CHAPTER THIRTEEN: THE PRIZE

1. There is evidence of this in the Communitarian movement in the US, which seeks to encourage family values.

2. The phrase is from Conor Cruise O'Brien, the Irish author and statesman. I find this the most credible way of explaining Germany's actions between 1933 and 1945.

3. World Nuclear Industry Handbook 1993.

Index